CW00554996

PUTTIN' ON THE STYLE
The Lonnie Donegan Story

Spencer Leigh
Illustrations by John Firminger

Copyright © 2003 Spencer Leigh
Published by Finbarr International

ISBN 0 9529500 2 2

Finbarr International, Folkestone, Kent, CT20 2QQ

PUTTIN' ON THE STYLE
The Lonnie Donegan Story

CONTENTS

p 31, 51, 59, 61, 62

PUTTIN' ON THE STYLE
The Lonnie Donegan Story

FOREWORD
by John Firminger

This is the third book that Spencer and I have been involved in together and it has been a labour of love. We both love Lonnie Donegan's records and putting together the various clippings took me back to when I used to mutilate my weekly pop papers and put the pictures of my favourite performers in my scrapbook. I would be reading 'New Musical Express', 'Disc', 'Record Mirror' and 'Melody Maker' as a matter of course, but I would also peruse the girls' weeklies, 'Valentine' and 'Mirabelle', if they were featuring rock'n'roll.

Compiling all the pieces for this book, inspired by the constant playing of Lonnie's records, was a wonderful trip back through the career of a most interesting man (to say the least!), Lonnie Donegan. Introducing elements of the blues, folk and gospel into pop music, he ignited the fire in a generation of music fans. Through the years, Lonnie also embraced music hall, country and even soul, something that he had plenty of.

Spencer has presented Lonnie's story in his usual entertaining and enlightening way, and there are several surprises along the way. How fortunate I feel for having seen Lonnie in action just three weeks before his death. He was still a superb performer and stylist and I felt I was witnessing a great British institution. Here's hoping you enjoy our efforts as Lonnie rides again.

PUTTIN' ON THE STYLE
The Lonnie Donegan Story

NOW THIS HERE'S A STORY
Introduction

"Lonnie Donegan was the Messiah and we all followed him." (Adam Faith, 1999)
"He still thinks he's Jesus." (Joe Brown, 1999)

Lonnie Donegan was very talented, very colourful and very important to the development of the UK music scene, and yet no one has written a book about him. The stumbling-block was Lonnie himself. For years, he had been promising to write his autobiography but whenever he started, he was soon bored or distracted. No publisher would give him the advance he wanted - in 1990, he was asking for £100,000. This was an outrageous figure - even with serial rights, no publisher could hope to recoup it, much less make a profit - and so Lonnie had no motivation for writing his book. Bringing in a ghost writer compounded the problem as the advance and the subsequent royalties would have to be split in proportions to suit Lonnie but not the writer.

Lonnie had a title though - 'All Roads Lead To Lon', which was how he saw himself. In his estimation, every significant British musician owed something to him. By the time of his death, he had drafted several chapters, and his wife, Sharon, and his manager, Mel Roberts, will be using this as a basis for a biography. This book, 'Puttin' On The Style', contains relatively little about his private life and asks whether all roads did, in fact, lead to Lon or whether Lonnie had too high an opinion of himself.

Even if he had influenced no one, the records he made during the 1950s are a testimony to his creativity and drive. No matter how primitive some of the recordings are, Lonnie and his group always sound as though they are enjoying themselves. One thing is certain: there has never been anyone like Lonnie Donegan. Lonnie Donegan was unique.

As well as being a top flight entertainer, Lonnie was a brilliant interviewee. It is one thing to print his conversation and it is quite another to hear him talk. He was a brilliant raconteur and he had a terrific knack of capturing voices and accents. When Lonnie describes hearing Kenny Ball for the first time, he mimicks the voices of the BBC panel with great hilarity and, presumably, accuracy. I have been laughing, sometimes uncontrollably, as I have been transcribing his conversation and writing this book.

Interviewing Lonnie could be an ordeal. He could be awkward, he could be frivolous, he could be pompous, but often when he was being tetchy, he was having fun. He despaired of being asked the same questions again and again. A telling moment occurred when he was interviewed by the promoter Gary Atkinson for 'Lead Belly Letter' in 1995. Lonnie says, "What you're doing here is giving me a little lecture on folk music and I don't need this. I just want to answer the questions. You put the questions and I'll give the answers. I know all about folk music." A little later he says, "This hindsight stuff is a bit bloody stupid, isn't it?"

A cautionary word: Lonnie embellished his anecdotes so that they are not always strictly truthful. In some instances where I think just his memory has been at fault, I have corrected his speech, but in others, I have left his words unchanged and it will be clear from the surrounding text that he is exaggerating.

Like 'Halfway To Paradise' and 'Baby, That Is Rock And Roll', I am delighted to be doing this book with John Firminger and his astonishing store of music newspapers. Lonnie was not handsome but he had very distinctive features, especially in profile, and looking through the cuttings, I can see that it was impossible to take a bad photo of Lonnie. He always looked good and he always looked young.

Spencer Leigh
May 2003

Thanks to all the interviewees and to 'New Musical Express', 'Melody Maker', 'Country Music People' and 'Liverpool Daily Post' for permission to copy articles from contemporary magazines. We cannot trace the copyright owners for 'Disc', 'Record Mirror' and a few US magazines but we acknowledge their contributions here. Our thanks to Ron Mason, who took the photos of Lonnie and Adam Faith at the Royal Albert Hall and to Tony Barrow for keeping his wonderful photos of Lonnie Donegan in Crosby in the 50s, which are being shown here for the first time.
Some of the text has appeared in different guises in 'Record Collector' and 'Now Dig This' and thanks for reproduction is given here. Many of Spencer's interviews with Lonnie Donegan and others have been broadcast on BBC Radio Merseyside and we are grateful to Mick Ord for permission to put them in print. Thanks also to Raphael Callaghan, Geoffrey Davis, Keith Firminger, Charlie Gracie Jr, Bob Groom, Michael Heatley, John Ingman, Carl Jones, the late Malcolm Jones, Anne Leigh, Derek Mason, Mick O'Toole, Keith Parkinson, Dave Radcliffe, John Reed and Hugh T. Wilson for their invaluable input. Above all, we would like to thank James Cullinan at Finbarr International for his faith in this book.

DECCA

JAZZ   JAZZ

7B   RPM

(68261 X/BD)

ROCK ISLAND LINE
(Traditional)
THE LONNIE DONEGAN
SKIFFLE GROUP
(Lonnie Donegan—guitar and
vocal; Chris Barber—bass;
Beryl Bryden—washboard)
Exempt

FJ.10647

Songs Of The Dustbowl; Woody Guthrie

Huddie Ledbetter, 'Leadbelly'

Jimmie Rodgers meets The Carter Family.

McKinley Morganfield,
a.k.a Muddy Waters

Triumph

The most outstanding triumph in recent years has been Russ Hamilton—with his very first disc. "We Will Make Love", on Oriole exceeded 250,000 in sales here, while the reverse side composition "Rainbow" hit the million mark in America. Throughout the world, this record must have chalked up a figure of 1¼ million; combined artist and composer disc royalties alone must have yielded Russ a minimum of £17,000.

During the past three years, a consistent series of hit parade entries have earned Lonnie Donegan colossal sums as a performer—plus his revenue from composing of a different kind. Lonnie searches for suitable material of a "public domain" nature—usually folk songs, which are non-copyright, where the identity of the original writer is unknown.

Lonnie then devises suitable titles with alterations to the lyrics and his own adaptation of the musical arrangements considered acceptable to the record buying public.

However, just recently, the music of a Donegan disc, "Nobody Loves Like An Irishman" was en-

RUSS HAMILTON and LONNIE DONEGAN, great friends and wonderful songwriters.

Lonnie Donegan

Real Name: Anthony Donegan. **Birthdate:** 29th April, 1931. **Birthplace:** Glasgow, Scotland. **Height:** 5ft. 6in. **Colour of Eyes:** Brown. **Colour of Hair:** Black. **Present Home:** London. **Where Educated:** London, Glasgow and Manchester. **First public appearance:** Stoll Theatre Concert on return from first U.S.A. Tour. **Other career details including awards; films; TV and radio shows:** Three Gold Discs (Only British Artist). Films: "Light Fingers" and "Six Five Special". Own A.T.V. Series "Putting on the Donegan". **Outstanding Discs:** "Cumberland Gap", "Putting on the Style", "My Old Man's a Dustman". **Position in charts:** Top. Albums include: "Lonnie Donegan Showcase", "Lonnie Rides Again", "Lonnie", "Tops with Lonnie", "More Tops with Lonnie". **Pet Likes:** Music, steak and kidney pudding, driving the car. **Pet Hates:** Cocktail parties, giggling girls. **Favourite Food:** Steak and kidney pudding. **Hobbies and recreations:** Collecting records, photography. **Where letters can be sent:** 34 Greek Street, London, W.1. **Other personal details of interest:** Lonnie's old man is not really a dustman—he's a Company Director.

PUTTIN' ON THE STYLE
The Lonnie Donegan Story

1. WHOSE ROCK ISLAND LINE IS IT ANYWAY?
I. Carter Family - Leadbelly - Woody Guthrie - Hank Williams
II. Songwriting credits

"In the beginning was the Word,
And the Word was made Lon."
(Lonnie Donegan, 1994)

I.

It could be said, somewhat uncharitably, that Lonnie Donegan was the world's first tribute act. It would be unfair because, almost by definition, tribute acts have to be subservient to the originals, and Lonnie Donegan brought a great deal of his own personality to the songs he performed. However, regarding him as a tribute act is a good starting-point for this book. As any rock history will tell you, the rock'n'roll of the mid-1950s was an amalgam of black rhythm and blues and white country and western. Lonnie Donegan also took the music of impoverished America, but his interest was primarily in folk music, notably the songs of Leadbelly and Woody Guthrie. Although he liked them, he shunned the more sophisticated Tin Pan Alley songs, but, right from the start, he added elements of British music hall. The obituaries were wrong: this did not enter his psyche with 'My Old Man's A Dustman' in 1960.

The first professional writer of the three-minute song was Stephen Foster. In 1850 he noticed that the Negro communities often lived in shacks and tents on the outskirts of town, hence 'Camptown' and his song, 'Camptown Races', which, incidentally, added 'doodah' to the English language. Although he had never seen the Swanee River, he wrote 'Way Down Upon The Swanee River' (1852), and a tender love song for his wife, 'I Dream Of Jeannie With The Light Brown Hair', followed in 1854. They had an unhappy marriage due to his drinking - Foster's lager, anyone? - and he died in poverty at the age of 37 in 1864. However, he had created a body of work that is still performed today and although the copyright on the tunes has long expired (75 years after his death), they are usually attributed to him and not just the anonymous 'Traditional'.

In 1892 another songwriter, Chas Harris, wrote 'After The Ball' after seeing a couple arguing at a dance. He turned down $10,000 for the copyright, marketed it himself, and with his efforts, he effectively started Tin Pan Alley. From then on, songwriters were keen to protect their work and if the provenances of songs that had been handed down for generations were not known, they claimed the authorship for themselves.

In the late 1920s, the Carter Family and Jimmie Rodgers recorded their hillbilly songs and started country music as we know it. Rodgers was a fine songwriter (his 13 'Blue Yodels', for starters), but A.P. Carter was more inclined to claim credit for the Appalachian songs he either knew or collected in his travels. Although a competent songwriter himself, he preferred to find material he could add to the group's repertoire. As a result, there has been much learned discussion as to just how creative the inappropriately named Alvin Pleasant Carter was. It seems unlikely that such a bad-tempered man would exhort us to 'Keep On The Sunny Side'. The authorship of many famous songs is in doubt, but even in later years, he refused to be questioned on the matter. However, he was as much the cheated as the cheater as RCA and Southern Music kept the bulk of the monies. Even in a good year, Carter might get no more than $1,000 a year and rather than continue performing, he preferred to see out his working life in a grocery store. He died in 1956 owing $2,000 and three years later, the Kingston Trio took 'A Worried Man', a song he had collected - if not written - in 1930, into the US Top 20.

Carter often used songwriting to articulate the feelings he had for his wife, Sara - 'My Virginia Rose Is Blooming' or 'Dark-Haired True Lover'. Unlike Woody Guthrie who used songwriting to point out America's wrongs, A.P. regretted writing 'The Fate Of Dewey Lee' about a murder in Richmond, Virginia as he felt it could only cause more pain to the families involved. The Carter Family's work has much in common with black blues, and 'See That My Grave Is Kept Clean', came from Blind Lemon Jefferson and was amended by Carter. However, there are antecedents for Blind Lemon's song in the 19th century shanty, 'Stormalong', and indeed, even 'Who Killed Cock Robin'.

A poster advertising a Carter Family concert in 1930 describes their music as 'morally good'. Morally good perhaps, but much of their work is mournful and the songs are scattered with final kisses and visits to graveyards.

Josh White was born in South Carolina in 1914 and from the age of eight, he was leading blind blues performers around and organising their street-corner collections. He was well known for 'The House Of The Rising Sun'. His son, Josh White Jr, says, "I have a tape of Woody Guthrie, Josh White and Leadbelly in their early years and all of them were singing their rendition of 'The House Of The Rising Sun', which they learnt from some hillbilly singer. At the time there was no minor chord in the song, it was all in a major chord. My father, being an interpreter and not being a prolific writer, heard it more as a lament and he put in the minor chord. The very first chord in the song is an A minor. My father's contribution to the song was giving it that minor chord. My old man always told it from the female's point of view, he never used verses that would take you away from the fact that this woman was telling her story."

Huddie Ledbetter, known as Leadbelly, was born in 1889 and called himself the King of the 12-String Guitar. He partnered Blind Lemon Jefferson for a time, but he was a fierce, uncompromising man who was incarcerated for both manslaughter and murder. In the climate of the times, he was lucky to escape with his life.

In the 1930s John Lomax and his son, Alan, were commissioned to make field recordings for the Library of Congress. They recorded the songs that had been handed down from slave plantations and from the Civil War. They went anywhere and everywhere and, in 1933, they encountered Leadbetter at the Louisiana State Penitentiary. He had amassed an unparalleled collection of prison songs. After his release, they employed him as their driver and he became the doyen for folk club sophisticates in New York. The songwriting credits on his various recordings differ but are generally 'Ledbetter, Lomax, Lomax' Play the recordings and his powerful voice is as forceful as ever, but he is best-known for his adaptation of a beautiful waltz for an unfaithful girlfriend, 'Goodnight Irene', which he had learned from his uncle. The song was a vaudeville tear-jerker written and performed by Gussie Lord Davis in 1886.

The folk singer, Oscar Brand, who is still performing in New York, knew Leadbelly. He says, "Leadbelly was a very proud man. He wasn't tall and he wasn't bulging with muscles but he was powerful in a way that I have never been able to understand and he could throw you across the street from one side to the other and you would never touch the gutter. He had that strength, and although I never saw it shown in actual combat, I saw him stare down many persons, white or black. He was very careful about white people. He knew that he could go back into jail, and it was sad because if he had been brought up in the north or in Canada, he might have had a much better chance of being an honest man. On the other hand, we wouldn't have had so many songs, so we have to trade for it.."

The jazz trumpeter and one-time skiffler, Ken Colyer, commented, "Leadbelly claimed he was the King of the 12-String Guitar and he was pretty good, almost a one-man band. He got a much fuller sound because of those 12 strings. Some of the strings were strung in octaves and the top two were in unison, and so you got this unique sound, which is pretty difficult to play. Nobody knows who wrote many of the songs he did, but he was able to add himself to them and the results were marvellous."

Oscar Brand: "Leadbelly didn't write songs, he sang them. We did a programme in a club in Boston and some man in the audience was heckling him, he was a southerner, and he said, 'Hey, boy', (when you say 'boy' to a black man that is as insulting as you can get, you're half a man, in other words), 'Sing us something from down home, sing us something about the cotton fields.' This went on for a little while and Leadbelly sang a song I had never heard before and I suspect he was making it up, (sings) 'When I was a little bitty baby, My mama would rock me in the cradle, In them ol'cotton fields back home.' That became one of his greatest songs and I am sure that he made it up right there."

This is typical of the way Leadbelly created his songs. Oscar Brand: "He would make up a song and change it as he went along. Many were songs that he had learnt at home as a boy, working in the cotton fields or being in jail, and then he put in a change here or a change there and gave it a power and excitement that it didn't have before. Whatever he sang, he never sang it the same way twice. If you hear two recordings of Leadbelly, neither of them will sound alike."

Woody Guthrie (1912 - 1967) was a left-wing radical, endlessly campaigning for the rights of workers and the common man. He wrote sharp, pithy lyrics but he plundered existing ballads for his tunes - 'Pastures Of Plenty' used 'Pretty Polly', and 'Roll On Columbia' resembled 'Goodnight Irene', but 'So Long, It's Been Good To Know You' and 'Reuben James' appear to be original melodies. Guthrie is a flat-toned singer and although I like it myself, I can appreciate that Donegan recorded more musical versions of his songs. Like many left-wingers, Guthrie hated the jingoism of Irving Berlin's 'God Bless America' (1938). Why should God bless America and nowhere else? Why should politics be interwoven with religion? Why should Americans feel that they need do nothing because God has blessed them? How he hated the song and, in 1940, he wrote a parody, 'God Blessed America (For Me)', to the tune of a Baptist hymn, 'Oh My Lovin' Brother'. Four years later, he amended his lyric to 'This Land Is Your Land'. Woody never sought commercial acclaim for his songs (although he was quick to copyright them), but 'This Land Is Your Land' became popular as the theme for his weekly show on a New York radio station. Even if you knew nothing of Woody's politics, this was a marvellous song about the beauty of America.

Lonnie Donegan never sang the more contentious political songs from Woody Guthrie's catalogue. The events described may have dated but the ideals behind them hadn't, and this is perhaps typical. He would not want to compromise his career by, say, supporting the Aldermaston marchers. When Woody Guthrie was inducted into the Rock And Roll Hall Of Fame in 1988, his son, Arlo, said at the glitzy ceremony, "I don't know where Woody would be tonight if he were alive, but I can guarantee you that he wouldn't be here."

Many of the Leadbelly and Woody Guthrie songs found mass acceptance in the States through the Weavers, who, ironically, found fame at the time of the McCarthy witch-hunt.. Indeed, the first published list of Communist sympathisers included Pete Seeger, who was a member of the Weavers with Ronnie Gilbert, Lee Hayes and Fred Hellerman. The Weavers had success with 'Goodnight Irene' (a US Number 1), 'Wimoweh', 'On Top Of Old Smokey' and 'So Long, It's Been Good To Know You'. Their records were prettified by Gordon Jenkins' string arrangements and so my recommended collection is 'Kisses Sweeter Than Wine' (Omega OCD 3021/2), which draws on their concerts at New York's Town Hall between 1950 and 1952. The songs include 'On A Monday', 'Old Riley', 'Bring A Little Water, Sylvie', 'Rock Island Line' and 'The Wreck Of The John B (I Wanna Go Home)'. Lonnie could have performed most of the songs without any problems - and frequently did.

Lonnie Donegan: "One group of people who should get almost sole credit for the public recognition for Leadbelly and folk music is the Weavers. The Weavers were responsible for almost everything and the leader of the Weavers was Pete Seeger. Those guys have all become totally forgotten now; and everyone is saying, 'Well, it was Guthrie who was the pure folk singer.' Guthrie was not a folk singer at all. He was a very well off, well employed, commercial singer who happened to sing in a certain style. He was hired all over the place to represent America. The Guthrie song that I get most results from is 'The Grand Coulee Dam'. Guthrie was employed to write that for the Federal Government, who were opening a big water project on the Oregon coast, on the Columbia River. They wanted PR for all the millions of dollars they had spent. They wanted a song supporting their project and they told him what to write. It's an anthem of the folk world, but it's not a folk song at all - it's an advertising jingle."

Although Hank Williams's songs hardly feature in Lonnie Donegan's recorded repertoire, the country singer is just as much an influence as Leadbelly or Woody Guthrie: "Hank Williams was one of my earliest influences. I loved 'Wedding Bells' and I loved the narrations that he did as Luke the Drifter. They are full of frank, honest emotions and truths. They are expressed in the language of the district, people do talk like that in the Southern states, they are overly religious and moral. There's nothing wrong with melodrama, nothing at all. I find that the people in the North of England are much more emotional and they love those songs. I can bring people in Liverpool to tears with 'Nobody's Child'. I'd love to make an album of Hank's songs as Luke the Drifter, like 'Pictures From Life's Other Side'. (Sings) 'Just a picture from life's other side'. Wonderful. Yes, I would love to record them."

Many of Hank Williams's songs such as 'Cold Cold Heart' and 'I'm So Lonesome I Could Cry' reflect his traumatic marriage to Miss Audrey, and he was an alcoholic, largely because of the pain from his back. He died, alone, miserable and drunk, on his way to a gig on New Year's Day, 1953, but could Hank have written those songs without the trauma in his life? Lonnie Donegan: "I don't think anybody can. Emotion doesn't come out of the air and that's what it's all about. We're all the same. No matter how ordinary performers may appear on the surface, you'll find a reason why they are up there. Everybody is on stage saying, 'Please love me', that's why we're there. Nobody on the stage is well-adjusted. They are all searching desperately for attention and affection. There is some form of emotional deprivation in every artist's early life."

II.

A common feature of Lonnie Donegan's interviews is how he recorded 'Rock Island Line' for a £3.10s (£3.50) session fee. Unquestionably, he had a right to be bitter over this, but morally he was hardly in the right as he was taking songs which were not his and claiming them as his own. By way of examples, here are some songwriting and publishing credits which appear on the original issues of his singles:

ROCK ISLAND LINE (Traditional) Exempt

Lonnie Donegan said, "'Rock Island Line' is the archetype of Afro-American folk songs - it has the slow rhythms, the ponderous feel, the growing excitement and the speeding up. It has the imagery and the storyline of this guy trying to smuggle stuff through on the train. That and 'Frankie And Johnnie' are probably the most interesting folk songs that I found." But who wrote it? Lonnie Donegan told me in 2001: "Up until quite recently I thought 'Rock Island Line' was an original by Huddie Ledbetter, but I find that it isn't so. Leadbelly very rarely composed anything. He was like me, a compiler and a perverter of folk songs, and this is one of the ones he collected himself."

'Rock Island Line' is one of many songs written about the symbol of the new twentieth century, the railway. Most, including 'Rock Island Line' and 'Wabash Cannonball', cannot be dated precisely and their authorship is unknown. An exception is 'Freight Train', known to be written by Elizabeth Cotton in 1905. The Rock Island Company had built a railway line across Arkansas and no doubt the workers devised this song around the same time about the ineffectiveness of its toll-gates. Leadbelly was to add a spoken introduction.

When the Lomaxes took Leadbelly to a prison farm as a performer in 1934, they heard the song being performed by inmates as they stacked logs. He learnt it immediately but did not record it until 1937. It became a staple part of his repertoire and he recorded it several more times before his death in 1949. His first introduction was about the use of pickaxes, but he developed this into a narrative about an engine-driver fooling the man at the toll-gate.

Anyone who hears Leadbelly's 1942 version will be struck by how closely Donegan has followed the arrangement. Lonnie has made the narration funnier and the ending more frenzied, but it is essentially the same.

Lonnie Donegan's Decca recording of 'Rock Island Line' was given a 'Traditional' songwriting credit at first, but once it was a hit, it became 'Traditional, arranged Donegan'. On the recent 'Rock Island Line - The Singles Anthology', the credit has become 'Ledbetter, Lomax, Lomax, arr. Donegan', yet none of the four had written the song.

STEWBALL (Traditional arranged by L. Donegan) Mecolico

Around 1830, an Irish horse called Skew Ball did well in America and was an example of the outsider beating the noble opposition. With a slight name change to Stewball and some symbolic significance, the horse became the subject of a work song for plantation workers. The melody is similar to the bluegrass song, 'Molly And Tenbrooks', which is about the Kentucky Derby and associated with Bill Monroe. Both Woody Guthrie and Leadbelly recorded solo versions of 'Stewball', but Donegan based his approach on an up-tempo version from Guthrie, Leadbelly and Cisco Houston, which they recorded together in 1946.

BRING A LITTLE WATER, SYLVIE (Traditional arranged by L. Donegan) Essex

A plantation song to be sure, but Donegan would not have heard it had it not been for Huddie Ledbetter.

DEAD OR ALIVE (Guthrie, Donegan) Essex

'Poor Lazarus' is a plantation song about a criminal who was pursued and shot by a posse. Woody Guthrie changed it to a gunfighter ballad in which the fugitive has a witty dialogue with the sheriff, saying he would rather be on the run than in a 'hard rock hotel'. He also tells his pursuer where he's going, which is hardly credible. Guthrie recorded 'Dead Or Alive' in 1944 and although Donegan hardly changes anything, he recognises that Guthrie's opening, "Dead or alive, It's a hard road.", can be worked into a commercial chorus. Both Guthrie and Donegan had their songs published by Essex Music and although Guthrie was ill by this time, an amicable arrangement was reached with Donegan and the Guthrie Children's Trust Fund.

I'M ALABAMMY BOUND (new words and new music by L. Donegan) Essex

'I'm Alabammy Bound', which dates from around 1905, is about the Negroes who left their farms and wandered around, looking for work and hoping to escape racial prejudice. The song's strong bass line is evident in Leadbelly's 1940 recording with the Golden Gate Quartet on which he sounds very like Lonnie. Lonnie adds a line about your hair curling, but otherwise what new words and what new music? And isn't that songwriting credit ridiculous - what about the old words and the old music?

GAMBLIN' MAN (Guthrie, Donegan) Essex

This is a traditional song with many, many verses - 'I wouldn't marry a railroad man', 'I would not marry a farmer' and so on. Vernon Dalhart was so delighted with this song that he recorded it for six different labels in 1925. Woody knew several variants and recorded his version in 1944. Lonnie upped the tempo, but he took both the lyrics and the melody from Guthrie's record.

MY DIXIE DARLING (A.P. Carter) Southern
The Carter Family recorded 'My Dixie Darling' in 1936. Southern Music had a firm grip on the Carter Family's work, so there was no funny business here.

GRAND COOLIE DAM (Guthrie, Donegan) Essex
Note the spelling. Reissues have been as 'Grand Coulee Dam', presumably to avoid offence, and as this spelling is used for the dam itself, I will use this throughout the book. Lonnie sings Guthrie's remarkable lyric word for word, and comments, "Woody Guthrie was much more of a lyrics man, a poet, than a music man. Most of his tunes are just begged, borrowed or stolen. He doesn't have any original tunes, and 'Grand Coulee Dam' is actually 'Wabash Cannonball'. The lyrics are beautiful, great phonetics, great to sing, and totally wonderful."

CAMPTOWN RACES (New words and music by Lonnie Donegan) Essex
Sounds exactly what I learnt at school. Stephen Foster, eat your heart out.

Being listed as the composer or part-composer of a hit song is very lucrative, and Lonnie added his name time and again although he was making few, if any, changes to the compositions themselves. It could be argued that Leadbelly and Woody Guthrie themselves were often not the original composers, but, again, Lonnie would not have heard the songs if it were not for them.

There are two aspects to being listed as the composer. The first is being seen as the writer and the second is receiving the royalties. A record collector is more interested in accurate credits, but the performers themselves are after the money. Al Jolson on his own accord and Elvis Presley through his manager, Colonel Tom Parker, had their names added to songs which they did not write, but it was more to get a slice of the action than to appear as a songwriter. When Colonel Parker's duplicity was uncovered, he went underground, still wanting a percentage of the songwriting royalties where he could but not listing Presley as a writer. Lonnie Donegan, I suspect, thought along similar lines - if I am recording these old songs and making them successful, I want some of the action.

Lonnie has often been criticised for taking credits, and comparison has been made with the Rolling Stones, who usually acknowledged the original composers when they recorded blues songs. The majority of their songs came from working bluesmen - Slim Harpo, Jimmy Reed, Muddy Waters - and so they didn't have much choice in the matter. They did, however, not acknowledge the Staple Singers' contribution to their own song, 'The Last Time'. In 2000 a US court determined that the Rolling Stones had "improperly borrowed" two of Robert Johnson's blues, 'Love In Vain' and 'Stop Breakin' Down' and that the royalties belong to a retired truck driver, Claud Johnson, whose mother had a brief romance with the musician in 1931. Someone even testified that she had seen them having sex! Confusingly, one of the critics of the Stones was Lonnie himself. Commenting on 'Juke Box Jury' in 1964, he complained that they were exploiting blues artists and making money out of them. John Berry in 'Record Mirror' sprang to the Stones' defence: "Mr. Donegan has got things the wrong way round. When the Stones record a number by a blues artist, the credit is given to him and he gets the royalties. They also seize every chance to make these artists more known here. In Mr. Donegan's day, the idea was to take a song of an obscure artist, adapt it to skiffle and record it as 'Traditional, arranged Donegan' or whatever name was involved. Surely, that's nearer exploitation." Ouch.

When the Animals' single for 'The House Of The Rising Sun' credited 'Traditional, arranged Price', Alan Price told the other Animals that they couldn't fit all the names on the label (oh yes) and he would share the royalties with them. According to drummer John Steel, as soon as there was a pay-out, he was off. Alan Price told me a different story: "I took the chords from Bob Dylan's record and as I used to rehearse the band, it was my arrangement. It's always been a subject of dispute, but it doesn't bother me. The record's been made, and that's that."

Lonnie Donegan: "In most of the cases I made what I think are quite effective changes. I rewrote lyrics and changed the chords to the choruses. I think I'm entitled to half the royalties. My reasons for making these changes were two-fold. One, being an English youth, there was no way I could be doing the same thing as an old American drunk. Two, my purpose was to get the English public interested in folk songs. Before me, an audience would boo you for singing folk songs because the songs were outside their experience. They didn't understand them. I picked out folk songs that were easy to assimilate and I changed whatever I thought was necessary. For example, 'Have A Whiff On Me' was a cocaine-sniffing song going back to the last century. There was no way you'd get played on the BBC and so I changed it to 'Have A Drink On Me'."

Although Lonnie had made little from recording 'Rock Island Line', he did admit that he had received several thousand in songwriting royalties. It smacked of sharp practice and I asked him in 1980 whether the composers or publishers ever objected to what he did. "No, not at all. The Richmond Organisation which is Essex Music here was thrilled when I recorded 'Rock Island Line'. The organisation published both Woody Guthrie's songs and Leadbelly's. We made arrangements about the songs that I'd record. Ten per cent of what I made from them was put into trust for Martha Ledbetter and for Woody's children. I've never met Arlo Guthrie but when I do, I'm going to rub into his face that I paid for his schooling." When I met Arlo myself and told him what Lonnie had said, he looked askance but didn't comment further.

Even though Woody Guthrie wrote Lonnie's Number 1, 'Gamblin' Man', Lonnie is a co-composer and on the basis of that admission, Lonnie took 90 per cent and Woody's family just 10. That seems scarcely credible, but how else can you interpret what he says? Maybe the publishers didn't mind as they were representing Lonnie's interest as well as Leadbelly's and Guthrie's, but, on the face of it, it seems a little like a solicitor representing both parties.

**19139731 Private Donegan
is on the right**

(Left) Folk Blues Troubadou
Josh White

(Right)
Ilford Blues;
Tony Donegan's
first
ensemble

Backyard Blues!

Before I became well known I had my own amateur band. Here we are putting in a spot of open air practice

What started it all is that we didn't have any rifles. I was eighteen at the time and just old enough for my first H.P. . . .

Hillbilly Heroes

**Ernest Tubb,
Tennessee Ernie Ford
Hank Snow**

**Lonnie with clarinet player
Jeff Kemp**

2. AND THE BAND BEGINS TO PLAY
Family background - Musical beginnings - Army life

Time and again, Lonnie Donegan was asked, "Is your old man a dustman?" He would respond, "No, my old man's a company director," but he never provided further details. Although often interviewed, Lonnie Donegan never said much about his family. Unlike many performers, he never said, "I owe it all to my mum" or anything like that, but he had more time for his mother than his father. Family details were rarely given but he did remark that his grandfather had been a colonel in the Royal Inniskillen Fusiliers.

When Lonnie stirred up attention in America in 1956, he was publicised as the 'Irish hillbilly'. On the other hand, when the BBC broadcasts, as it frequently does, programmes about Scottish rock, Lonnie Donegan is always the starting point.

Anthony James Donegan was born during the Depression on 29 April 1931 in the Strathclyde district of Glasgow. His mother, Mary Josephine, was Irish and his father, Peter, Scottish, but his old man did not work in the shipyards. He was a violinist with the Royal National Scottish Orchestra, which was then only a part-time symphony orchestra. Lonnie said, "That was only for a brief period. I was brought up on classical music and obviously it is still the main music in the world, but he was out of work. He didn't want me to follow in his footsteps so he discouraged me from learning a musical instrument at all, but I drifted into it."

The family came to London when Tony (Lonnie) was three as his father thought there would be more opportunities there. They settled in a single room in East Ham and so Lonnie's background became a mixture of Irish, Scottish and Cockney. Adding to the mix, his mother worked as a shop assistant while Lonnie was at school but later she taught English to foreign students, and all this helped with Lonnie's love of accents, turning him into an outstanding raconteur. His personality developed at an early age: he was not large and he used his guile to avoid trouble with other schoolboys. He said, "When I was a small kid, I would fight back with my tongue. It gave me my cockiness."

Rheumatic fever, which is unknown today, was common in the 1930s and was associated with poor housing conditions. Lonnie caught it when he was four and it left him with a damaged heart. Both Billy Fury and Bobby Darin were known to suffer from the after-effects of the disease, but, until Lonnie had problems in the 1970s, he did not go public on his heart condition. However, he faced the prospects of becoming an invalid. He said, "When I was 11, I made a decision. Rather than live my life doing nothing, I'd go out and have a short, sharp life. Since then, I've never stopped." His first sign of rebellion was to play football, and he played for show business teams until his thirties.

He regretted not having a good education, and he ensured that his own children were well educated. Even in later life, Lonnie's spelling was somewhat wayward, but he made no attempts to improve it in spite of criticising others for speaking badly.

Lonnie Donegan: "The only music I could hear was on the radio. I didn't have a gramophone when I was a kid, that was a luxury item. The first people who made my ears prick up when I heard them on the BBC were Hank Snow, Hank Williams, Tennessee Ernie Ford and Ernest Tubb. Frank Crumit also did some lovely things. I first heard 'Frankie And Johnny' from him." (Crumit was the Donegan of his day: capable of singing straight songs but known for novelties like 'Abdul The Abulbul Amir', 'The Prune Song' and 'What Kind Of A Noise Annoys An Oyster?').

His father had not been able to find permanent work in London, and he took playing violin in dance quartets on cruise liners and could be away the best part of a year. During the war, he joined the merchant navy and when he returned in 1945, he and his wife were almost strangers and had grown apart. Lonnie's mother learnt to live without him and, also without Lonnie, who was evacuated from London to live with relations during the early part of the

Second World War.

Lonnie said of his father, "I knew my father had musical talent, but the poverty we went through ate into his bones. He was so broke that in the end, he put away his fiddle. I've kept going with the music, no matter what, so I have succeeded where he failed."

Lonnie's parents divorced, and Lonnie and his mother moved to Altrincham in Cheshire. She paid for a year's education at a Catholic school, which Lonnie enjoyed. He wanted to be a naval architect and then, having been given a chemistry set for Christmas, he saw himself as a research chemist. His mother couldn't afford a second year at the school and, in 1946, Lonnie took a job as an office boy for a stockbroker in the City of London.

When Lonnie was four, an uncle had stayed at their house and Lonnie had been fascinated with his guitar. He liked the shape of a guitar, but his parents had not encouraged him. He did occasionally bang on tins and fancy himself as a drummer, but he had no musical ambitions until a fellow office worker showed him his guitar. He played guitar in an amateur dance band and he showed Lonnie the basic chords. When he bought a new guitar, he offered Lonnie his old one for £2.10s (£2.50). With a loan from his father, he acquired the guitar and started playing along to records and radio programmes.

Then the singer Beryl Bryden transformed his life: "Beryl was lovely, the first blues singer I ever saw. I was 16 and a friend of mine said he had heard a jazz band playing down the road. It was the Freddy Randall Jazz Band playing at the Cook's Ferry Inn in Edmonton. I went with him the next Sunday and I didn't know what to expect as I knew nothing about jazz. The band came on and it was a wonderful, exciting noise with trumpets and trombones and drums, and then out comes this queenly woman, she was in her mid-twenties, but she was quite tall and very imposing. When she opened her mouth to sing 'St. Louis Blues', I jumped on the table and my friends were most embarrassed. I remember saying, 'To hell with you, I'm enjoying it.' It was wonderful. That night catapulted me into jazz and blues."

He had a few guitar lessons from a music teacher, but he learnt 'St. Louis Blues' with a friendly trumpeter and developed an interest in jazz clubs, becoming particularly keen on Humphrey Lyttelton and his guitarist, Neville Scrimshaw. He rehearsed with an amateur band in Ilford and his first stage appearance was playing 'Muskrat Ramble' at a school dance some six weeks later. Soon he was coming in late to work and he left before he was sacked.

Lonnie took a job in the storeroom at a laboratory for Kings College in the Strand and enjoyed the academic environment. Lonnie told the 'Daily Express' in 1984, "There was absolutely no money in the civil service, and working hard was frowned upon by your workmates. It made them look lazy. I devised a filing system for the stores and when my boss found out that I'd done this in my lunch hour, he went potty. He ran around putting everything back higgledy-piggledy because he realised that if the clerk - this little 17 year old twit - could do this and put his hand on anything by just looking up his file, then he, the boss, had no job. Of course, he was quite right."

Lonnie left the storeroom after two years and sold men's clothes in a West End store, Meaker's, doing extra shifts in a suburban branch on a Saturday and doubling his salary. Lonnie told the 'Daily Express', "That's why I have no patience with people who claim they're out of work because they can no longer do what they want to do. Oh dear! What a shame! Go and find something else! Of course, there are some people who really can't find work and I do feel for them. But for the others, too bad."

After the men's store, Lonnie became a builder's labourer. Despite his slight figure (5 foot 8, 9 stone), Lonnie was heaving bricks and cement around from morning to night for £6.10s (£6.50) a week.

In 1949 Anthony Donegan was conscripted, becoming 19139731, which is surprising. Someone with a damaged heart would surely not be acceptable, but this inconsistency was not questioned, to my knowledge, during Lonnie's lifetime. Lonnie became an acting unpaid lance corporal in the Royal Army Medical Corps, but still singing and playing where he could. However, he soon became ill and his appendix was removed. Lonnie was sent to Southampton to recuperate and naturally sought out a jazz club. He could see that the Wolverines Jazz Band was not happy with its drummer. When he returned the next week, he found that the drummer had gone but left his drums behind. Not shy in coming forward, Lonnie took over but when he returned late, he was disciplined and lost his stripe. It didn't phase Lonnie and he said of his army life, "If you can put up with the discipline, it is the easiest job on earth." Probably was after being a builder's labourer and, more significantly, Britain was not fighting anyone at the time.

Posted to Woolwich, Lonnie became friendly on his nights out with the trombonist, Chris Barber, whom he had first met in Ilford. Barber ran an amateur band and asked Lonnie to play banjo. He had never played the banjo before but thought it a good idea. The banjo with its strident tone appealed to him. He bought one for £5 and played it with a guitar tuning: "I didn't know there was a banjo tuning so I tuned the first four strings like a guitar and threw away the fifth." Lonnie joined the band and as they launched into 'Tiger Rag', Chris realised that he couldn't play but had potential and encouraged him. Lonnie had difficulties travelling to gigs as he had no transport. Often he would walk back from the West End to Woolwich. He would stumble into his barracks at four in the morning and be up again at six-thirty.

One night Lonnie returned late to find the corporal waiting for him. He told Lonnie that that the next day he was designated for medical corps duty at the annual Trooping The Colour ceremony. Lonnie was apprehensive as he knew nothing about stretcher bearing, but the day passed off without too many troops passing out. Donegan returned and found himself facing another charge, this time for not sweeping under his bed.

Because of a ridiculous ban from the Musicians' Union on American musicians, blues musicians didn't visit Britain often, so the presence of Josh White in 1950 was something of a novelty. Lonnie was there. "I idolised Josh White. He sang blues and spirituals and all of a sudden he had a hit record with 'One Meat Ball'. They didn't know what to do with him and so they put him on Moss Empire variety shows. I met him backstage at the Chiswick Empire. He wasn't used to having admirers and he didn't know what to do. His dressing-room was full. He'd say, 'Have a drink' and he'd give you a tumblerful of scotch. That was how he drank it himself. He was also a rep for Martin guitar strings. He had some arrangement to help them flog strings and he handed out packets to us. In 1976 I was in Vancouver doing a big spectacular with the Irish Rovers, and Josh's son was on the show. It was uncanny because he had all his dad's licks."

Josh White Jr: "My old man played a Martin guitar primarily all of his life. It was one of the pioneer guitars and it had the best sound, but it is all subjective, it is how it feels to you. My dad always played a wide neck guitar, the neck was more like a classical guitar, his hands were rather big, and maybe Martin made a good wide neck guitar that fit his hands right. There were no 14 fret guitars then. The length of the neck from where you tune the strings to where the neck gets to the base of the guitar could only be 12 frets then. My father always played a 12 fret guitar."

Lonnie Donegan: "People went to the Chiswick Empire to see a comic and got a blues singer. He kept a very high proportion of blues in his act, so we were all totally delighted with him." Lonnie had missed seeing Leadbelly in Paris in 1949. Another blues enthusiast, Alexis Korner did see him but didn't see much as Leadbelly had draped a cloth over the neck of the guitar so that no one could copy his technique. In Paris, Leadbelly was diagnosed with a nerve disorder which killed him six months later.

In order to stay in London and so continue in the Barber band, Lonnie volunteered for a "special treatment" course. This turned out to be education in the treament of venereal disease. In 1970, when Lonnie appeared in Las Vegas with Vic Damone, he told him, "I've played around with V.D. before."

Like many of his contemporaries, Lonnie Donegan didn't want to pass army exams and be posted overseas. He wrote his name on the top of his paper and left the rest of it blank. For his insubordination, he was posted to Vienna. There he worked as a storekeeper, but still travelled around the city and enjoyed hearing zithers in cafés. He met his first Americans and some of the servicemen passed over their V-discs of special performances by US stars for servicemen. He loved hearing Hank Snow and many other country performers on the American Forces Network (AFN) and on records, and he also had his first live experiences of country music.

Lonnie was in Vienna for a year. He was demobbed in 1951: "My ambition was to become the best jazz banjo player in Europe, and I achieved that."

(Above) The Tony Donegan Band

My first experience of the Co-op — with Ken Colyer and his Jazzmen. This was a co-operative band, which means we all shared the hard times . . .

(Above) Lonnie, at left, with KenColyer's Band with Chris Barber seen at right.

When Lonnie was one of the band

A picture from the past—notice the banjo player on the extreme left of the picture. Yes, it's LONNIE, in the days when he played with Chris Barber's band. Clarinettist MONTY SUNSHINE is beside him and CHRIS and OTTILIE PATTERSON are on the right of the picture.

(right) Blues Inspiration
Lonnie Johnson

(Above) With Chris Barber's Band and is that George Melly on vocals?

n Colyer's
SKIFFLE
ALBUM

IN' HOME
RELESS LOVE
HN HENRY
OWN BY THE RIVERSIDE
HIS TRAIN
HE GREY GOOSE

26

A sight to gladden teen-age hearts — from left to right — Mickey Ashman; Monty Sunshine; Otille Patterson; Ron Bowden; Pat Halcox; Lonnie Donegan; Chris Barber — a right bunch of budding bandleaders . . .

e right) Lonnie & Maureen's
ing Day

ve) Monty Sunshine and Lonnie.
t) Chris Barber, Shelley Winters
Lonnie.

3. NEW ORLEANS JOYS
I. Tony Donegan Band - Lonnie Johnson
II. Ken Colyer - Chris Barber - 'Rock Island Line'

I.

Lonnie Donegan was demobbed in 1951 with £35 in savings. He worked at an electrical store and then at the stationers, Ryman, where he was in charge of the ink and watercolours. When a customer was unsure of what he wanted, Lonnie asked for details. One such customer was a manager at Millets Army Surplus Store in Oxford Street and he needed to write price tickets. He was also short of a window-dresser. Typically, Lonnie claimed experience in both subjects and within days, he was working at Millets. Lonnie taught himself window-dressing by looking at other shops in Oxford Street. However, Millets never subscribed to the 'less is more' philosophy and always wanted the windows stacked with their goods. The Army Surplus Stores were a feature of the 1950s and made the public wonder how the British forces won anything when they had no concept of how to order appropriate amounts.

The jazz promoter, James Asman, ran a club on Monday nights at Abbey Wood in south-east London. The resident band was led by the trumpeter, Bill Brunskill, and one night Asman asked Lonnie to perform while the band was at the bar. Asman wrote in 'Melody Maker', "He was by no means a great success. Our club members found his music too much like hillbilly for pleasure. But Lonnie could yodel fine."

Nevertheless, Lonnie soon joined Bill Brunskill's band. That this was immediately reconstituted as the Tony Donegan Jazz Band, and the name has been taken as an early example of Lonnie's ego. In point of fact, Lonnie was the one who was getting the band work, and Bill, described by Lonnie as 'a super guy', was happy as a band member. The Tony Donegan Jazz Band had residencies at Abbey Wood and at Freddy Randall's club in Tottenham. They made a recording at a small studio in Battersea and although the tracks have never been released, the titles indicate the band's repertoire - 'Ace In The Hole', 'Boll Weevil Blues', 'Cakewalkin' Babies From Home' and 'Yes Sir, That's My Baby'.

Lonnie was undoubtedly very busy. He kept his job at Millets, ran the band and, by law, had to spend time with the Territorial Army. He played two or three nights a week in his jazz band and he arranged their bookings. In addition, he was acquiring a taste for American blues and folk music. He said, "How I came to hear American folk music was a very slow process 'cause there wasn't much to be heard, very little, and it was all on the BBC because that was our total media output. It took many years but I have always had a natural ear for that kind of sound. I have natural leanings towards folk music of all kinds. I was the first one to try and purvey it as a commercial project."

A lucky find helped Lonnie Donegan in his quest to find this music. He discovered that the field recordings made for the Library of Congress were available at the American Embassy. Lonnie Donegan: "A lot of people asked me where I got the records from because in those days American folk records weren't available on the market and the answer is, I used to go to Grosvenor House, where the American Embassy was. They had a small section of the Library of Congress recordings in there - most people don't know that they have a record library of ethnic American music and you can go in and listen to things, or you can borrow them. That's where I discovered Woody Guthrie doing 'Gypsy Davy', which is an old English song from the North-East, and I was knocked out with it and I went to Collett's Bookshop which was a Communist bookshop in those days and said, 'Has anyone heard of Woody Guthrie?' Woody was involved in American labour unions which I didn't know about, and he was in touch with the bookshop and would write to them regularly. He used to write fabulous letters on great big long pieces of paper and he would do a washed drawing over the top of a gazelle or a deer. The drawings didn't block out the words, which were also for keeping and were semi-poetry. It was like he wrote in blank verse. I hope somebody kept them because they were super."

With Lonnie around, the American Embassy couldn't hold on to their records. "I borrowed the first record that Muddy Waters ever made, and I told the library that I'd lost it. I was probably the only person in Britain to hear that record."

Much of the employment in the UK was unionised and operated a closed shop where somebody couldn't work if they were not a union member. The Musicians' Union was particularly left-wing and both part-time and full-time musicians found themselves caught in their rulings. Frank Robinson, the pianist with the Merseysippi Jazz Band, recalls, "We have been in the union since 1951 and we had no choice because it was a closed shop. We had to be in the union as we could not have broadcast otherwise, and the union was very strict. We were not allowed to play with other musicians unless they were in the union. We would get a list every month of people who had been blacklisted." Being a member had the advantage of receiving a minimum wage of £3 if the venue was of a reasonable size.

The Musicians' Union had very strict rules about the employment of American musicians. They could only appear in the UK if an exchange with a British act had been arranged. As very few British acts had a following in the US, this was a non-starter, and this is why, for example, Leadbelly played in Paris, but not London. John Lawrence, who plays cornet with the Merseysippis, remembers, "The Union didn't agree with American musicians coming over here and had this odd theory that it was putting British musicians out of work. I don't know where we could have found a guitar player who could sing and play like Lonnie Johnson but the Musicians' Union didn't see it like that. They could only come if we sent someone in return and who could we send that they would want to listen to? You couldn't expect the Musicians' Union to take a realistic view about anything connected with music: they were more interested in union matters than musical matters. When the American players did come here, they gave additional work to a lot of local players, like us with Louis Armstrong. Every one of his concerts was a gig for an English group."

Lonnie Johnson, who was born Alonzo Johnson in New Orleans in 1899, hence the 'Lonnie', was a superlative blues guitarist and vocalist, who recorded with both Duke Ellington and Louis Armstrong in the 1920s. His popularity stretched over many years as he topped the US rhythm and blues charts in 1948 with 'Tomorrow Night'. In 1952 he came to Europe with the ragtime pianist, Ralph Sutton, and contrary to expectations, some UK dates were arranged. They received work permits from the Ministry of Labour.

The Americans were to be supported at the Royal Festival Hall by Humphrey Lyttelton and John Dankworth and their bands. However, they were threatened with union expulsion if they went ahead, and the promoters looked for non-union musicians to replace them. The Tony Donegan Jazz Band was not in the union as they were not making enough in part-time employment to justify the fees. The promoter took a chance on them and George Webb, who had left Humph and reformed his Dixielanders.

To hell with the union, Anthony Donegan was delighted to be on the same bill as his hero: "Lonnie Johnson had a nice clear melodic voice that was easy to follow. He had a beautiful guitar technique and he picked some nice tunes: 'Old Coals Will Kindle' is a really lovely song. I loved Leadbelly and Woody Guthrie but I couldn't play guitar like them and I couldn't sing like them. Leadbelly for a start had a cleft palate so nobody could sing like that. Lonnie Johnson was someone I could follow, but he wasn't the only one." Unable to resist a joke or a good line, Lonnie continued, "I got to finding blind blokes who could only play one chord and that was fine, and I could sing through my nose anyway."

But Lonnie was frustrated by Lonnie Johnson's performance that night: "He was a bitter disappointment. All we had were these old records and we expected the Americans to sound like them, which they didn't. Johnson had become rather smooth, singing 'Stardust' with an electric guitar. He was no longer in the gin mills."

Nevertheless, the evening made a lasting impression on Anthony James Donegan. The MC, wanting to acknowledge the performers, meant to refer to Lonnie Johnson and Tony Donegan, but in the heat of the moment, it became 'Lonnie Donegan and Tony Johnson'. Donegan liked that and so became Lonnie Donegan.

Chas McDevitt was in the audience and he recalls the Tony Donegan band in their yellow jumpers and was very taken with their version of 'Sweetheart Of Jesus'. Lonnie said, "We were very well received by everyone, except the Musicians' Union." But the Musicians' Union won as Lonnie decided that he would have to join and become a full-time professional. The rest of the band was reluctant to follow him, so Lonnie had to find a new outlet for his talent. He rekindled his friendship with Chris Barber, and they established a new Jazz Band with Monty Sunshine on clarinet.

After Lonnie Donegan, Bill Brunskill became part of Bob Dawburn's Barnstormers and also continued his own band with a residency at the Fighting Cocks in Kingston, a regular booking which lasted 16 years. In 1984, he was the subject of a TV documentary, 'Whatever Happened To Bill Brunskill?', which was narrated by George Melly.

In 1953 Lonnie was invited to appear as a solo act on a jazz concert at the Royal Albert Hall, where, incidentally, he met Kenny Ball for the first time. He chose one of his own compositions, 'Lonesome And Blue'. He was well received but the reviewer for 'Melody Maker' asked why he hadn't brought his band along.

When Chris Barber's band was playing on the 'Jazz Saturday' series at Battersea Pleasure Gardens. A pretty girl tripped and fell in front of the band. The band members laughed and she said, 'What about a request?' Lonnie retorted, 'What about a date?', to which she said, 'Play me a number and we'll come to an agreement.' The girl was Maureen Tyler, whose father owned a pub in Mile End. Chris Barber had his band and Ken Colyer, the Crane River Band and, following Lonnie's instigation, the keenest of the musicians would jam there on after hours sessions.

II.

Ken Colyer, who was born in Great Yarmouth in 1928, was a jazz trumpeter. He had been a merchant seaman but he took unenviable, temporary jobs such as a cleaner on the London Underground. He formed the Crane River Jazz Band in 1949 and was very strong-willed and a purist when it came to music: "So much happened in a short space of time. The Crane River Jazz Band achieved good audiences, but two or three of us left and I formed the Christie Brothers Stompers with Keith and Ian Christie. That didn't last long, although it was potentially a very good band. I went back to sea because I was sure that there must still be jazz men in New Orleans playing the music. And I was right. The peak for me was seeing George Lewis's band, which was absolutely superb, out of this world."

Of course it wasn't as easy as that. As a merchant seaman, Ken Colyer joined a ship going to New York. Once in New York, he jumped ship and boarded a series of buses until he arrived in Louisiana and reached his goal, New Orleans. He was there three months but then he was gaoled for deserting his ship.

Meanwhile, Chris Barber's Jazz Band had problems with its trumpeter, Pat Halcox. He wanted to remain in his day job and not go professional. The band needed a good trumpet player. Bill Colyer told them that his brother was imprisoned in New Orleans and so they wrote and asked him to join them when he got out. Ken Colyer said, "It was Chris Barber's band initially. Pat Halcox dropped out and I took over and we became professional. I had just come back from New Orleans and we called it Ken Colyer's Jazzmen, which was a name they accepted. I got a lot of publicity from being the first British musician of any note to get to New Orleans and play with the men I idolised. I was better known than either

Chris Barber or Monty Sunshine."

It would be a cooperative band, so everyone would be paid equally, but even in a cooperative, and rather like 'Animal Farm', there are leaders. The band was formed in March 1953. Ken Colyer's Jazzmen went to Denmark for a month and found they could each earn about £5 a week. They came back and secured a residency at the Crypt in Marble Arch.

Chris Barber: "Lonnie's style of dress was not imaginative. He had been a window-dresser at Millets, which specialises in having very crowded displays. First thing he tried to do was to take everything out of the window and make it artistic. He was almost fired on the spot. It was rumoured that when he left Millets after we had turned professional, he was wearing four jackets and two pairs of trousers. I cannot vouch for this and I will not accuse him of it but he was wearing clothes that looked like the ones Millets sold for quite a while later."

Lonnie Donegan: "I don't know what he's talking about but then one seldom does know what Chris Barber is talking about." Looking at pictures of Ken Colyer's Jazzmen, it must be said that their check shirts look very similar to what was being sold at Millets.

The argumentative Ken Colyer - who was as much into scuffle as skiffle - believed that the best music was made by amateurs and he was against the band making much more than subsistence wages. He didn't want to compete with the more established bands. He was also a superlative trumpeter - "I could cry listening to him sometimes, he had so much music in him," said Lonnie.

Both Ken and Bill Colyer had extensive record collections and Chris Barber would ferret around in junk shops for Duke Ellington 78s and Leadbelly records. This guided their repertoire which included both modern jazz and ragtime amongst the more traditional numbers. The band members appreciated Lonnie Donegan's excursions into blues songs and folk songs, and realised that this could be a distinctive part of their performances. Lonnie would sing a few songs, such as 'Midnight Special', often with Barber on double-bass, Colyer adding a second vocal and guitar and Ken's brother Bill on washboard. Bill Colyer, who worked as an assistant manager at Collett's bookshop, had a record by Dan Burley and his Skiffle Boys, which amalgamated blues and folk music in an entertaining way. As a result, they called Lonnie's spots a Skiffle Session. "I didn't invent the word," says Bill Colyer, "but I sure as hell put it in the language." "I wish we had called it Lonnie Donegan music," Lonnie reflected, "and then I wouldn't be asked all these questions all the time."

Diz Disley: "I came to live in London in 1953 and I became very interested in the original Ken Colyer band and I would listen to them a lot. I met Lonnie Donegan and eventually I shared a flat with him in Archway. For years, the bugger told people that I owed him £4.10s which wasn't true. The whole skiffle thing was started by Ken and Bill Colyer, and it was Bill who called it skiffle. I joined Ken Colyer later on and we did the same sort of things as Lonnie in the skiffle group, but I always felt that Ken was a better singer than Lonnie."

Chris Barber: "The word 'skiffle' was taken from an old Dan Burley record. He was an American Negro who edited a black newspaper in Chicago and was a very good rent party pianist. It was back-room music, rent party music, casual and not self-conscious." Dan Burley's 'Skiffle Blues' dates from 1946, but there are earlier examples of the word, 'Chicago Skiffle' (1926) by Jimmy O'Brien's Washboard Band and a compilation of snippets from other records, 'Hometown Skiffle' (1929), featuring Blind Lemon Jefferson and the Hokum Boys.

Lonnie Donegan: "Skiffle was originally associated with rent-house parties. If one of the guys was short of rent, he'd hold a party and people would come round with bottles and guitars for a bit of a whoop-up. He'd pass the hat round during the proceedings, just like Phil the Fluter's Ball 400 years earlier. The kind of music they would play was very improvised, very folky and a bit jazzy. This was roughly parallel to what we were doing so we called it 'skiffle', but we just did it for variety. We enjoyed it, we liked singing the songs and the public liked hearing them." Lonnie also liked the friendly approach of the western swing recordings by Bob Wills and his Texas Playboys, which was another ingredient. Lonnie also said, "If everybody was a nervous old man, nothing would happen. You need these young idiots who know no fear to attempt new things." Unfortunately, Lonnie's first attempts at recording skiffle music, made for Storyville Records in Copenhagen in April 1953, remained unissued until the Bear Family box set in 1993, and the tracks were 'Hard Time Blues', Nobody's Child', 'You Don't Know My Mind' and 'Midnight Special'. The inclusion of a country music weepie, Hank Snow's 'Nobody's Child', is, as we shall see, particularly significant.

One day Lonnie was doodling with his banjo on a train and discovered an augmented chord. "I like that," said Ken Colyer, "it sounds like Duke Ellington." Lonnie used it for the blues 'Early Hours', which was one of the eight tracks on Ken Colyer's Jazzmen's 10 inch, 'New Orleans To London', in 1953 and it includes a clarinet break from Monty Sunshine as well as Lonnie's banjo. Monty Sunshine: "I still think that 'New Orleans To London' is a magnificent album, and I am very proud of 'Harlem Rag'. To be honest, I used to laugh when Lonnie did his skiffle songs, but it caught on and became a great success."

Ken Colyer: "You cannot tell what will catch the public's ear and become a hit. We recorded 'Isle Of Capri' and it topped the hit parade in Denmark. If a pop song has good, adaptable music, you can use it and that has always been done in jazz." 'Isle Of Capri' was also released as a single in the UK, but the song is associated with Gracie Fields, who had the added advantage of living there.

The band was doing well but it had its problems, often related to Colyer's heavy drinking which made him moody and argumentative. When a fan told him that they played better than the Americans, Colyer hit him for being so stupid. How the band folded depends on who you believe, but the band certainly had its own Battle of New Orleans. Bill Colyer: "We had a swinging thing going with these skiffle sessions, but Lonnie was drifting off into country and western songs and we wanted to get it into the blues, and that led to the break up of the band."

Whatever, after one show in May 1954, Colyer sacked at least one of the musicians, possibly Lonnie, but possibly the whole rhythm section of Lonnie, Ron Bowden and Jim Bray. Barber retorted that the band was a cooperative, it was not his band, a cooperative band did not have a leader, and so a person could only be removed with the agreement of the whole band. Colyer shouted, 'You're all sacked', and the next day, when tensions had cooled, everyone decided to leave Colyer. They rang Pat Halcox and asked him to replace Ken on trumpet. The unit again assumed the name of the Chris Barber Jazz Band. The band, still a cooperative, was immediately more organised. Lonnie said, "Chris is able to be a business man, a publisher, a record dealer and then play like Kid Ory on trombone, and not many people can do that."

With Colyer gone, the atmosphere considerably improved. Said Lonnie, "It was like a family. The atmosphere in the band was wonderful, it probably still is my happiest time, that's what I like about a band. We worked last night and we're going to work again tonight, and again tomorrow. We were like family, brothers, and it really was fantastic."

I should have stood well back when I asked Lonnie what he thought of George Melly's exposé of the jazz world in the 1950s in 'Owning Up'. "I don't care for George. I think it's rather sad the way he's still doing gigs. He couldn't sing then and he can't sing now. But he knows how to get attention. George is a professional outrager. We were all quaking when we knew his book was coming out as we didn't know what he'd been saying about us. Fortunately, he or his publisher saw sense and only put about a quarter of it into print. It's people like George who make me glad that there are still libel laws. I didn't think much of the book anyway. It isn't particularly funny and considering that George is meant to be a writer, it was very badly written."

commented to Lonnie that the final part of 'Owning Up' was sad because those wild jazz musicians had settled down to day jobs. "Not all of them. If you'd met the Mick Mulligan band, you'd never have thought that any of them were capable of holding down a nine-to-five job for even a week. I thought of them as a bunch of psychopaths. No, I'd better not say that. Let's say they were very eccentric."

In 1954 Chris Barber's Jazz Band received a contract to make a record for Decca, a 10 inch album, which would be called 'New Orleans Joys'. During a break in the sessions at Decca's West Hampstead studios on 13 July 1954, history was made as Lonnie recorded some songs with his skiffle group. Skiffle group is a misnomer as there are only three musicians on these tracks - Lonnie on guitar, Chris Barber on double bass and Beryl Bryden on washboard. Although only two and a half minutes long, 'Rock Island Line' includes a one minute narration, three verses and five choruses. The three musicians are evidently having a great time as evidenced by Chris and Beryl's campy harmonising towards the end of the recording. 'John Henry' is more predictable, but very well executed. The band got £60 between them for recording the LP and Lonnie got a bonus, roughly equal to a day's wage, for his vocals.

Lonnie Donegan: "We went into the studio to make a band album and Chris said, 'We want to cut some vocals now.' The engineer said, 'We don't want vocals, we just want an instrumental album', but Chris insisted that Lonnie Donegan and the skiffle group was an integral part of the repertoire, and fans would be disappointed if something wasn't included. The engineer reluctantly said, 'Okay, you want to sing something. There's the mike, the tape's running, I'm going for a cup of tea. When I come back, I'll hear what you've done.' We did five folk songs, 'Rock Island Line', 'John Henry', 'Nobody's Child', 'Wabash Cannonball' and 'The Wreck Of The Old 97', although only 'Rock Island Line' and 'John Henry' were included on the album. 'Rock Island Line' was released as a single after Decca had gone through every other track, all with some success. It sold three million in six months and it's still selling today. I had only been paid £3.10s (£3.50) as a session fee but it did give me a career."

It defies logic that the Musicians' Union should be so strict in some areas and yet permit such measly payments here. Lonnie Donegan had recorded five skiffle performances, and he was effectively being paid 70p (14 shillings) a song with no royalty payments.

(Left) Lonnie with Dickie Bishop, Chris Barber.

(below) The Decca LP by Chris Barber's Jazz Band which included Lonnie's recording of 'Rock Island Line'.

DELIGHTFUL

LONNIE DONEGAN with CHRIS BARBER'S JAZZ BAND

"On a Christmas Day"/"Take My Hand, Precious Lord."

COLUMBIA DB. 3850

I MUST ADMIT THAT after the efforts of some of the artistes I have reviewed this week, our old friend Lonnie Donegan sounds quite tuneful, and the neat and tidy Barber band lilting and pleasing to the ear.

This Columbia release was originally made available on the EMI Overseas catalogues and it is probable that quite a few enthusiasts have so far overlooked it. "On a Christmas Day" is taken from the Leadbelly repertoire whence so much of this present day skiffle output has sprung unbidden. It is a delightful song, simple and effective. The original Leadbelly version (obtainable, by the way, on CAPITOL LC. 6597) is immensely superior, but I am sure that the Donegan version will sell better. The reverse is a sentimental religious ballad and offers ample scope for the plaintive accents of Lonnie Donegan.

THEY MADE HISTORY

CHRIS BARBER'S JAZZ BAND
"Storyville" / "I Never Knew Just What a Girl Could Do".

Decca F-J.10790

SINCE DECCA ALLOWED BARBER AND DONEGAN to slip through their fingers they have been releasing one at a time the items recorded by them in 1954 and '55. "Storyville" is from a Royal Festival Hall concert held in January, 1955, whilst the reverse comes from a similar venue in October of the previous year.

The band consists of its more famous sidesmen, Pat Halcox on trumpet, Barber trombone, Monty Sunshine clarinet, Donegan on guitar, Jim Bray bass and Ron Bowden drums. This, as a matter of fact, was the group that made British jazz history under the leadership of Colyer, who was later replaced by Halcox. It still possesses the initial verve of the Colyer reign and makes pleasant going of the two titles.

There is a lilting and melodic vigour about the Barber band which attracts so many young enthusiasts, but one should not be deceived into believing that behind the clean-cut accents, there is any real depth. I think that, whilst Barber and his colleagues mean very well indeed, they are steadily slipping away from the first fine ambitions and conceptions.

At the time I write the band, by virtue of its recent recordings, seems to need a major upheaval to revert the musicians within it to a healthier attitude towards the music they wish to recreate.

Guy Mitchell
SINGING THE BLUES
Crazy with Love
PB650

ALMA COGAN

Frankie Laine
MOONLIGHT GAMBLER
Only if we Love
PB638

Hit Parade Stars of 1956

Shirley Bassey
AFTER THE LIGHTS GO DOWN LOW
If You Don't Love Me

Frankie Vaughan
THE GREEN DOOR
Pity the Poor, Poor Man
PB640

Rockabilly Lonnie and Johnny Burnette & The Rock'n'Roll Trio, (L. to R.) Johnny Burnette, Dorsey Burnette and Paul Burlison

★ *ANNE SHELTON enjoying a private session of skiffle from her co-topliner, LONNIE DONEGAN, in between houses at the Prince of Wales Theatre.* —R.M. Picture

SUCCESSFUL SKIFFLERS

One of the highlights of this year of fast, gimmicky music was the success of LONNIE DONEGAN and his Skiffle Group. They were house-packers at every music-hall in which they introduced their unique interpretations of song and rhythm. Here's a fine shot of Lonnie and his Skifflers in action at the Prince of Wales Theatre, London. — R.M. Picture.

☆☆☆☆☆☆☆☆☆☆☆☆☆

The New Show At The Prince Of Wales

'SKIFFLERS' JUST LOVE LONNIE

I THINK THERE ARE ENOUGH SKIFFLE FANS to ensure some measure of financial success for Messrs. Val Parnell and Bernard Delfont during the three weeks' run of Lonnie Donegan and his Skiffle Group at the Prince of Wales Theatre, London.

At both houses on Monday the Lonnie loyalists filled all parts of the house, from the back row of the 'gods' to the front row of the stalls, and they applauded just as heartily as Lonnie and the group played.

There's no disputing the fact that 25-year-old Glasgow-born Lonnie is a terrific worker and a terrific showman. He 'gives' with heart and soul and he is probably the greatest 'skiffler' of his kind. I'm not going to present myself as a top expert on this form of musical entertainment, nor will I attempt to criticise it. In any event, criticism is completely out of the question because nobody who loves Lonnie or skiffle would pay the slightest attention to detractors.

4. GOING FOR GOLD

1956 - Lonnie Donegan's year

Nobody at Decca Records spotted the commercial potential of 'Rock Island Line' and nor, it must be said, did Lonnie Donegan. The 8 track, 10 inch album, 'New Orleans Joys', by Chris Barber's Jazz Band was released in 1954.. Two of the tracks, 'Chimes Blues' and 'Merrydown Rag' were released on a single in December 1954. 'Bobby Shaftoe' and 'The Martinique' followed on a single in March 1955, but neither record sold enough copies to make the charts. That appeared to be that. Because the band was working regularly, 'New Orleans Joys' was a catalogue album that would be assured of steady sales over the years. Chris Barber's Jazz Band only had a one-off recording contract with Decca and so could record elsewhere, and they certainly did. In September 1954, Lonnie Donegan led the Barber band for a seasonal release, 'On A Christmas Day', for EMI's Columbia label. In October, live performances were recorded in Copenhagen for the Storyville label, although little was issued. They include concert performances of 'Rock Island Line', 'Bury My Body', 'Frankie And Johnny' and 'Wabash Cannonball'. Returning to the UK, Lonnie sang 'Take My Hand, Precious Lord' for Columbia, while Decca recorded a concert with other performers, which was released as 'Jazz At The Royal Festival Hall'. Lonnie performed two skiffle songs on this concert, 'Bury My Body' and 'Diggin' My Potatoes'.

Lonnie took time out from the Barber band to record a film theme at Elstree Studios, 'The Passing Stranger', with Ken Sykora on electric guitar and Bruce Turner on saxophone. It was a low budget film for the home market, but the theme was released as a single by Oriole.

Chris Barber's Jazz Band made several appearances on BBC's 'Jazz Club', which fortunately have been preserved. The skiffle songs no longer feature just guitar, double-bass and washboard. Dickie Bishop has been brought in as a second guitarist, Ron Bowden adds drums and Chris Barber harmonica. The performances featuring Lonnie's lead vocal (and not all are skiffle performances) are 'Take My Hand, Precious Lord', 'On A Monday', 'Midnight Special', 'When The Sun Goes Down', 'Railroad Bill' and a duet with Chris's wife, Ottilie Patterson, 'When I Move To The Sky'.

Chris Barber: "On the record of 'Rock Island Line', we used Beryl Bryden on washboard and then we decided to put drums on it. We added drums, bass and guitar and so our skiffle music became more country, rather like Bob Wills and the Texas Playboys - western swing mixed up with country blues and whatever else there was. Lonnie liked English comic songs so Max Miller came into it as well."

Dickie Bishop: "I had worked in bands when I was very young with Pat Halcox. Pat joined Chris's band, and about a year later, Chris said, 'Pat tells me that you sing American folk songs. Would you come along to the Royal Festival Hall tomorrow night?' There was just Lonnie, Chris´and me doing it as a trio. It was a knockout, so Chris invited me to join the band and the skiffle group would be a bigger thing. I used to more or less live with Lonnie as I didn't have the transport to get home and he lived near the centre of London. We used to sit up all night playing guitars and swopping songs, and his landlord, luckily enough, was a Greek guy who played mandolin and wanted to sit in. Denny Wright who was one of the loveliest guys you could ever meet heard about our sessions and he turned up one night at the 100 Club and asked if he could come back with us. He became a regular at our late-night sessions and he was a wonderful guitar player."

When considering Donegan's early career, the most intriguing release is the EP, 'Backstairs Session', by the Lonnie Donegan Skiffle Group for Polygon. Lonnie Donegan, aided by Dickie Bishop, is to the fore and there is a full sound, but no drums. Dickie Bishop: "I can remember the 'Backstairs Session' EP well. We had to teach Bob Watson and Pete Korrison the parts. Chris Barber insisted on playing harmonica on it and Denis Preston, the record producer, kept on saying, 'Chris can you move a bit further away from the microphone?' He was almost in another room, and Denis was right. Chris wasn't very good on the harmonica!"

'Midnight Special' is both a train song and a penitentiary song - it was said that you would be pardoned if the Midnight Special shone its light on you. Nice thought, but I'll bet it didn't work. Lonnie took 'When The Sun Goes Down' from the repertoire of Big Bill Broonzy and 'New Burying Ground' from a Library of Congress recording and it is by no means as miserable as it sounds. 'Worried Man Blues', often called 'It Takes A Worried Man', is performed by Lonnie and Dick in the style of Woody Guthrie and his sometime partner, Cisco Houston. The worried man, incidentally, is condemned to travelling on the Rock Island Line. As an aside, none of the early train songs I've heard suggest that they are behind schedule or subject to cancellation. Maybe services were more efficient back then.

Thanks to the Decca manager, Bob Crabb, the third single from 'New Orleans Joys', 'Rock Island Line', was released by Decca in November 1955. Possibly he spotted its potential, but he did release it on their jazz imprint (the light, as opposed to dark, blue label), indicating, perhaps, that only normal jazz sales would be expected. Attributed to the Lonnie Donegan Skiffle Group, the single was 'Rock Island Line' and 'John Henry'. Lonnie was not happy and asked for the record to be withdrawn: "I don't think it's a particularly good recording," he said.

The Decca label was doing well at the time. It specialised in British acts and had any number of good-looking balladeers on its books. Dickie Valentine had the Christmas Number 1 with 'Christmas Alphabet', while David Whitfield ('When You Lose The One You Love') and Jimmy Young ('Someone On Your Mind') were having hits with forgettable ballads. For your Christmas party, you could choose between the jaunty piano medley of Winifred Atwell ('Let's Have A Ding Dong') and the Johnson Brothers' harmonies ('Join In And Sing Again'). Decca's Stargazers were competing with the Coronets and Alma Cogan on the novelty hit, 'Twenty Tiny Fingers'. The pop hits of the day were competent and pleasant, but something earth-shattering was making its way to the top - Bill Haley and his Comets with 'Rock Around The Clock', released on Brunswick and distributed through Decca. As it happens, the song's nonsensical couplets with a chirpy chorus have much in common with 'Rock Island Line', and one song could almost be sung to the tune of the other.

Rock'n'roll was coming and popular music would never be the same again. 'It Came From Outer Space' was a scary 50s sci-fi film but the title could have referred to Elvis Presley and Little Richard, both of whom were having UK chart success by the middle of 1956.

Decca would not undertake much promotion on jazz singles as fans were more likely to buy albums. The singles were unlikely to be hits, but radioplay could encourage album sales. The promotion team realised that 'Rock Island Line' was different. Although attributed to Chris Barber's Jazz Band on the album, it now had the strange billing of the Lonnie Donegan Skiffle Group and the very title, 'Rock Island Line' sounded like a novelty. The first disc-jockey to play the record was Eamonn Andrews on his 'Pied Piper' programme. He had just recorded a narration, 'The Shifting, Whispering Sands', so he warmed to Lonnie's spoken introduction. Helping this record into the charts might increase his own chances and, indeed, he made the Top 20. The bandleader, Jack Payne, who became a staunch opponent of rock'n'roll, promoted Lonnie's single on the BBC programmes. Complementing the Americana in Lonnie's song was Tennessee Ernie Ford's 'Sixteen Tons', a deep voiced novelty that told of the injustices of company stores in the south of America, and a song which would have been ideal for Lonnie.

When 'Rock Island Line' made the charts in January 1956, Lonnie told the 'New Musical Express' that he had no plans to go solo: "We work sometimes as much as seven engagements a week, and as we are a cooperative band, we're all quite well off financially.

In any case, I don't want to be swept along on the tide of the latest gimmick and then left high and dry when it wears off." Lonnie's comments on his earnings are so uncharacteristic that I wonder if he said it. Lonnie knew little about the charts at the time and the jazz musicians were snobbish about it. "I would have a sly look at the charts and sometimes chuckle to myself," said Lonnie.

At the time though, Lonnie was still committed to Chris Barber's band. He did occasional promotions on his own: "My first solo broadcast was doing 'Rock Island Line' with Cyril Stapleton and his Orchestra. I was very embarrassed because I couldn't read music and I didn't have any parts for the musicians. However, Bert Weedon was playing for Cyril and he came up and congratulated me. He said, 'You're the first man to have made any money out of the guitar. Bloody well done!'."

The freight train on the 'Rock Island Line' sped its way to Number 8. It was regarded as a humorous record because most listeners would not know the song's background and, in any event, half the records on the charts were either adult novelties - including rock'n'roll dance songs, 'Pickin' A Chicken' with Eve Boswell, and the craze for crew cuts with Frankie Vaughan's 'My Boy Flat Top' - or children's novelties - 'The Ballad Of Davy Crockett' and 'Robin Hood'. 'Rock Island Line' apart, the only song on the Top 20 to have endured as a standard is 'Only You'. Another peculiar statistic is that, in April 2003, there are hardly any survivors from that chart. Don't become a pop singer if you want a long life.

John Lennon bought the 78rpm of 'Rock Island Line' and played it incessantly. A year or two later he had moved to rock'n'roll and he sold his copy to another Quarry Man, Rod Davis. Rod, who still has the single and loaned it for display in The Beatles Experience at the Albert Dock in Liverpool, says that the centre was chipped because John had been taking it on and off the spindle. "My copy was the same," says Gerry Rafferty, "It was a great record and I used to play it to death. Skiffle was a very primitive form of music, and it gave working class kids with no musical education the opportunity to perform simple songs with simple instruments."

Chris Barber's Jazz Band was now signed to Pye's Nixa label, and Decca realised that Lonnie would be following up his hit with a rival company. "It wasn't entirely Decca's fault because the whole British recording scene was a cottage industry. There were three big companies and their prime function was to make American records available over here. No one knew what to do when a British artist started selling."

Decca looked at the tracks that they had featuring Donegan and came to the extraordinary conclusion that his live performance of Washboard Sam's ribald 'Diggin' My Potatoes' would be suitable. There was no way a song about marital infidelity could be played on the BBC in 1956, especially the way it was expressed:

"I crept up to the window, thought I heard a moan,
I heard somebody say, 'Oh, you're suckin' my sweet bone',
You're diggin' my potatoes, trampling on my vine,
I had a worried feeling resting on my mind."

When I heard 'Diggin' My Potatoes' as an 11-year-old in 1956, the imagery was totally lost on me and I had no idea why the BBC had banned it. Probably because of the ban, the record failed to make the charts. In 1965 the song was a Top 50 entry for Heinz and the Wild Boys.

As usual, the band recorded prolifically. Over the next few weeks, the Lonnie Donegan Skiffle Group recorded six tracks at their sessions. Four of them made the EP, 'Skiffle Session'. Lonnie tells the story of 'Railroad Bill', whom he plans to assassinate for stealing his wife. 'Ol' Riley' is about a fugitive prisoner from a chain gang: the song is sometimes known with different verses but the same holler, 'Here Rattler', as recorded by Grandpa

Jones. The fugitive has immersed himself in the river so that the bloodhounds would lose his trail. Dickie Bishop is subdued on 'Stackalee', later recorded by Lloyd Price as a raucous rock'n'roll record, and 'The Ballad Of Jesse James', a glorification of the American outlaw. When Jesse went legit, he used the pseudonym Mr. Howard, hence the reference in the song's chorus.

A significant session was on 20 February 1956 when Donegan, Dick Bishop, Chris Barber and Ron Bowden recorded 'Lost John' ("Now this here's a story about an escaped convict called Long Gone Lost John) and 'Stewball' ("Now this here is a story about a racehorse called Stewball"). These are two of Donegan's best sides, although Lonnie is hoarse towards the end of 'Lost John'. It is told with much good humour:

"If anybody asks you who sung the song,
Tell 'em Lonnie Donegan's been here and gone."

Lonnie said, "Folk singers personalise the songs all the time, so why not?" The song also brought a new word to England: Lost John's shoes look the same front and back and "You couldn't tell which-a-way Lost John gwine."

The interplay with the backing vocalists (Barber and Bishop) is particularly good on 'Stewball' and the speed generated by the song gives an example of the control exerted by Donegan's voice. Maybe that explains the hoarseness. Ron Bowden played drums: "Lonnie loved 'Stewball', he thought it was a great song, and it was terrific being on those records. I can't remember any hassle about the sessions at all. My part certainly was very straightforward, but Lonnie gave his all, all the time. He worked bloody hard when he was on stage and he was always pushing the tempos."

Several American artists covered 'Rock Island Line', notably the veteran New York balladeer Don Cornell ('Hold My Hand', 1954), Grandpa Jones and a young Bobby Darin, but despite what some sources say, not Johnny Cash. Darin's cover included an annoying train whistle and he ruined his chances by forgetting the words on a TV show hosted by Tommy and Jimmy Dorsey. Lonnie made Number 8, Don Cornell 59, and Stan Freberg 79, although it is Freberg's 'Heartbreak Hotel' side that is listed.

Johnny Cash somehow believed that Lonnie had deprived him of a hit: listen to how he acknowledges Lonnie's presence in the audience on his 1976 album, 'Strawberry Cake': "I heard Lonnie Donegan is in the audience tonight, so will you take a bow, Lonnie, wherever you are out there. In 1958 Lonnie Donegan was all we heard and so too was this 'Rock Island Line' song. We recorded it on Sun Records before it came out by Lonnie Donegan, probably nobody heard it because it didn't get played on the right stations, so we'll do it for you tonight." Johnny is mistaken: he recorded 'Rock Island Line' after Lonnie Donegan and it was the B-side of his March 1957 single, 'Next In Line'. Good version but judging by Cash's narration, he had been listening to Donegan, although he has different verses. The Sun version of 'Rock Island Line' by Johnny Cash did make Number 35 on the US Country Charts in 1970.

Lonnie says, "You get the same story from Frankie Laine. He'd been bashing the earholes of his record company trying to get them to let him record 'Rock Island Line'. No one would listen to him and when he discovered that my version had come out, he was very annoyed."

Don Cornell had come to the UK to tour the Moss Empires. His manager, Manny Greenfield, thought it would be a good press story to put the two recorders of 'Rock Island Line' together and they met at the Finsbury Park Empire. Greenfield was surprised to discover that Lonnie didn't have a manager. Sign here, kid...

Don Cornell had hoped for the US hit with 'Rock Island Line', but Lonnie won through and Manny Greenfield arranged for Lonnie to appear on 'The Perry Como Show', which had colossal viewing figures. The show's producer did not want Chris Barber's band as the record was essentially Lonnie with Chris and Beryl. Lonnie discussed it with the band, who said his job would be there when he returned and he took a fortnight's holiday: Chris Barber said, "Lonnie, this is the jam, but the band is your bread and butter." It was a traumatic time to go away. Lonnie had married Maureen Tyler on 31 March 1955, and their first child, Fiona, was born on 13 March 1956.

When Lonnie arrived at rehearsals, the Musicians' Union would only allow him to perform as a singer. He had never performed without something in his hands before, but Perry Como gave him some helpful advice. Donegan, still looking uncomfortable, was backed by the studio orchestra, many of whom were jazzman. The single climbed to Number 8, the same position as in the UK, and this was at a time when British records rarely made the US charts. Jerry Allison of the Crickets recalls that Buddy Holly loved the record and they would perform their own version in small clubs around Lubbock, Texas. "We thought it was a rock'n'roll record," said Jerry.

Indeed. In the 1950s Lonnie had been amazed when some journalists had described him as a rock'n'roll singer. "But you sing 'Rock Island Line', don't you?" said one reporter. "Yes, but if it was 'Rock Of Ages'," responded Lonnie, "would you still call me a rock'n'roll singer?"

Whatever, Lonnie Donegan knew he was lucky to have a hit in America: "It was a freak hit as British performers didn't have hits in America. To be asked to go to America and sing American songs to the Americans in American was a weird experience. I appeared on 'The Perry Como Show' with guest star, Ronald Reagan. Being a film star, he was a distinguished guest and he had to take part in a little sketch that involved us together. Ronald Reagan said, 'Well, what is a Lonnie Donegan?', and silly gags like that. He was a romantic actor so you couldn't expect him to be hilariously funny or do dances or sing songs. I was asked to do all sorts of television and rock'n'roll shows. 'Time' magazine came for an interview. I was also extremely flattered when Stan Freberg did 'Rock Island Line'. He did a parody of Elvis on the other side and they were both very funny. He did others afterwards, some of which were funny and others that were not. Nobody is without sin, some work, some don't work, but 'Rock Island Line' was particularly good."

After the Como show, Lonnie returned to his hotel in Times Square with just £5 in his pocket "and they said they would call me." The next night, Lonnie was booked to perform at a large night club, the Town And Country, in New York. Again he could not play guitar and he gave an expressive performance, basing his presentation on Harry Belafonte's. Lonnie recalled, "The next job was in a rock'n'roll show in Detroit. It was ridiculous and I felt like a human sacrifice. All the coloured acts were backed by an orchestra but I had no parts as I'd come from a jazz band. I was alone with a little Martin guitar and I had to sing 'Rock Island Line'. We would do five shows a day, the audience would sit down with a bunch of sandwiches, put their feet on their stage and sit there for 12 hours. In between the performances, they screened a terrible English thriller to get people to leave. When it got to the third show of the day, one girl shouted out to me, 'Cut out all that shit, man, just get on with the song.'

The rock'n'roll show opened at the Fox Theatre in Detroit on 21 June 1956 and featured LaVern Baker, Frankie Lymon and the Teenagers, the Cleftones, Johnny 'Guitar' Watson, Lonnie Donegan and several other acts. Lonnie Donegan: "The Johnny Burnette Rock'n'Roll Trio was on the show and on the second day, Johnny said, 'We love what you're doing, man, can we come out and play out with you?' I said, 'Thank you very much, but my money won't run to that.' He said, 'Who said anything about money? Man, we just want to play with you.' I said, 'Great', and from then on they were my backing group. Dorsey Burnette played slap-bass and the guitarist, Paul Burlison, played like the guy who played with Elvis, Scotty Moore. Johnny slashed the guitar like me and sang like a cross between me and Elvis. We enjoyed ourselves after that."

A succession of dates followed on rock'n'roll package shows with Chuck Berry and Frankie Lymon and the Teenagers, night clubs, dance halls and television variety. Usually, it was not hard work - if he was on a rock'n'roll show, he would only perform 'Rock Island Line' and 'Lost John', although he might have to do it five times a day. When he played in one casino, he had to compete with the noise of one-armed bandits. He said, "Aren't you Americans ashamed of yourselves?" Everyone turned and looked and he said, "All this beautiful American folk music that you don't want to listen to belongs to you." He went down well after that.

Lonnie soon tired of the bookings and felt lost and alone. He asked Maureen to come over, so she left their baby with her parents and flew to America. They took a holiday in Memphis and New Orleans. Manny Greenfield wanted him to join a ten week tour, but he had no inclination to do this and besides, "I had a telegram from Pye saying, 'Come home. You're Number 2 in the charts with 'Lost John'.'"

Lonnie didn't mind leaving America, telling Alan Clayson in 'Record Collector': "I didn't see success over there as long term. The main incentive for me going over was to see all the jazz musicians I admired live in Birdland and New Orleans, all expenses paid. I had every intention of coming back and rejoining Chris Barber, but the agent booked me for all sorts of rock'n'roll shows." Reading between the lines, Lonnie was looking for songs he could record.

It became difficult for Lonnie to remain with Chris Barber's Jazz Band. Chris Barber: "When Lonnie got a hit, he got offers to go solo and earn enormous amounts of money. Our band was a cooperative and he had the cheek to ask for more money if he was to stay in the band. He said, 'Look, I'm bringing so much more to the band so I should be paid more.' I said, 'Lonnie, skiffle is bringing in more money now, but next time it might be clarinet solos - ha, ha.' Next thing I know, 'Petite Fleur'. The point I was making was that if you're going to have all for one, then it's one for all. If you then say that somebody's more equal than somebody else, then it's 'Animal Farm'. We were happy when he decided to go. He was getting £400 a week at the Glasgow Empire just to play 'Rock Island Line' and 'Midnight Special', which is what he liked doing anyway."

Ron Bowden: "It was inevitable that Lonnie would leave but I am sure he missed playing the banjo. I had the impression that it was his first love and he was a terrific player."

Dickie Bishop: "He was an extremely good banjo player, he had an incredible right hand, he was almost as good as George Formby. They both had fantastic rhythm in their right hands."

Guitarist Diz Disley: "Donegan asked me to join his skiffle group when he went off on his own but I didn't want to. I didn't like him very much and we didn't get on too well. I'm not alone in that. A lot of people didn't like him, he was too big-headed, and success didn't change him! I didn't think much to his banjo playing and he knew that."

Chris Barber might have expected to put Dickie Bishop in Lonnie's role, but he jumped ship and went with Donegan, albeit briefly. However, Chris had little trouble in finding a replacement for Donegan: "We played The 100 Club and in walked a bloke looking just like Lonnie, wearing the same clothes, and we did a double-take. It was Johnny Duncan, an American serviceman who'd married a British girl and stayed over here. He'd been in Bill Monroe's Bluegrass Boys and he could play both a mandolin and a Jumbo Martin behind his head. The mandolin's okay but it's hard work to even reach the Jumbo. Lonnie's voice was a bit nasal, country and western sounding, and Johnny's voice was the same thing raised to the n'th power. It was very squeaky indeed but people were expecting skiffle from us so he was just right."

Dickie Bishop: "Lonnie asked me to join his band, but I preferred to stay with Chris and I took over on banjo. Johnny Duncan and I got a completely different thing going with

country music. We were like the Everly Brothers, we got a lovely thing going there."
Not everyone was pleased with Lonnie's success. James Asman, a key figure in the
promotion of traditional jazz, in London savaged him in 'Melody Maker'. He condemned
'Lost John' and 'Stewball', saying, "Both sides carefully ape the style of the original hit
single with Lonnie wailing vigorously throughout to a skiffle accompaniment by members of
the Barber group. As a jazz record, it can only be described as phoney." He suggested that
Lonnie was an Irish country singer, whose appeal could be compared to the yodelling Slim
Whitman. Asman advised, "Lonnie might do well to discard his incursions into the dead
Ledbetter's library of folk ballads, and let the husky Negro folk artiste rest more easy in his
grave. Jimmie Rodgers, Hank Williams, Montana Slim, the Carter Family and many of the
great hillbilly singers offer songs as well as a style of singing which might pay very healthy
dividends."
'Lost John' had entered the charts in April 1956 and was in the Top 3 throughout June. It
only made Number 58 in the US. It was a favourite of the young John Lennon, perhaps
regarding himself as long lost John. He performed it with his group, the Quarry Men, a year
later and he also recorded a fun treatment with Klaus Voormann and Ringo Starr in 1970,
which was produced by Phil Spector. John doesn't remember all the words and goes into
'Railroad Bill', ending with the words, "I'm defunct."
Lonnie had to form a new group quickly, both for recording and touring. Mickey Ashman
from the Barber band joined him on bass, and Monty Sunshine recommended his friend,
Nick Nicholls. Nick had no intention of playing the washboard, saying, "Why should I play
the washboard when I can afford to play the drums?" Lonnie saw the Vipers at the Cat's
Whiskers and invited their acoustic guitarist, John Booker, to join them for a recording
session the next day, which was 2 August 1956. Unfortunately, he overslept and so the
producer, Denis Preston, called their friend, Denny Wright. Denys Justin Freeth Wright was
born in Bromley in 1924 and was noted for playing jazz guitar like Django Reinhardt and
for Latin-American rhythms with Edmundo Ros. He was still in bed, but he threw on his
clothes (actually over his pyjamas!) and arrived at the session within half an hour. He
brought a Hofner electric guitar, so Lonnie only went electric because someone had
overslept.
Because of the delay they could only get two songs down, but they were good ones -
Leadbelly's 'Bring A Little Water, Sylvie' ('Now this here is a story about a man a-workin'
in a field') and Woody Guthrie's Dead Or Alive'. 'Sylvie' was another example of
Donegan's frantic vocalising and his picture of the desperado in 'Dead Or Alive' was vividly
captured. As with 'Lost John' and 'Stewball', both sides were listed on the charts and it
became a Top 10 single.
Nick Nicholls: "There is a thing in traditional music called controlled acceleration. It was
done to create excitement but we held the tempo, we increased the excitement by repetition.
I never considered Lonnie to be an excellent singer but what he did was excellent. As a
vocalist he had a whine to his voice, the sort of whine you can hear it in cowboy music. His
voice was a distillation of the different artists that he had listened to."
John Peel: "Lonnie beat Elvis to the charts by five or six months and he was unlike anything
we had heard before. Lonnie Donegan let you know that there was a mad joy to be had
from popular music where you could shriek along with his stuff and let go. I also loved his
voice. I love that nasal whine which nobody has really done since. It is terribly dramatic
like that very high guitar-playing on Gene Vincent's records." A comparison can also be
made with the high-pitched vocals on bluegrass records.
On the other hand, Ken Colyer was unimpressed with skiffle's popularity and told me, "I
viewed it all with great distaste. I have never flown under false colours." Umm, yes, what
about those Decca singles of 'The Grey Goose' and 'Take This Hammer'?
In August 1956, Lonnie made his performing debut with his own group and they were the

star turn on variety shows. An Irish comic said to him, "You bring 'em in, son, and we'll entertain them." Lonnie said, "He was partly right. Lots of people went to see a variety show every Friday night, no matter who the artists were. I had to adapt, I had to learn how to present an act."

Lonnie also made the album, 'Showcase', in two days. That sounds extremely hurried now, but it was normal for 1956. The highlight is Lonnie's dynamic 'Frankie And Johnny': he relates the story very well and although it would have made a great single, it was considered too long at five minutes. The arrangement blurs any distinction between skiffle and rock'n'roll, although Denny was more a jazz guitarist.

Marty Wilde: "A lot of the skiffle songs were silly, they didn't make much sense to me. Not that the early rock'n'roll songs were a lot better but there was a certain amount of honesty in rock'n'roll. Skiffle was just like folk songs tarted-up. I loved Lonnie's 'Rock Island Line' though - it's a classic - and I also love his version of 'Frankie And Johnny', which is the best blues singing I have ever heard in this country from any white singer, it's great."

Lonnie Donegan: "God bless Marty for saying that. It was the first piece of heavy rock, and it was designed with that in mind. We did play heavy. We didn't have a sound for wimps. Way, way back, I was always a shouter and a screamer and a thumper and banger and I have never been accused of over-finesse." So it's official - Lonnie Donegan invented heavy metal.

Lonnie travels the rock island line with two more train songs, Roy Acuff's 'The Wreck Of The Old '97' and a whooping, hollering 'Wabash Cannonball', which could easily have been a hit single. In a more restrained mood, Lonnie performs two blues, Leroy Carr's 'How Long, How Long Blues' and Lonnie Johnson's 'I'm A Ramblin' Man'. He puts the country weepie 'Nobody's Child' on record and has a playful interchange with Denny Wright on 'I'm Alabammy Bound'. The spiritual 'I Shall Not Be Moved' is based on the Weavers' arrangement.

Two more tracks were recorded at the session - a remake of 'Rock Island Line', although Pye could not, by copyright law, release that until at least five years after the Decca release. In fact, Pye did not issue it until a 'Golden Hour' compilation in 1971. The other track was 'Don't You Rock Me, Daddy-O', which became the next single with 'I'm Alabammy Bound' on the flip.

Adam Faith told me in 1997: "Lonnie is the great hero of almost everybody who was around in that period. When you listen to his records, they are still fantastic. He had an amazing voice, and he and Paul McCartney are the best singers that this country has ever produced. Lonnie was way ahead of us all, he was singing black music before we even knew it existed. If Lonnie had been born now, he would be revolutionising music in some way."

After 10 drab years of rationing , austerity and living with the constant reminders of bomb sites and injured servicemen, the country was becoming optimistic. The youth had spending money and wanted to enjoy themselves. They enjoyed music that their parents couldn't identify with. 1956 was, quite simply, an extraordinary year. Lonnie Donegan himself had had a hit single in America with 'Rock Island Line' and won a gold disc. He had had three hit singles in the UK and both an EP ('Skiffle Session') and an LP ('Showcase') had sold enough to enter the UK singles chart. And the new rock'n'roll was skiffle.

VIPERS SKIFFLE GROUP
ou Rock Me Daddy-o"/
000 Years Ago"
LOPHONE R.4261.

OB CORT SKIFFLE GROUP
ou Rock Me Daddy-o"/
a Worried Man to Sing
Worried Blues"
ECCA F-J.10831.

NNIE DONEGAN KIFFLE GROUP
ou Rock Me Daddy-o"/
Alabammy Bound"
NIXA N.15080

RYL BRYDEN'S KROOM SKIFFLE
Jones"/" Kansas City
Blues"
ECCA F-J.10823.

SIGNIFICANT FEATURE ABOUT THIS f skiffle pottage is that f the releases, from companies. all fight to one " pop " hit. " Don't k Me Daddy-o ".

just for the record I Bob Cort version the h the Vipers running it second. But, in the manner of commercial rs, I have little doubt Lonnie Donegan will lot of them on sheer ures, that is, providing nage to get out sufficient to the retailers. At the nearly every Nixa, Van-Mercury and Emarcy er is hard to get. The s hopelessly behind the which must be infuriat-the Nixa publicist who blood trying to promote tes and Top Ten record only to find that all this neutralised by a factory 't keep up with the rush. is no doubt, too, that ers and the Bob Cort re indebted to this situa-or when the Skiffle fans , wherever they go, shops of supplies of Lonnie n they often listen to his the field, buy them, and s lost. I calculate that in this fashion, must ot thousands of fans, plus mount of percentage

however, is just another awful headaches public-nagers and agents must in every day business recourse to Aspirin, or Aspro—or arsenic. does explain, in a small why the record shops en't got supplies of some e popular Rock 'n' Roll kiffle numbers—and it t be your chance for a while to go out and our money on something worth while like a Jelly orton, a Louis, an Oliver eadbelly.

LONNIE WILL LICK THE LOT!

Meanwhile this sort of half-hillbilly-half barbecue music is making headway, even against my firm disapproval! And there is no doubt, I must admit, that jingles like " Don't You Rock Me, Daddy-o " will take on. They have a lively attraction which makes even my reluctant foot tap slightly.

But one ought to consider the meaning of titles such as these. The Top Ten these days is filled with suggestive tune titles. " Rock ", my tender little chickens, refers by no means obliquely to sexual intercourse, and a " Daddy-o " could be a dirty old man.

It all goes to show, doesn't it?

CHAS. McDEVITT SKIFFLE GROUP
with NANCY WHISKEY

le Direction: BILL VARLEY, 6 Denmark St., London,
E 7934

The Vipers Skiffle Group

LONNIE DONEGAN AND HIS SKIFFLE GROUP

Lonnie Donegan showcase nixa

Wabash Cannonball / How
Long, How Long Blues/
Wreck Of The Old '97/I'm
A Ramblin' Man/ Frankie and
Johnny / Nobody's Child / I
Shall Not Be Moved / I'm
Alabammy Bound

LONNIE DONEGAN'S 'LOST FILM' MYSTERY IS SOLVED by KEITH GOODWIN

FOR thousands of his fans, I have solved the mystery of Lonnie Donegan's "lost film". It is "Light Fingers", in which Lonnie is prominently featured. After a "disappearance" of two years, it will be premiered in London this month!

Parkside Film Productions completed work on "Light Fingers" early in 1957, but unforeseen technical difficulties resulted in a long screening delay that has been a constant source of puzzlement in pop music circles.

However, the film in which the Donegan skiffle group are co-featured with screen stars Roland Culver, Guy Rolf, Ronald Howard, Eunice Gayson, Hy Hazell and Avril Angers, is now set to open at the Cameo-Royal, Charing Cross Road, next Saturday, May 9.

How do Lonnie and his boys fit into the story? The singing guitarist interrupted rehearsals with his group at his father-in-law's public house in Mile End, London, on Monday to explain in detail.

"The group and I are quite extensively featured," he began. "We sing the title song, a slow blues, our past hit ' Gamblin' Man', and also play all the incidental background music, which we composed too.

"**Over the opening credits, I narrate the plot and the group appear in night club settings a couple of times.**

"Then, as the final scene comes to a close, I relate the moral of the story. That's about as much as I can tell you—we did it so long ago that I've forgotten," Lonnie chuckled.

This news comes barely a week after our announcement that towards the end of next month, Lonnie begins shooting a new film which promises to be a notable milestone in his advancing screen career.

Some details of the movie were revealed in our news pages last week. Tentative title of the film is "The Hellion," to be shot by Hughie Green Productions. Appropriately enough, Lonnie portrays a skiffling bandleader, starring opposite former "Expresso Bongo" principal James Kenney.

The Villain

"I'm the real villain of the piece," Lonnie announced, with a wicked grin on his face and a merry twinkle in his eyes. "Actually," he continued " the film doesn't involve too much singing, and really doesn't offer much scope for comedy. My role is more of a straight, dramatic part."

What's the extent of Lonnie's previous acting experience? "None whatever," he said quite frankly. "I've never had a dramatics lesson in my life, but believe me, I'm willing to learn."

Mind you, although Lonnie is a newcomer to acting, he's already a " veteran " of four films, including " Light Fingers." Pop music fans, for example, will remember him in the screen version of " 6.5 Special," in which he performed two smash hits—" Grand Coolie Dam " and " Jack O'Diamonds."

Before that, however, he went before the cameras for two other movies with the Chris Barber Band, with whom he played banjo before the advent of the skiffle boom. One was " The Hypnotist," starring Paul Carpenter; the other was " Jazz Club," a semi-documentary featuring Barber's group which gave a brief insight into jazz bands and fans.

" You know," said Lonnie, " I've never seen myself on the screen. No, not even ' 6.5 Special.' I suppose most people will think that rather odd, but really, I've never had the time or opportunity to see the films."

How does Lonnie feel about entering the film world? " I'm looking forward to it," he told me. " You see, so far, I've really enjoyed what little I've done. It's not particularly easy work, but I find it very interesting.

" Of course, filming presents problems. One of the biggest to me is the lack of personal contact with an audience. Even when I do TV shows, I've always had an audience in the studio. It makes me feel more at ease.

" Put it this way," said Lonnie, warming to his subject. " When I'm on stage facing a live audience, I can see how things are going and can change my approach accordingly. With filming, it's very different. You simply face a dead camera, and apart from contact with the producer and director, there's no way of knowing how things are shaping."

I asked Lonnie how a possible career in films would interfere with his other activities in the music world. " In the first place," said Lonnie, " you've got to realise that I'm still a beginner as far as films are concerned. The success or otherwise of the film for Hughie Green is going to have a lot of bearing on my future, but whatever happens, I'm not going to give up my regular stage work.

" Filming interests me a lot. It's a whole new realm of show business which I have yet to explore, and I'm very keen on the idea. If the film does well, then I'd like to do more and more screen work, not simply in dramatic roles but also light comedies with musical interest.

" Now if this happens, and I'm cast for more films, naturally I'll have to reduce my stage appearances. But I'd like to be able to do both in equal proportions, since I wouldn't like to lose contact with variety and concert audiences," he declared.

Finally, I threw the obvious question at Lonnie—are you a regular cinemagoer? " Well, I'm not a film addict," he replied. " I go as often as I can, but I like to pick and choose the films I see.

His likes

" My favourites? Well, I like the classic comedies featuring people like Fernandel, Charlie Chaplin and the Marx Brothers.

"**I thought Jacques Tati's ' Monsieur Mulot's Holiday ' was one of the funniest films I've ever seen.**

" Then I also enjoy Shakespearian films, and serious stories when they've got great actors like the late Humphrey Bogart. But I don't like musicals too much—they seem too false to be true. Marlon Brando? I'm told he's good, but I've never seen him !"

Lonnie gave a good deal of consideration to the question of influences on his screen career. " For slapstick comedy, Chaplin is the obvious influence," he said. " From the light comedy angle, Dirk Bogarde impresses me very much, and in the serious field, I think the late Leslie Howard was excellent."

So there, in a nutshell, you have a brief résumé of Lonnie Donegan's film career to date and his aims for the future. So far, Lonnie has mastered every field of entertainment he's entered; screen success seems destined to be another feather in his cap !

New Skiffle Rival

DICKIE BISHOP

"Cumberland Gap"
"No Other Baby"

(DECCA F. 10869)

■ **L**ATEST DECCA DISC recruit to the Skiffle ranks is Mr. Bishop who works with a group differing from its contemporaries in the addition of western fiddles.

There is, in fact, a strong western flavour about the entire recording—Bishop himself working with something of an A[?] can accent.

He romps through " Cum[?]land Gap " in a manner l[?] to prove serious competiti[?] both the Vipers and Done[?] If Lonnie isn't careful, he'll [?] his pet stage number runni[?] the top on rival sides !

The echo effect is [?] throughout Bishop's disc, ar[?] successful for a while, but [?] throwback palled on me be[?] I finished hearing " No O[?] Baby." This is a slower [?] from the mock cowboy [?] western fields.

The KING of Skiffles
latest and greatest

LONNIE DONEGAN

Recorded during his fabulous
London Palladium Performance
" Putting on the Style "
"Gamblin' Man"

Photo-flair
Photography

nixa N 15093

LONNIE on LP
' LONNIE DONEGAN SHOWCASE '

Distributed by Pye Group Records (Sales) Ltd., 66 Haymarket, London, SW1

A SKIFFLE 'CERT'

LONNIE DONEGAN

"Gambling Man"
"Putting On The Style"

(NIXA N. 15093)

THE SKIFFLE STAR'S latest pairing was actually recorded during a performance at the London Palladium on May 9.

But if you saw Lonnie's act at any other of his Palladium appearances let me warn you that the lyrics of "Putting on the Style" have been abbreviated. On the disc, they do NOT (naturally!) include Donegan's cracks apropos Tommy Steele! The number still emerges as a comfortable breeze for Lonnie's lot, however.

"Gambling Man" is a furious skiffler in the Nixa boy's true colours. Frantic repetition of the title, the groaning intakes of breath and the wild instrumental antics are all there.

It builds to fever pitch for the run-out audience applause. Commercially, I should think it's home and dry.

ve) Lonnie on '6-5 Special with Pete Murray
o Douglas. (Below) Performing "Jack O'Diamonds"
5 Special film.

As Wishee-Washee in Panto at Chisick Empire

LONNIE DONEGAN

PYE nixa

I'M JUST A ROLLIN' STONE
(Extra, Donegan)
LONNIE DONEGAN
and his Skiffle Group

Skiffle ace LONNIE DONEGAN, caught by RM cameraman DAVID LOUIS, give of enthusiasm over the fact that he has both an LP and a "single" out this week on is a ten-incher. "Lonnie." "Single" is "Betty, Betty, Betty"/"Sally, Don't You Grie
Dave Gell's review, page 14).
Lonnie is in the Royal Command show at Glasgow on July 3. Two days later, he's i panel game on ABC TV, "Can Do." Then, on July 7, he starts his summer seaso
Palace, Blackpool.
Reports from America say dee-jays out there are looking eagerly forward to the rele
Donegan discs on the DOT label. (Lonnie told the RM this week that the deal is now
final stages of negotiation). —RM Picture.

Viewers of Granada's "Chelsea at Eight" on Tuesday saw LONNIE DONEGAN without his group. It played off-vision for the first number, but for "Grand Coolie Dam," Lonnie sang and accompanied himself. He's been asked to return as "a folk singer," which is how he was introduced by Bernard Braden on Tuesday.

5. SINGAWAY, LONNIE, SINGAWAY
1957 - Skiffle's year

n 1957 the comedians, and I use that word loosely, Morris and Mitch released an EP called 'Six Five Nothing Special'. It included a 'narration with music', 'What Is A Skiffler?'. It was nowhere near as sharp as Stan Freberg's 'Rock Island Line', but it indicates how skifflers were regarded at the time - adolescent male bohemians frequenting Soho coffee bars and playing two chords on makeshift instruments. A skiffler, the plum-voice narrator says, is a "bearded, chick-chasin' bundle of noise." The record's best moment is when a toff makes his record and breaks into a phoney American accent for 'Don't You Rock Me, Daddy-O'.

The record, presumably aimed at parents, states that "You can lock him out of your record collection, but you can't lock him out of the hit parade." The irony is that the skifflers were locked out of the hit parade. Lonnie Donegan aside, hardly any skifflers made the charts. None of the other acts had a skiffle hit before 1957 and none of them had a hit after 1957. This is the sum total of the skiffle hits, including Lonnie's, in 1957.

Vipers - Don't You Rock Me, Daddy-O' (Highest position: Number 10: Entered chart: January 1957)
Lonnie Donegan - Don't You Rock Me, Daddy-O (Number 4, January 1957)
Vipers - Cumberland Gap (Number 10, March 1957)
Lonnie Donegan - Cumberland Gap (Number 1, April 1957)
Chas McDevitt Skiffle Group featuring Nancy Whiskey - Freight Train (Number 5, April 1957)
Vipers - Streamline Train (Number 23, May 1957)
Lonnie Donegan - Puttin' On The Style / Gamblin' Man (Number 1, June 1957)
Chas McDevitt Skiffle Group featuring Nancy Whiskey - Greenback Dollar (Number 28, June 1957)
Johnny Duncan and the Bluegrass Boys - Last Train To San Fernando (Number 2, July 1957)
Lonnie Donegan - My Dixie Darling (Number 10, October 1957)
Johnny Duncan and the Bluegrass Boys - Blue Blue Heartaches (Number 27, October 1957)
Johnny Duncan and the Bluegrass Boys - Footprints In The Snow (Number 27, November 1957)
Lonnie Donegan - Jack O'Diamonds (Number 14, December 1957)
Scarcely an album's worth of hits and the very name of Johnny Duncan's group indicates that he wasn't playing skiffle at all, but who knew any better in 1957?

Wally Whyton took a shanty, 'Sail Away, Ladies', and used the contemporary expression, 'Daddy-O', to create 'Don't You Rock Me, Daddy-O'. He explained, "Lonnie Donegan came to the Coffee Pot one night and he heard us sing it. He went away and recorded it and his publisher asked him who wrote it. He told the publisher to ask me. I said that the rewrite was mine so he gave me a publishing contract. George Martin said, 'If Lonnie's going to have an enormous hit with this, we should jump in with our own version.' We recorded the same song and put it out."

The Vipers, featuring Wally Whyton, were the new kids on the block and, given the vast numbers of folk songs to choose from, it is strange that Lonnie Donegan should have taken something from their repertoire, 'Don't You Rock Me, Daddy-O'. It looked mean-spirited, and if he had lost the chart race, his career would have been damaged.

To an extent, Donegan was being generous. Wally Whyton retained the shanty's chant, "Sail away, ladies, sail away", which occurs 10 times. There are five short verses, describing how his girlfriend is buying a dress, and the title line is repeated 40 times. Donegan has three verses (all different from the Vipers), changes the chant to "Sing away, ladies, sing away" (12 times) and halves the chorus so that the title only occurs 16 times. To add colouring, Denny Wright takes a guitar solo, and it is a far better record.

Strangely, the Vipers had one advantage over Lonnie Donegan. Pye had no truck with the new-fangled 45rpm records. Even though 'Rock Island Line' had been pressed on both 78 and 45 for Decca, his Pye singles up to this point were resolutely 78. Pye was using pliable vinyl rather than brittle shellac, but that was no improvement as a mixture of the two types of 78s didn't respond well on auto-change machines, and two 78s would come down at once. All in all, it was a curious decision and one which must have harmed Donegan's sales. This also explains why Pye was keen to issue a series of extended plays called 'The Lonnie Donegan Hit Parade'. A collector who rejected 78s as old-fashioned could purchase his hit songs, several months too late, in this form.

Although Lonnie was choosing commercial songs for his singles, he returned to his roots for a concert at the Conway Hall, Kingsway, London in January 1957. It was recorded by Denis Preston, who was experienced in recording jazz bands live, and his assistant was Joe Meek, who was later to make his mark with 'Telstar' and 'Johnny Remember Me'. Donegan is on tremendous form and he includes an electrifying version of Leadbelly's 'Black Girl', admittedly only after a prompt from Preston. Also included is an excellent version of 'Ella Speed'. Dickie Bishop takes the lead competently enough on 'Precious Memories', but it only emphasises how distinctive Lonnie's voice is. Although a 10 inch LP was proposed, only an EP, 'Donegan On Stage', was issued, but it included an exciting 'Muleskinner Blues' and a rousing gospel medley, 'Glory'. The full concert was released as 'Live! 1957' by a specialist label, Zircon, in 1999.

A few years before the release of that album, Lonnie said, "There was an invited concert at the Conway Hall in London and the audience got so excited that they rendered the recording impossible, and it was the first rock'n'roll riot that they had ever had in Britain. A few chairs got thrown and they managed to rescue six tracks and they issued four of them as a live EP." That being the case, Lonnie must have been as surprised by 'Live! 1957' as anybody else. If not more so: when he stayed with Carl Jones in 2001, his Number 1 fan showed him a copy. He claimed that he had not seen it before, threatening to sue the record company for issuing it without his knowledge. (This is typical Lonnie behaviour and the way he would act whether he knew about it or not.)

A week after Conway Hall, Lonnie was asked to appear on the 'Festival Of Jazz' at the Royal Albert Hall, which was being broadcast live by the BBC. That night Denny Wright was as bad as he had been good at Conway Hall. He was drunk and sadly, the adrenalin charge from performing did not knock him into shape. He plays shambolically, even causing Lonnie to ask his bass player, Mickey Ashman, to take a solo instead. The broadcast must have been disastrous and it is remarkable that Zircon obtained permission to include it on their 'Live! 1957' CD. Presumably Lonnie's permission did not have to be sought.

Ever the professional, Donegan sacked Wright after the concert, although he would remain under sufferance until a replacement was found. He was featured on the single of 'Cumberland Gap', which was recorded three weeks later and was a vast improvement over the live recording. Lonnie's new guitarist was a dance band guitarist, Jimmy Currie. He had been with Tony Crombie and his Rockets, mostly a group of jazzmen who were cashing in, not too effectively, on rock'n'roll. Most listeners knew they were slumming it and didn't buy their records. He was by no means as distinctive as Denny Wright but he was, as will be seen, a fine songwriter. His first job was taking part in the film, 'Light Fingers', starring Guy Walsh and Eunice Gayson, in which the Lonnie Donegan group performed the title song and 'Gamblin' Man'.

Lonnie Donegan: "The film was a disaster. I told the director that it wasn't funny. It was

British front parlour stuff. I suggested that it would be funnier if my face appeared in the corner of the screen commenting on the action. It was turned down but when they saw the reaction to the completed film, they were begging me to do it. I said, 'No way.' I sang in a night-club scene and it was the whole Machiavellian bit. The director had written the song I was to sing and he expected me to record it. I also said 'No way' to that'." The acetate of the song was rescued from the producer, Roger Proudlock's garage by Carl Jones and included in the 1993 Bear Family set. It is a pleasant novelty and Lonnie was a little light-fingered himself as he borrowed the theme for 'Lively!'.

Writing in 'Reveille' on 23 May 1957, Lonnie said, "The present interest in skiffle has coincided with the popularity of rock'n'roll' and is mistakenly believed by many people to be connected with it. Skiffle is as different from rock'n'roll as jazz is from dance music. The essential of skiffle is continual improvisation, which is opposite to rock'n'roll with its monotonous repetition."

He also told 'Picturegoer' in 1956: "Nothing makes me madder than to be bracketed with these rock'n'roll boys. Like all gimmicks, it is sure to die the death." The TV producer, Jack Good, said, "Donegan hated rock'n'roll with a passion. He was a musical snob. Rock'n'roll to him was trash and had no pedigree."

The opinion didn't really change. He told the 'Liverpool Daily Post' the day before he played the Cavern in 2001, "I disliked rock'n'roll because in its first incarnation, it was a bastardisation of the folk music I was doing. It was the 12-bar blues played in an exaggerated manner purely for commercial benefit."

The rock writer and musicologist, Mike Brocken, comments, "The whole concept of skiffle is very interesting from a sound perspective. Because it is not rock'n'roll, it is not so loud and not so right up front. It bridges what came before and what was to come. Lonnie Donegan was the lynch pin between sound levels."

George Melly: "The first rock breakthrough was simultaneous with skiffle, and programmes like '6.5 Special' tended to mix rock'n'roll, skiffle and revivalist jazz. Lonnie himself did that to some extent. I loved what Lonnie based his stuff on - Leadbelly especially - and Lonnie's trick was to speed everything up. 'Rock Island Line' is a good example, and I had recorded that myself some five years earlier to no effect whatsoever. Lonnie's skilful enough and he certainly found a formula, but I wasn't potty about him, no."

Alexis Korner had known Lonnie for sometime and Lonnie had heard records in his London flat. Alexis wrote an article, 'Skiffle Is Piffle', for 'Melody Maker' in July 1956: "It only bears a superficial resemblance to the music which inspired it. British skiffle is, most certainly, a commercial success, but musically it rarely exceeds the mediocre and is, in general, so abysmally low that it defies proper musical judgement." He said that the music had become "a fair source of income for half the dilettante three chord thumpers in London." Lonnie struck back with the criticism that Alexis himself was on the skiffle trail when he said that he wasn't. Intriguingly, when Chris Barber played Lonnie's version of 'New Burying Ground' to the blues musician, Sonny Terry. Sonny Terry said, "That's Lead, man."

Unlike Pye, the much smaller Oriole label issued its singles in both formats. Their hitmakers, the Chas McDevitt Skiffle Group featuring Nancy Whiskey, underlined the music's preoccupation with American railways with 'Freight Train'. Chas recalls, "I was incensed that it wasn't a hit earlier. I saw everybody else in the charts and I thought I should be there as well. We were doing the same songs but Oriole wasn't doing any advertising at all. It was a very parsimonious record company, so we had to promote it ourselves. Luckily, we got some television and it started to happen. Oriole had its own factory which was unusual, but it was so busy pressing records for other companies that we couldn't get ours done. The shops couldn't get enough copies of 'Freight Train'. Somebody latched onto it in Canada and it was then heard in New York and became a hit in the States." The record made the US Top 40 in June 1957 and led to an appearance on 'The Ed Sullivan Show', where great play was made of the fact that they had a washboard player, Marc Sharratt, whose fingers were insured for £5,000.

Lonnie returned to the States for a second tour, this time with his group and as an exchange for Bill Haley and his Comets. This time was even more bizarre as he recalled, "The Americans don't see me as a skiffle artist. To them, I am a singer of novelty songs and as such I was something a bit different. There were union problems in that I couldn't just go with my skiffle group to the States. The only way to do it was to effect an exchange. Bill Haley and the Comets were wanted in Britain and so we went over there. I was on tour with the Harlem Globetrotters, who were a very popular and highly-priced presentation. The Globetrotters were at their peak and I appeared before 150,000 at Madison Square Gardens. They had a comedy game first and then there was an hour of visual acts before the game itself. They had the best circus acts in the world and I was the opening act, more vocal than visual really. It was terrifying because the crowd was all around me and I had to walk a quarter of a mile to get out to the middle. We had a ten minute spot and the place broke up. The reaction was so fantastic that we topped the bill the following night."

Lonnie undertook 16 cities in 19 days with the Globetrotters, playing to an average of 30,000 people a show and even joining them on the cover of 'Time' magazine. He enjoyed it as he met some of his heroes - Count Basie, Louis Armstrong and Duke Ellington. When he was in Louisville, Kentucky, he received a telegram to say that his new record, 'Cumberland Gap', was in the charts. When he looked out of the window, he could see the Cumberland Gap itself.

Few English listeners would know of the Cumberland Gap, and Lonnie used to say that most people thought it was in the Lake District. In actuality, the Cumberland Gap is a natural pass through the Appalachian Mountains, and the area is rich in natural resources, timber and coal. The residents were exploited as the rights to timber were bought for a few dollars. Strip mining ruined much of the countryside.

Donegan took the American civil war song and turned it into a frantic chase, for some unstated reason, to get to Cumberland Gap. There are few words to the song, just a few rhyming couplets. It is an extraordinary performance, equal to anything from the rock'n'roll stars, and is a contender for the most exciting British record until the Beatles. (Other candidates would be 'Move It!', 'Shakin' All Over' and 'Wimoweh'.) Donegan rushes through the chorus six times and each time he does something different with his voice. In the final moments, he goes quiet and climaxes with a thunderous 'Cumberland Gap'. The verses are nonsensical but it does include one of his favourite couplets, which, in later years, he used in 'Linin' Track':

"Two old ladies sitting in the sand,
Each one wishing that the other was a man."

One of Lonnie's later musicians, Sticky Wicket recalls, "My dad bought a lot of his records and I loved 'Cumberland Gap'. I loved the energy that came out of it. He never did it in later years. He used to say, 'I'm 70, are you a sadist?'"

Lonnie's record is less than two minutes long but it is a tour de force, loosely based on the Riley Puckett and Gid Tanner original from 1924. It was futile for anyone else to cover it, but it happened. For some crazy reason, Lonnie previewed the song on the 'Festival Of Jazz' broadcast for the BBC in February 1957. Rival skifflers heard the song and decided to record it. Without a Lonnie Donegan in the group, the Vipers didn't do a bad job and their more staid performance made the Top 10. Dickie Bishop, who had been playing with Lonnie at the Festival of Jazz, released it on a Decca single, while the Cranes Skiffle Group, actually Chas McDevitt, covered it for Woolworth's Embassy label. Lonnie: "You did a record and somebody else would cover it. That was the name of the game in those days.

Dickie Bishop's an old mate of mine but he covered 'Cumberland Gap' for Decca and took about 60,000 sales from me."

Dickie Bishop: "That's not true. Lonnie and I used to do 'Cumberland Gap' together and I didn't know he was going to record it. If Lonnie's going to say that, I could say that he stole about four of his hits from me."

When 'Cumberland Gap' reached the top in April 1957, Harry Belafonte was Number 2 with 'The Banana Boat Song', then Tab Hunter with 'Young Love' and Little Richard with 'Long Tall Sally'. The four records are a microcosm of pop music at the time - skiffle, calypso, teen ballad and rock'n'roll. Belafonte is to calypso what Donegan was to skiffle - he towers over it and his records, like Donegan's, have more tension and melodrama than his competitors. He also adds his name to the songwriting credits in some cases.

Once it was a hit, Morris and Mitch recorded a parody of 'Cumberland Gap', arranged by Harry Robinson, Lord Rockingham himself. Robinson recalls, "We did a mickeytake of 'Cumberland Gap', and to make it easier, I hired Lonnie's lead guitarist, Denny Wright. I had taken a whole day to transcribe his guitar solo into music and it looked horrendous. I don't even think Segovia could have played it! I put it down in front of Denny and a whole load of expletives came out. He said, 'How on earth do you expect me to play that?' I said, 'Denny, that's what you played on Lonnie's record'."

The B-side of 'Cumberland Gap' was a further indication of Lonnie's versatility. He took Mickey and Sylvia's US rhythm and blues hit, 'Love Is Strange', and gave a hypnotic performance that, in my opinion, surpasses the original. It is only marred by all the instruments crashing in at the end! Lonnie Donegan was releasing up-tempo A-sides, but this could have been a Number 1 in its own right.

Denny Wright left Lonnie Donegan after 'Cumberland Gap', telling the press that he was going to do studio work. He was soon on the road again. Johnny Duncan had left Chris Barber and he now formed the Bluegrass Boys, bringing in Denny Wright on lead guitar. Denny's solo on Johnny Duncan's 'Last Train To San Fernando' undoubtedly helped it to become a hit.

Lonnie Donegan was asked to support the Platters at the London Palladium in May 1957, and then a month later, he was topping the bill in his own right at London's biggest theatre, the Hippodrome. Much of the Lonnie Donegan edition of Fans' Star Library (1959) was PR hype, but one sentence rings true. Lonnie says, "You may think I made a lot of money out of that, but believe me I did not. A lot of money was made, but Lonnie didn't see much of it."

This is true. After the first year, Lonnie asked his accountant if he could buy a new Jaguar for £900. The accountant told him No, he couldn't. His earnings after tax were £1,125. Lonnie had learnt a lesson, but it had been an expensive one.

Denis Preston was asked to record Lonnie's five song spot at the London Palladium and this resulted in two new titles, Woody Guthrie's 'Gamblin' Man' and an old pop tune, 'Puttin' On The Style', recorded first by Vernon Dalhart in 1924. 'Gamblin' Man', on paper a much better song than 'Cumberland Gap', was given an equally frenetic treatment and Lonnie introduces his new guitarist with the words, 'How about Jimmy?' His solo is indistinguishable from that on a rock'n'roll record.

'Puttin' On The Style', with just banjo, bass and tambourine accompaniment, mocked its potential record-buyers as much as 'What Is A Skiffler?' did, but not to alienate them. Lonnie is also acknowledging that he is no longer young:

"As I look around me, I sometimes have to smile,
Seeing all the young folks puttin' on the style."

The implication is, I've seen it all before and isn't it boring. Lonnie Donegan was giving out contrasting messages as Princess Margaret was known to be a fan. 'Puttin' On The Style' went back several decades and, indeed, the young man in a hot-rod car had been riding a horse in the original. The song had been updated by Norman Cazden, a Harvard graduate like Tom Lehrer who had studied piano under Aaron Copeland. Donegan's love of music hall was coming through - note his camp, "With a pair of yellow gloves he's borrowed from his dad." Dickie Valentine, who was far better placed to scoff at the youths of the day, recorded a cover version with different verses. Although no one bought Valentine's version, it was invariably played on the BBC and on Radio Luxembourg's chart of sheet music sales. Lonnie's flippant verse about religion nearly caused the record to be banned completely.

As if to emphasise the music hall content of the song, the squarest of square bandleaders, Billy Cotton, included 'Puttin' On The Style', on the Top 20 charity single, 'All Star Hit Parade, Volume 2'. The record also included the Beverley Sisters with 'Freight Train'. Lonnie parodied his own song in 'Lonnie's Skiffle Party' (1958), an ill-advised and unsuccessful attempt to regenerate life into skiffle, which with 'Knees Up Mother Brown' and the occasional gay joke is more like music hall.

'Gamblin' Man' / 'Puttin' On The Style' itself was a great double-header and it topped the UK charts. Lonnie Donegan: "I loved doing live recordings. They were good fun and exciting. These days what you hear on records may not be a group at all." But the reason was mostly expediency: Lonnie was on the road so often that it could be difficult to get him to a studio.

With 'Cumberland Gap', 'Gamblin' Man' / 'Puttin' On The Style' also gave Lonnie consecutive Number 1's. No artist had scored three consecutive Number 1's and his follow-up, 'My Dixie Darling', although very pleasant, lacked excitement and only reached Number 10. The B-side, 'I'm Just A Rollin' Stone', was too bluesy to attract many sales in its own right. The songwriting credit was given to Lonnie Donegan and Jimmy Currie, and the song is not a direct crib of the Muddy Waters' original.

Lonnie Donegan had often appeared on the teenage TV show, '6.5 Special', directed by Jack Good, and if only Good had been asked to direct the film version. '6.5 Special' was the first rock'n'roll film to appreciate that you didn't need a dopey plot - in fact, you didn't need one at all. Two girls (Diane Todd and Avril Leslie) board the 6.5 Special from Glasgow to London and find, for no apparent reason, that the train is full of British singers performing their latest singles. They end up at the BBC and Lonnie is already there, in evening dress and performing 'The Grand Coulee Dam' and 'Jack O'Diamonds'. Although Lonnie always looked youthful, he rarely dressed in the fashions of the day. Nick Nicholls; "Wearing dinner jackets was very unusual for us and I don't know why we did it. It was usually suits or handmade outfits for all of us. Lonnie was very particular about presentation. We would never be sloppily dressed."

And why wasn't Lonnie on the special itself performing his train songs? Jim Dale, of all people, performs Johnny Burnette's 'The Train Kept A-Rollin'' and the film is so lame that you wonder why the girls didn't pull the communication cord.

The film includes the '6.5 Special' regulars - Josephine Douglas, Pete Murray, the supremely unfunny Mike and Bernie Winters, and the boxer Freddie Mills. The music, like the programme, covers many bases and includes John Dankworth with Cleo Laine, Joan Regan (wonderfully made up - and she is going to bed), Dickie Valentine, Petula Clark and Russ Hamilton. The penny whistle man, Desmond Lane, is presented as a teenage idol - in your dreams, mate. The closest we get to rock'n'roll are Jackie Dennis in tartan trews with 'La Dee Dah', Don Lang with the theme song, and the King Brothers with '6.5 Jive'. On the basis of this film, rock'n'roll as well as skiffle was a spent force, but far more imaginative performances were happening elsewhere.

By the end of 1957, it was unlikely that anyone else would get a skiffle hit, so why did skiffle fall down? The homemade quality of the music was its own downfall - musicians were becoming more competent and wanted to play electric instruments, rock'n'roll had more passion and excitement, and the songs were about teenage love and preoccupations. In the end, despite Lonnie's histrionics, skiffle music was too tame to last, and it was inevitable that it would be supplanted by the more exciting and vibrant rock'n'roll. Like Lonnie's role in 'Aladdin' at the Chiswick Empire that Christmas, it was Wishee Washee.

SPECIAL FOR SKIFFLERS!

Whenever Lonnie plays a new town, he likes to form a club there, and to date there are Lonnie Donegan Skiffle and Folk Music Clubs operating in Bristol, Cardiff, Birmingham, Liverpool, Manchester and Leeds. Each member pays a shilling a week subscription and this money goes to meet the many expenses to be met.

The Skiffle Clubs have their own committee, which is responsible to the main London office, and they meet once a month or fortnight. When Lonnie happens to be in one of the towns where there is a club in operation, he holds a meeting and invites all the members for an informal get-together.

Each time Lonnie waxes a new record, he sends a copy to each club. In this way they have built up their own library of Lonnie Donegan records.

In addition to the main clubs there is a club in Shrewsbury which is run in a college for the blind by a blind girl.

As most of Lonnie's clubs have not been functioning very long and are still in their infancy, Lonnie pays the rent for the hire of the halls they use, and will continue to do so until each club is well-established and able to pay its own rent. The clubs run their own Talent Contests, visit local hospitals and altogether have tremendous fun. If you are interested in joining a branch of the Lonnie Donegan Skiffle and Folk Music Club, write to Sylvia Simmonds, 34, Greek Street, London, W.1. Please enclose a stamped, addressed envelope.

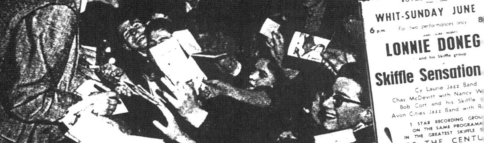

PARTY SKIFFLE

LONNIE DONEGAN and his group got into a party mood to make their latest "Skiffle Party" record which has just been released by Nixa. In the picture (l to r): LONNIE, NICK NICHOLLS, LES BENNETT and PETER HUGGETT.

(Above) Lonnie takes d of his new car, a gleami Riley Pathfinder

onnie goes on and on

LONNIE DONEGAN—Puttin' On The Style, My Dixie Darling, Gamblin' Man, I'm Just A Rolling Stone (Nixa NEP24067).

Volume Three of the Donegan Hit Parade, a series which looks like running for ever.

LONNIE DONEGAN.—Nixa have hit the jackpot with their Donegan Hit Parade series. It looks like running for ever.

LONNIE DONEGAN
"Times Are Getting Hard Boys"
"Lonesome Traveller" N.15158 (78 & 45)

There ain't gonna be no war

LONNIE

HARRY

DISC THE NEW RECORD & MUSICAL WEEKLY

the "MONARCH OF SKIFFLE" **Lonnie Donegan** SINGS TWO GREAT SONGS "JACK O' DIAMONDS" and "HAM..."

nixa DISTRIBUTED BY PYE GROUP RECORDS (SALES)

AMERICA is not the only spot with problems in scdom. Lonnie Donegan ently recorded for Nixa number entitled "Times Getting Hard." Then news flashed around the master hit-maker ry Belafonte had also ed it. The bets were cast onnie or Harry for the Ten?

ell, you can replace the s in your pocket—there not be a contest. Oh yes, y Belafonte has recorded

the number—but his disc is not coming out until 1959, I am told.

So Lonnie's v e r s i o n, coupled with "Lonesome Traveller," will continue its climb to the top unchallenged. Incidentally, for the folk with fact-and-figure brains, both sides of the Donegan disc were composed by singer Lee Hayes. He is a member of The Weavers, America's top folk-vocal (or s h o u l d it be folkal?) group.

NOBODY LOVES LIKE AN IRISHMAN

Recorded by LONNIE DONEGAN on NIXA Records

2/-

**LONNIE ON
MERSEYSII**
At St. Luke's
Hall, Crosby.

(All photos cou
of Tony Barrow

(Left) Lonnie fac
fans as he makes
Personal Appear
for Disker Music
Tony Barrow.

(Above right) Lonnie is so used to signing autographs, he can do it with his eyes shut! Seen backstage at St. Luke's Hall with Lonnie are Tony Barrow (centre) and Derek Vaux who is now the bass-player with Liverpool's veteran Merseysippi Jazz Band

(Above) Lonnie prepares to draw the winning tickets in a charity raffle during a jazz band ball at Crosby, promoted by Tony Barrow's Disker Music.

(Right) Lonnie gets Police escort with one sergeant and one shy constable

6. LONNIE'S SKIFFLE PARTIES
I. Skiffle clubs
II. Lonnie in 1958 - 'Tom Dooley'

Coming from a jazz rather than a pop background, Lonnie Donegan was uneasy with screaming fans and did not want a Fan Club, per se. He hit upon the idea of Lonnie Donegan Skiffle And Folk Music Clubs and so he was encouraging amateurs to form their own groups. They opened in many major cities - Birmingham, Bristol, Cardiff, Leeds, Liverpool and Manchester - with the headquarters being in London. A special branch was set up at a college for the blind in Sheffield. The members would pay a shilling (5p) a week, which was largely to cover expenses such as the hire of halls. When Lonnie went to a city for a week's variety, he would go to the club on a Saturday morning, signing autographs and listening to the local talent, but not playing because his contract with Moss Empires would not permit it.

Mick Groves, who became a member of the Spinners, was the Merseyside president of the Lonnie Donegan fan club. "You didn't call it a 'fan club', it was a 'skiffle club' or a 'folk club'. Lonnie's secretary was a girl I'd known in Salford and she said, 'You're singing and playing a bit and Lonnie's looking for people to run this club for him.' I said, 'Lonnie's great but I can't be bothered sending out signed photos of him.' She said, 'No, he just wants somewhere in each of the main cities that will be a focus, like a local skiffle club.' The Cavern was available and so we had a few meetings there. Lonnie Donegan came down with a young comic who was just starting his career and that was Des O'Connor."

The Liverpool solicitor David Deacon recalls going to the meetings: "They were wonderful and I remember both Clinton Ford and Des O'Connor attending. I got an invitation to meet Lonnie at 1.30pm at the Cavern and when I got there, he was at the bottom of the steps, shaking hands with everyone as they came in. It made me think, If I can meet a star like this when I am 15, I can meet anyone - and indeed it has worked out that way. The club moved to Sampson and Barlow's in London Road, but the skiffle element fizzled out. Many people wanted rock'n'roll but Mick Groves and some of the others wanted folk and that became the Spinners' club."

Lonnie is convinced that he saw the Beatles as the Quarry Men play at that function but that is unlikely. Even if he had, why would he remember? However, the Quarry Men were great fans and George Harrison borrowed money from his parents to go to the Empire to see him. Paul also saw Lonnie at the Empire, and the Quarry Men included many of Lonnie's songs in their repertoire. Lonnie wasn't sure what he had started: "I was shocked by all the skiffle clubs that opened everywhere, and the thousands of guys trying to imitate Lonnie Donegan. It was uncanny how much John Lennon sounded like me on the Quarry Men tape that turned up a few years ago."

Mick Groves joined the Gin Mill Skiffle Group and became the first washboard player to join the Musicians' Union. "I was the world's worst washboard player and I don't know how I got away with it - probably because Lonnie Donegan couldn't be everywhere. Groups were wanted for skiffle concerts and we thought we should be in the Musicians' Union. I got a letter which said, 'Thank you for joining but we don't think we're going to place a lot of work your way as a washboard player'."

And what exactly was skiffle? Wally Whyton of the Vipers: "It had to be acoustic. The flavouring was essentially three guitars, an acoustic bass and if you could slap the bass as well that was even better, and a washboard that was played with thimbles. Some people used banjos and mandolins instead of guitars and when we toured with the National Skiffle Show, we used new groups every night and they were all different."

John Pilgrim, also from the Vipers: "We were the first punk folk band - in fact, skiffle was punk folk. When you hear the Vipers' records, you hear the band that played in coffee-bars. Lonnie used session musicians on his records so that was a very different thing."

Jack Bruce, later with Cream: "I was in a skiffle group like everybody else of my age. It was a very important thing as it meant that everyone could be in a band. I was learning cello and I took my school cello and played it as a bass. (Laughs) I also got a white shirt and dyed it black."

Primitive times. Johnny Guitar played with Ringo Starr on Merseyside in the early days of Rory Storm and the Hurricanes: "Our transport used to be the 61 bus to the Stanley Road junction where we would meet Ringo Starr standing by the roundabout with a snare drum or washboard. We'd all jump on the L3 bus to St. Luke's Hall in Crosby. We'd have problems fitting the tea-chest with the broom handle under the stairs. When we got there, the stars of the show, we'd have to disgorge from the bus, complete with the tea-chest bass and snare drum."

Dave Lovelady from another Liverpool band, the Four Jays, later the Fourmost: "One bus conductor was very loath to take our tea-chest bass on the bus. After we pleaded with him, he agreed to let us stand it on the platform, right on the edge. As the bus was pulling out from the stop, a chap came running up at full pelt. He made a frantic leap for the platform but grabbed the broom-handle instead of the pole. He went sprawling on the street and the tea-chest bass went all over the road."

Folk singer Martin Carthy: "When I look back, I can see how important Lonnie Donegan was. Skiffle represented ordinary people making music. There had been this idea that music was played by trained musicians, and ordinary people didn't have anything to do with it. It enabled certain people to keep control of the music business. The music business continues to reassert its stranglehold over music and every now and then, the people take it back, which is what they did with Lonnie Donegan, which is what they did with the Beatles, which is what they did with the Sex Pistols."

Jazz musician Johnny Barnes: "You could make a double-bass out of a tea-chest with a broom handle and a piece of string, and the guitar was the most expensive instrument in the group. Nobody bothered about having a PA, you used whatever was there, and the bass or the guitar wouldn't be amplified. It was largely home-made instruments."

Ironically, Lonnie himself didn't have this primitive sound: "When we started, Bill Colyer played washboard for us and then Beryl Bryden, but we never had a regular washboard player in the line-up. It wasn't an elastic enough instrument and we soon switched to drums. We were always very professional but the songs were so simple that this encouraged the kids. Kids could bang them out with a few chords on a guitar and bashing mum's washboard and dad's suitcase. Legions of kids followed us. Nobody was playing guitars before us and you could say that rock'n'roll was the son of skiffle. If you go back far enough, nobody was playing any guitars in Britain of any nature until I started All the guitar-players have come, if not directly from Lonnie Donegan, then from one removed, maybe Chas McDevitt or Bert Weedon or the Shadows."

R&B singer Cliff Bennett: "Lonnie Donegan was certainly a great influence. It got us altogether but we played skiffle as a joke. When rock'n'roll started to take a grip on the country, we wanted to be taken seriously and so we progressed to rock'n'roll. We got banned from the traditional jazz clubs for throwing rock'n'roll songs into the act."

Lonnie felt that he played with more integrity than the first UK rock'n'rollers. He said, "Cliff, Adam and Tommy were puppets on a string. They did what their record companies told them and they covered the latest hits from America. They were not serious musicians at all and if one of them had a shiny new suit, that was it for the week."

Pete Oakman of Joe Brown's Bruvvers: "The changes happened quite quickly but gently. The instrumentation changed as the tea-chest bass went and a double-bass player moved in.

Joe elbowed him out and asked me to go from rhythm guitar to double-bass, which Dad bought for me. About two years later Joe wanted me to get a bass guitar, but we didn't realise that we needed amplification and speakers. We had the guitar and then we went to a market in the East End and bought 15 small speakers. We put holes in some plywood and attached the speakers. It sounded awful and was so embarrassing as it sounded like I was farting all the time. We got more amplification for the guitars so the whole thing was slowly moving away from skiffle. There were still skiffle numbers in the set but we started doing 'Bird Dog', 'Hula Love' and some Buddy Holly stuff."

The teenage fans usually enjoyed rock'n'roll as well as skiffle, and they would see the American stars when they came to the UK. Undoubtedly, seeing Buddy Holly live in March 1958 was akin to St. Paul's vision on the Road to Damascus for many skifflers. Lonnie himself was impressed and befriended Buddy, quizzing him about his instruments: "I spoke to him about his solid electric Fender and his new state of the amp amplifiers and he had a strange style, a fingering electric style. The only fingering you could see in Europe at that time was Spanish or classical. Buddy was like a one-man orchestra and so was the drummer, Jerry Allison, he was a one-man percussion unit, and the bass player, Joe Mauldin, had the most perfectly hit bass sounds filling the hall. Just the three of them and they were so efficient."

Buddy, Joe and Jerry were a three-man band, and Lonnie was the first in the UK with the now-standard line-up of lead guitar, rhythm guitar, bass and drums. Before Lonnie, it did not exist. All roads do lead to Lon, but all roads lead away from him as well. The roads can lead in different directions. It is not correct to say that all the skiffle groups turned to rock'n'roll. Some shunned it, and the Gin Mill Skiffle Group became those folk group entertainers, the Spinners. The Watersons, a more ethnic folk group, also played skiffle first. The Spinners sometimes recreated their skiffle days with Deryck Guyler on washboard and revived several of Lonnie's hits on the LP 'Last Night We Had a Do' (PRT N 6553) in 1984.

II.

Lonnie Donegan's high-spirited 'Jack O'Diamonds' at the end of 1957 can be seen as the death throes of skiffle. The original song, printed in a book in 1910, was about a tough prison guard but in Lonnie's hand, it is about a game of cards. The title line is not as inviting as "Cumberland Gap, 15 miles to Cumberland Gap" and the instrumental break is nowhere near as inspired as Denny Wright's. The single, which was the first to be issued on 45rpm as well as 78rpm, only reached Number 14, which was poor by Lonnie's standards. I suspect that Woody Guthrie's 'Hard Travellin'' had been the intended single, but Donegan's performance was disjointed and not released at the time. There is also an hilarious outtake where Donegan fluffs his words and the band members play what they like. The B-side to 'Jack O'Diamonds', the blues-tinged 'Ham'n'Eggs', was very good but not commercial. The song is attributed to both Lonnie and Woody Guthrie and there's no doubt that Lonnie is singing about something that passionately interested him: food.

His following single was recorded at the same session: 'The Grand Coulee Dam' and 'Nobody Loves Like An Irishman'. Woody Guthrie's poetic lyrics ("In the misty crystal glitter of the wild and windward spray") are in a class of their own. Donegan, although upping the tempo, ensures that all the words can be heard perfectly. Indeed, on his last concert tour, Lonnie took to reciting the chorus so that the audiences could appreciate the words. The song restored Lonnie to the Top 10, perhaps helped by the controversy surrounding the B-side. Lonnie and Jimmy Currie (though his name was not on the first pressings) updated a nineteenth century song, 'Nobody Loves Like An Irishman', admittedly not too thoroughly as the girl is still looking from behind her fan. He had found the lyrics in Carl Sandberg's American Songbook and added his own melody. The BBC banned the song on the grounds that Turks might find it offensive. It was the first time that a record had been banned by the BBC on racist grounds. The song was innocuous as you have to be very sensitive to be offended. These are the controversial words:

"The turbaned Turk who scorns the world
May strut about with his whiskers curled,
Keep a hundred wives under lock and key
For nobody else but himself to see.
Yet long may he pray with his El Koran
Before he can love like an Irishman."

The song also has a go at the English, the French, the Spaniards, the Dutch, the Swedes, the Russians and the Prussians. Prussians? In 1958?
Woody Guthrie had written 'Sally Don't You Grieve' in 1944 about a soldier going to war:

"I'm gonna cross that ocean wide,
Army rifle by my side,
When Hitler's beat, you can be my bride,
I told her not to grieve after me.

"When I'm gone, Sally, don't you grieve,
When I'm gone, Sally, don't you grieve,
When I'm gone, Sally, don't you grieve,
I told her not to grieve after me."

In the 1950s, the folk singer Malvina Reynolds, who wrote 'What Have They Done To The Rain', changed the words so that they applied to any boy/girl situation and it was recorded by the Gateway Singers of Iowa. Without claiming any composing credits, Donegan took their arrangement and recorded it himself, making the charts in July 1958. It is surprising that it didn't climb higher than Number 11 as Lonnie was the only Pye artist on the charts at the time and presumably their promotional staff would be pushing it all they could. Coincidentally, the Kingston Trio recorded 'Sally Don't You Grieve' with a different story (this time about under-age sex) again in March 1958, but they weren't happy with it and tried again in November, when it became the B-side of 'Raspberries, Strawberries'. The B-side of Donegan's version of 'Sally Don't You Grieve' was also listed on the charts. It was 'Betty Betty Betty', a folk narrative better known as 'Betty And Dupree' and in the style of 'Frankie And Johnny'. Dupree wants to steal some jewellery for his girlfriend., but the robbery goes wrong and he is arrested for murder. An R&B version by Chuck Willis made the US Top 40.
Lonnie Donegan made his records with Denis Preston for Record Supervision Ltd, often with Joe Meek as the recording engineer, and the results were then passed to Pye. In January 1958, Lonnie moved directly under the control of their in-house producers and the 'Daily Herald' reported that there was a £10,000 compensation fee of which Preston received 75%. Preston considered the article libellous as it would appear that he had taken unfair advantage of Donegan and the newspaper apologised in High Court.
Around this time Lonnie talked about his earnings to the 'Daily Telegraph': "Out of every £500 of takings some £450 has to go out again in the form of expenses. I have to pay my band. I pay them well to keep them happy. They are probably the highest paid band in this

country. On my payroll, I have a business manager, an agent, an accountant, a road manager, a secretary, an office girl, three musicians and a photographer. That gets rid of a lot of money. In my first year, I estimate that I earned about £35,000. Now I'm glad to say it is going up a little all the time. I probably earn now about £45,000 to £50,000 a year." He continued, "What have I done with my money? The main thing is to have a home. I've been working for that. We never really had a home before. It's always been furnished rooms. The nearest we got to having our own home was four unfurnished rooms in East Ham. That's what I'm doing with my money - building a house which should be finished soon at Woodford. By the time it's finished, the land paid for and the garden landscaped, I reckon it will have cost me £15,000. That's taken care of all my money."

He was still upbeat about skiffle: "Skiffle is the first folk music that we had in this country since the madrigals. It is amateur music and though the Tin Pan Alley moguls might like it to die, they'll be disappointed. In fact, it is growing all the time."

In 1958 Pye were releasing singles by Lonnie Donegan as though they were going out of fashion - well, he was. 'Lonesome Traveller' the fourth single of the year with two more to come, was another frenzied rave-up. By now, Lonnie had discovered the duo, Miki and Griff, and he brought them in for the harmonies. The record was both exciting and tired and barely made the Top 30. Pye should have gone with the B-side, an exquisite ballad from the Weavers' repertoire, 'Times Are Getting Hard'. Donegan shows his ability to sing a tender ballad and his performance is helped, or possibly hindered, by his whistling. "The Humphrey Lyttelton band and ourselves went to Germany, and there were about 7,000 people in Hamburg in 1958. We were doing very well until I got to 'Times Are Getting Hard'. I do a whistling bit in that and even if I say so myself, I do a lovely bit of whistling. I am not a man who whistles and I don't know why I did it on the record. The Germans hated it and started to shout and boo and in the end they were throwing chairs. I said to the boys, 'Quick, 'Gamblin' Man' and off.' I was in tears backstage as I couldn't work out what had gone wrong. Someone told me later that the Germans considered whistling on stage to be extremely rude. Probably now they are more civilised, but then they were son of Adolf." Those two tracks were included on Donegan's second album, another 10 inch affair, called 'Lonnie'. Lonnie made the record with his skiffle group with backing vocals from Miki and Griff and harmonica from John Cole. The slow and dramatic interpretation of Leadbelly's work-song, 'Ain't No More Cane On The Brazos', was outstanding, and a very bluesy tribute to Lonnie Johnson, 'I've Got Rocks In My Bed' wasn't far behind. The two songs about sloth, 'Lazy John' and the repetitive 'Long Summer Day', could, ironically, have done with more time spent on them. Some of the songs came from meeting the folk song collector, Alan Lomax, at the 100 club in Oxford Street. Once again Lonnie's memories were uncharitable: "He simply wanted to make money out of it. The Lomaxes had copyrighted Leadbelly's songs with a publisher and that's where their alleged protectiveness was. They were only concerned with making a buck." It would be good to have heard the conversation - was Alan Lomax complaining about not getting enough of a cut from Lonnie's previous hits?

The LP contained three spirituals - 'The Sunshine Of His Love' (a soft-shoe rave-up), 'Ain't You Glad You've Got Religion' (a gospel rave-up) and 'Light From The Lighthouse' (a Sally Army rave-up usually called 'Let Your Light Shine On Me'). There was no crusading reason for this as no artists emphasised religion until Licorice Locking of the Shadows convinced Cliff, Hank and Brian to become Jehovah's Witnesses in 1962. Licorice was to Cliff what the Maharishi was to the Beatles.

In the middle of 1958, Lonnie had some personnel changes: Les Bennetts came in for Jimmy Currie and Pete Huggett for Mickey Ashman. 19 year old Bennetts came from Les Hobeaux skiffle group and was a good guitarist and backing vocalist, fitting in well with the former jazz musicians. Their first outing, though, was a sign of total desperation, 'Lonnie's Skiffle

Party', and few were impressed with such nonsense. However, the record is not without interest as it blurs the distinction between skiffle and music hall with its feeble jokes, forced good humour and 'Knees Up Mother Brown'. This record shows the way Lonnie Donegan's career was heading.

Meanwhile, following Lonnie's success with 'Rock Island Line' in the States, there had been a small interest in the folk music, giving rise to the Kingston Trio in 1957. American youth had more money than their English counterparts, which obliterated the need for makeshift instruments. The Kingston Trio were good-looking American lads with crew cuts and smart acoustic guitars.

The sixth and final single of the year was a classic, 'Tom Dooley' and 'Rock O'My Soul', which reached the Top 3 and was Lonnie's biggest hit since 'Puttin' On The Style'. In 1868, in the Blue Ridge Mountains, Tom Dula killed his girlfriend, Laura Foster, for giving him a sexually transmitted disease. He was caught and sentenced to die, hence the folk song which was written by Frank Warner and became 'Tom Dooley'. The first version was recorded by Grayson and Whitter in 1929, and Grayson was related to Sheriff Grayson himself.

The US folk group, the Tarriers, who included Alan Arkin, revived the song in June 1957. The Kingston Trio heard a floor singer performing it at the Purple Onion in San Francisco and they included it on their first album. It topped the US charts and someone at Pye thought that it would be ideal for Donegan. He covered the song and scored an immediate advantage by performing it on 'Sunday Night At The London Palladium'. Both versions spent a long time in the charts, but Donegan had the edge making Number 3, whilst the Trio reached Number 5. He said, "I tried to come up with songs that nobody else had thought of. Other people did covers of mine and I did theirs. My version of 'Tom Dooley' is different from the Kingston Trio's." Donegan was also helped by his breathless performance of a gospel song, 'Rock O'My Soul', on the B-side.

When 'Picturegoer' criticised Lonnie for stealing a song from the Kingston Trio's repertoire, he retorted, "Frankly, I didn't want to do 'Tom Dooley', but I was persuaded to record it and I made quite a different version from the Kingston Trio. A folk singer would be crazy to ignore material that is right up his street. I have created a style - and a big following for it. I have to be on the lookout for songs that are suited to my idiom. I can't afford to pass up songs just because they may have been recorded by someone else, but I always aim to do something different. I am no copycat."

In 1959, Peter Sellers released his comedy album, 'Songs For Swingin' Sellers', which was produced by George Martin. Sellers had parodied skiffle with 'Any Old Iron' (1957) and now he launched into Donegan on 'Puttin' On The Smile'. Lonnie admired his talent for impersonation - "it's hard to get the speed and the breathing right" but he thought the best impersonation came from Ron Moody.

'Puttin' On The Smile' is a very funny track where Lennie Goonigan (Peter Sellers) talks of going to the Deep South ("Brighton, Plymouth"), but it savagely satirises his authenticity. Lennie Goonigan is asked, "You have a song that is Number 1 over here at the very moment. Where did you discover that one?" Goonigan replies, "It was an obscure folk song at the top of the American hit parade." Lonnie told 'Picturegoer' that it was "very amusing", but inwardly, he was seething and he couldn't understand why Peter Sellers had recorded such a cruel parody. Little did he know that it had been written under a pseudonym by that most benign of skifflers, Wally Whyton.

...E GIVES the factory girls a hand; believe us, this is ...ally-arranged picture. The skiffle star, who knows ...about the technical side of pressing records, really ...d help in getting those "Dooley" discs out!

Rock 'n' Variety (left)
American stars tour the
UK along with big bands,
comedians and singers

Below) Despite his apparent
hatred of rock 'n' roll Lonnie
appeared on the two popular
weekly British TV rock shows.

LONNIE DONEGAN was a happy addition to last week-end's
"Drumbeat". He is pictured here at the piano with JOHN BARRY
(centre) and BOB MILLER.

LONNIE DONEGAN'S versatility knows no bounds. Here he is playing
pianist to vocalists BILL FORBES (l), MIKE PRESTON and NEVILLE
TAYLOR, after last week's "Oh Boy!" show.

Lonnie Donegan found 'Gum' in Boy Scout book!

MOST of Lonnie Donegan's speciality numbers are the produce of his own extensive memory—songs he has kept stored up in his mind for years, and which he has a habit of bringing out into the daylight of this modern beat age, adapting them to suit his own unique style.

There are exceptions to the rule. Some of them, for instance, he finds by intensive research through old folk-tune books.

And his current hit, this week riding high at No. 3 in the hit parade, was found—of all unlikely places—buried within the yellowed pages of an old Boy Scouts' song book!

It wasn't completely new to him, though. The printed copy only served to refresh his memory of the song he used to sing when a boy as " Does Your Spearmint Lose Its Flavour ? "

Suspecting that there might be some proprietory difficulties, with a consequent BBC ban, it was decided to substitute the words " chewing gum " in this up-to-date version.

When Nixa a-and-r man Michael Barclay travelled to Glasgow to record " Tom Dooley," Lonnie told him about the oldie he had unearthed.

On the spot, they decided to do a preliminary recording of the number, which so impressed everyone concerned that it was immediately earmarked for the next Donegan release.

Lonnie always enjoys working to an audience, and his recording managers believe that they get the best out of him when he is so doing. So, it was decided to make the " Chewing Gum Song " a live session.

Stage try-out

Lonnie tried it out in his stage act for three or four weeks, and one night that livewire Nixa twosome, Messrs. Barclay and Alan Freeman, arrived with all their equipment at Oxford's New Theatre, and duly recorded the number.

I remarked to Alan that, at a live performance, there is no opportunity for a re-take.

" Well, we always record at both houses, so that we can get the better of the two," he explained. " And in this case we had also taken the precaution of waxing the number in our studio, just in case the theatre session didn't work out satisfactorily."

For the other side of the record, " Aunt Rhody," the Freeman-Barclay team whizzed up to Hull's Regal Cinema, though this time they didn't record during an actual performance. They waited until after midnight, and recorded on-stage during the small hours of the morning—with the safety curtain lowered to improve acoustics.

This is all part of what Alan calls " Nixa's policy of decentralisation of recording." Which is another way of saying that they like to get out of London to record some of their titles—provided that the amenities offered are adequate.

" It creates tremendous local interest," says Alan. " And it does us a power of good, by way of publicity in the local papers."

Four million

Alan tells me that since Lonnie has been with Nixa he has sold close on four million records—and it would be difficult to produce evidence to refute his claim that Lonnie is the most consistent British seller of recent years.

We can also expect another Donegan LP in the near future. I understand that there is sufficient material already recorded for another album release.

Alternatively, as Alan put it, " Lonnie is welcome to go into the studio at any time he likes to cut an LP straight off the cuff—but the difficulty is pinning him down to times."

The latest news I hear is that Lonnie's " Chewing Gum " opus is being released in the States this week on the Dot label.

And the next Donegan record ? Well, it seems that during the " Aunt Rhody " session at Hull, Lonnie suddenly snapped his fingers with delight when, completely out of the blue, he remembered another old number which would be well-suited to his idiom.

Then and there, he became wildly enthusiastic about it, dashed off a trial recording—and this number is now set aside awaiting release, as soon as the demand for the present record has subsided.

DEREK JOHNSON.

LONNIE DONEGAN

Does your chewing gum lose its flavour on the bedpost overnight?

TWO SIDES OF A DISC HIT

🐖 The artist and his a-&-r managers 🐖
ALAN FREEMAN and MICHAEL BARCLAY

write about their top Pye star

LONNIE DONEGAN

LONNIE sends his vocal "all" into the mike and . . .

. . . ALAN FREEMAN (l) and MICHAEL BARCLAY twiddle the control knobs and see that the recording apparatus captures the best of Donegan for you.

is never happier than when he is surrounded by his family—and Harry Hammond found him in ....lest mood when he called at the Donegan home this week. Lonnie is seen with his wife, Maureen, ...met him through being one of his first fans, and his daughters, Fiona (3) and Corrina (9 months).

7. PALACE OF VARIETIES
I. Music Hall
II. 'Chewing Gum' and 'Dustman'

I.

In the 19th century, entertainers could be found in taverns up and down the country, and gradually, when theatres were built, they performed in music halls to larger audiences. The shows were brassy and vulgar and great fun and the legendary names include the Liverpool comic Dan Leno, George Robey (the singer and comedian who wrote 'If You Were The Only Girl In The World') and Marie Lloyd (a specialist in rousing novelty songs such as 'Don't Dilly Dally On The Way').

When the male impersonator Vesta Tilley appeared on the first Royal Command Performance in 1912, Queen Mary instructed the ladies in her party to look away as she did not consider a male impersonator to be ladylike, which, I suppose, was the whole point. The comedian Harry Lauder ('I Love A Lassie') found royal favour as he was the only music hall star to be knighted and also the first comedian. The second was Norman Wisdom.

The golden age of the music hall was before 1920, because after that time, there was a much wider choice of light entertainment - jazz musicians, dance bands, ballrooms and the cinema. But right up to the mid-1950s, wonderfully bizarre bills would be touring the UK - the top of the bill might be a straight singer (say, Donald Peers) or a singing whistler (Ronnie Ronalde), but you would have to watch comedians, instrumentalists, magicians, ventriloquists and all kinds of novelty acts - remember Nat Jackley with his rubber neck and Leslie Welch, the memory man - before you got to the star turn. It was tacitly assumed that none of the audience had any attention span and few acts performed for more than 20 minutes.

Music hall was more of a mixed bag than American vaudeville, and much more parochial - so many of the songs and so much of the humour related to Britain itself and it was particularly popular in the East End of London ('Down At The Old Bull And Bush', 'Burlington Bertie From Bow', 'Knocked 'em In The Old Kent Road'). Vaudeville had fizzled out in the US by 1950, and the US country star Slim Whitman was surprised to find that he was on a show with comedians and acrobats because he was only working with other country performers in the States. Guy Mitchell was so amused that he added a cartwheel to his own act.

It wasn't video that killed the radio star but radio and then TV. Many of the comedians had toured for years on the same 15 minute act and if they did not have anything in reserve, their careers were over once they were heard nationally. Those who could adapt - Max Bygraves, Harry Secombe - became radio stars who occasionally worked the halls. Secombe also was part of the Goons, who changed the nature of comedy in the UK.

Max Wall, notoriously, ruined his career with a live joke on the Light Programme when he hadn't appreciated that a radio audience was not as crude as a music hall one. "I was walking on a tightrope when I met Marilyn Monroe coming towards me," he said, "I thought she was going to toss me off but I blocked her passage." Wall did not appear on another BBC programme for years.

The first American rock'n'roll stars to visit the UK including Buddy Holly and Charlie Gracie had to perform on variety shows, where their fans would be impatient to see them. The British impresario, Larry Parnes, taking a lead from Alan Freed in America, realised that rock'n'roll fans would prefer two hours of their music. He promoted shows featuring the artists he managed (Marty Wilde, Joe Brown, Billy Fury) and his concert tour starring Gene Vincent and Eddie Cochran, although noted for its tragic ending, broke new ground. In 1960 Bobby Darin, Duane Eddy, Clyde McPhatter and Emile Ford toured together, and music hall was effectively over.

Vestiges of it remained, notably with the TV variety show, 'Sunday Night At The London Palladium', which invariably featured a US singing star, the 'Beat The Clock' quiz game, a comedian, a wise-cracking compère and the Tiller Girls.

If it was time to Roll Over George Formby, nobody told Lonnie the news. The East End entertainers - Tommy Steele, Joe Brown, Lonnie Donegan - and also Salford's Clinton Ford performed their new music, but they kept returning to music hall. When Tommy Steele's father, a real live Alf Garnett, told him that he would never be as good as the Two Bills From Bermondsey, Steele recorded their theme song, 'What A Mouth' and took it into the Top 10 in 1960. Lionel Bart wrote a special Cockney song for Joe Brown, 'Jellied Eels', and he also recorded 'The Darktown Strutters Ball' and 'I'm Henry VIII, I Am'. Lonnie Donegan loved music hall songs - the best ones were witty and had instantly memorable melodies. Commentators say that Lonnie Donegan spurned American folk and replaced it with music hall. The truth is that there is a strong strain of music hall throughout Lonnie Donegan's work, but from 1959, he was just as likely to pick a music hall song as an American one.

Lonnie loved music hall. Whenever I interviewed him, he would speak as enthusiastically about Max Miller or Hutch as he would about Leadbelly or Woody Guthrie. He loved the corny jokes, the knockabout humour and especially the nonsense songs that were often performed. He considered George Formby's songs to be as well crafted as Woody Guthrie's, an opinion that, years later, was to be shared by Pete Seeger. (I thought for many years that George Formby was a tragic figure, browbeaten by his aggressive wife, but a recent biography reveals he had an affair with the lovely singer, Yana, so it did turn out nice again on occasion.)

Lonnie more than anyone was a music hall entertainer. He said, "The platform for working at that time was the variety theatre to a very general public. I was headlining over dancing girls, comedians, jugglers, whatever, and couldn't just stand there like one of Lowry's matchstick men. I had to learn to back-project, announce, get laughs and use a PA system that 'were good enough for George Formby and good enough for you'. You had to perform, not just play. Otherwise, you died and got no work.'

Carl Jones: 'I remember Lonnie staying at my house one night and taking a book about music-hall by Roy Hudd from the bookcase. I was surprised at all the people he had worked with - Hylda Baker, Jewell and Warriss, and so on. He was flicking through it, reminiscing on these names, when he came across a section on himself. He was very pleased about that."

II.

Men have been chewing nuts and leaves for centuries, but William Wrigley created a new fad with his Spearmint Gum, which was introduced in 1893. Within 20 years, it had become an enormous industry and Wrigley was looking for suitable investments. The Wrigley family sponsored the baseball team, the Chicago Cubs, but the club was rocked by scandal in the 1920s which made the gum an object of satire.

In 1924 Billy Rose wrote 'Does Your Spearmint Lose Its Flavour On The Bedpost Overnight?' for his Broadway musical, 'Little Miss Puck', and he described it as "the first singing commercial". It was first recorded by Ernest Hare and Billy Jones. Rose, the husband of Fanny Brice, became a Broadway impresario and wrote several impressive songs including 'Happy Days And Lonely Nights', 'Without A Song', 'Me And My Shadow' and 'Don't Bring Lulu'. He railed against the stupidity of rock'n'roll music so presumably he had forgotten 'Does Your Spearmint Lose Its Flavour'. Another song, 'Chewing Gum', was written and recorded by the Carter Family in 1928 and although Lonnie didn't record this song, some of its verses parallel 'Gamblin' Man'.

Lonnie knew the song as a boy scout. In his hands it became 'Does Your Chewing Gum (Lose Its Flavour On The Bedpost Overnight)?', the answer to which is probably yes. Donegan recorded it live at New Theatre, Oxford and although it is far more music hall than skiffle, Nick Nicholls' percussive contributions are 100 per cent skiffle. Lead guitarist Les Bennetts was well suited to his secondary role as Lonnie's stooge. Note how enthusiastic the audience is, they are even screaming for Lonnie. Lonnie saw off a cover version from the puppet piglets, Pinky and Perky, but its very presence was rather ignominious, to use Donegan vocabulary. The B-side, a recording from the Regal ABC Theatre in Hull but not live, was another childhood song, usually known as 'Aunt Rhody' but sometimes as 'The Old Grey Goose'. Very skiffley with even a washboard in the band.

Lonnie Donegan: "I didn't decide to move into variety, these things aren't cut and dried. I'm not into making market strategies and plans. We're not ICI and I'm sure that 95% of all show business is completely accidental. 'Chewing Gum' is a good example of that. I was just singing a snatch of a song that I had learnt in the boy scouts, and the boys said, 'Hey, that's fun. Let's put it in the act.' I was sure it was a folk song because that's what boy scouts sang. Pye recorded it live at Oxford and when they were researching the writer and the publisher, they found it had been written by Fanny Brice's husband for a musical, 'Little Miss Puck'. I thought, 'My god, I'm in trouble. The Spinners won't speak to me for a week.' Now it's a folk song again."

'Chewing Gum' went to Number 3 and Lonnie should have given more thought to the next single, 'Fort Worth Jail'. Nothing wrong with the song which was written by the western actor, Dick Reinhart, but Lonnie takes it too fast and it loses its meaning. Nick Nicholls's torrid drum solo is out of place. The B-side was Leadbelly's 'Whoa Buck', which had been in the can for a year and featured an unusually restrained performance from Donegan. Good track. Another Ledbetter song, 'Shorty George', from the 'Whoa Buck' session was unissued at the time - note the verse from 'Matchbox' in the middle of the song, there was a lot of mixing and matching in these blues songs.

Jimmy Driftwood was an Arkansas teacher who entertained his charges with historical ballads. In 1936 he wrote a song about the Battle of New Orleans on 8 January 1815 in which General Andrew Jackson, known as 'Old Hickory' and a subsequent American president, surprised the British and prevented them from capturing New Orleans. (Ironically, the Treaty of Ghent had been signed at the end of 1814 but the news had not reached the troops.) Driftwood took a fiddle tune commemorating the battle, 'Eighth Of January', and it became 'The Battle Of New Orleans'. Driftwood was not to be discovered until 1957 when he recorded the song for his first RCA album. He refers to the 'bloody British' and he also refers to giving them 'hell', both words being daring for US radioplay in the 1950s.

'Tom Dooley' had started a fad for nineteenth century historical songs - remember Larry Verne with 'Mr. Custer'? 'The Battle Of New Orleans' was given an upbeat treatment by Johnny Horton in 1959, topping the US country charts for 10 weeks and the pop charts for six. 'The Battle Of New Orleans' was perfect for Lonnie, who was asked to cover it. Lonnie maintained that it was not a cover as Johnny Horton had wanted "a Lonnie Donegan sound" on his original recording.

Lonnie took 'The Battle Of New Orleans' surprisingly slowly - the British are, after all, running away, but Lonnie doesn't turn the song into a rave-up. He adds a spoken introduction - a return to 'This here's a story' - and to avoid a BBC ban, he changed Johnny Horton's 'bloody British' to 'blooming British'. Horton also recorded a new vocal for radioplay. Strangely, both Horton and Donegan are reluctant to say the word 'hell'.

Lonnie's 'We stood quite still' merited another take, but Pye thought the rest so good that they overlooked a minor slip - or they couldn't be bothered.

Finbar Furey: "Many people would cringe in England when they heard Lonnie sing 'The

Battle Of New Orleans' as it was about a British defeat, but they loved the record in Germany and Ireland. It was as popular as any of the rebel songs in Ireland!" (The charts in Ireland didn't start until 1962 so we don't know if it would have been Number 1.)

On the B-side was an Appalachian song, 'Darling Corey', which Lonnie had heard from the Weavers. One of his later band members, Nick Payn, comments: "I loved that B-side, I just adored 'Darling Corey' as a seven year old. I couldn't understand it though. I thought the 'steel house' was a house made out of metal as I had never heard of a whiskey still. The thing that came across was the urgency and the excitement. Lonnie was gasping for breath and I can see now that he was crossing the boundaries between jazz, country, blues and folk."

This battle of New Orleans was won by Lonnie who went to Number 2, while Johnny Horton reached Number 16, still his highest UK chart placing. Pye thought it would be a good idea for Lonnie to cover Johnny's next song, 'Johnny Reb', written by Merle Kilgore. Lonnie received the single but by mistake, learnt the other side, 'Sal's Got A Sugar Lip', again written by Jimmy Driftwood. He took it much faster than Horton and it went into the Top 20. Lonnie's B-side was the jazz standard, 'Chesapeake Bay', with his discoveries, Ian Menzies with the Clyde Valley Stompers. A second track recorded with the trad band was 'Ace In The Hole', which was associated with the Yerba Buena Jazz Band, and it is a pity that Lonnie didn't consider playing on an entire album with them.

In any event, Lonnie had his own 'Johnny Reb' to contend with. In order to boost his following in Ireland, he recorded a rebel song, a curious move from someone who had shunned the political songs in Woody Guthrie's repertoire. He chose 'Kevin Barry', the story of an 18 year old rebel who refused to inform on his comrades and was shot by the English in 1921: his dying wish was to be shot 'like a soldier'. The B-side was a lovely tribute to an Irish river, 'My Lagan Love', which was written by a leading poet, Patrick Kavanagh. The song was subsequently recorded by Kate Bush. Another rebel song, 'My Only Son Was Killed In Dublin', remained unissued until the Bear Family box-set in 1993.

Finbar Furey: "'Kevin Barry' was one of the top rebel songs, it is an absolute corker. 'My Only Son Was Killed In Dublin' is some song as well, it is about a 15 year old kid who was blown away years ago in Dublin. I recorded 'My Lagan Love' myself. It is about a man so in love with this woman that he is like a 'lovesick fairy child'. He doesn't know what to do with himself. The girl in the song grew up beside the River Lagan, probably on a farm. Lonnie was a wonderful musician who had a great spin on history. Not only was he a great skiffle artist but this guy knew his history on the songs. There are a lot of freaks out there who don't even know what they are singing about, but Lonnie did and, boy, could he sing."

Despite its sentiments, 'Kevin Barry' was a beautiful acoustic performance from Lonnie and so was placed on an EP called 'Relax With Lonnie'. The EP also featured Amos Milburn's bluesy 'Bewildered', a superb ballad which had topped the US R&B charts. 'Bewildered' is a sensitive, jazz-slanted performance with a fine solo from Les Bennetts. Lonnie might have known Lonnie Johnson's version of 'Bewildered' better because he also recorded Johnson's B-side, 'I Know It's Love', now retitled 'Baby Don't You Know That's Love'. The balance on 'It Is No Secret' is unusual as the song becomes a duet for Lonnie and Les's guitar.

In October 1959 Lonnie Donegan made his third album and his first 12-inch LP, 'Lonnie Rides Again', in two days, seven tracks one day and five the next with 'The Golden Vanity' left over. The album was released three weeks later with a jokey cover implying Lonnie was a rocking horse cowboy and this must have hurt its sales. I didn't buy it myself because my 14 year old self didn't want to be seen carrying what looked like a children's album. Particularly one with a kid's song, 'Mr. Froggy', on it. A great pity as it was a superb album, and, incidentally, 'Mr. Froggy' shows that Lonnie could have made a great children's album.

Packaging apart, 'Lonnie Rides Again' is a total success. I asked Lonnie if he was allowed to choose the songs: "They would have me play songs that I thought might be right for records and then they would pick out the singles. As far as the albums were concerned, the LPs were entirely my own choice. I just tried to give as wide a coverage to folk songs that I knew as possible."

Lonnie had been very impressed with Josh White's repertoire, taking 'The House Of The Rising Sun' for himself. The song about a young girl being condemned to a life of prostitution had been around for a hundred years and was first recorded by Texas Alexander in 1928, but even in 1959 it would not be considered for a commercial single. It is an excellent performance with an eerie guitar solo from Les Bennetts. Lonnie must have smarted when the Animals took it to Number 1 in 1964 as he could have performed it brilliantly with their arrangement.

'Fancy Talkin' Tinker' was a rewrite of 'Kassie Jones', a 1929 recording by the bluesman Furry Lewis and it is as close to autobiography as Lonnie got. In later years, Lonnie performed a fiery version of this song and the fact that it wasn't released as a single marks a lost opportunity.

Lonnie returns to Leadbelly for a fine 'Take This Hammer' and 'John Hardy', a gunfighter closely related to the engineer, 'John Henry,. 'Gloryland', a favourite of the New Orleans marching bands, needs backing vocals (did Miki and Griff not turn up?), and as Lonnie shouts 'Sing' at one stage, he must have expected their voices to be overdubbed.

Country music is featured with two Hank Snow songs, the B-side, 'You Pass Me By' (1951) and his country hit, 'The Gold Rush Is Over' (1952) as well as the Carter Family's 'Jimmie Brown The Newsboy' (1929), which was a contemporary US country hit for Mac Wiseman. "I have heard many versions of 'Jimmy Brown The Newsboy'," says country music writer Hugh T. Wilson, "and Lonnie's is easily the worst. Paper boys should approach the house quietly and drop the paper completely through the letter-box. Lonnie sounds like a paper boy who would bang the gate, rattle the letter-box and leave the paper protruding so that it gets wet and lets the wind in." Cole Porter's pastiche of country music's 'death songs', 'Miss Otis Regrets' is very well performed.

Despite disliking Peter Sellers' 'Puttin' On The Smile', Lonnie himself was happy to lampoon the craze for forming skiffle and rock'n'roll groups by updating 'Talking Guitar Blues'. This has been thought to be an update of an Ernest Tubb record in which the young lad now buys a guitar and ends up like Tommy Steele. However, Ernest Tubb recorded no such song and probably Lonnie derived his performance from Woody Guthrie's friend, Ramblin' Jack Elliott, who had been living in London.

The album included the American version of 'Talking Guitar Blues', but he assumed a Cockney accent for a second version for the B-side of 'San Miguel'. "That is typical of my modus operandi at the time," said Lonnie, "I was taking American folk material which is quite esoteric and presenting it to Mrs. George in Warrington, who had heard about it from her friend in Eccles. If you presented it exactly the same as this negro jailbird was singing it back in Mississippi, it wouldn't make much sense. When it came to this particular track, I sang it as per Ernest Tubb and then thought, 'Well, I dunno, dunno how this is going to go in Essex', so I did it again, in English and reviewed the two to see which would be the best to present to the public." The reference to Woodford is well-chosen as Lonnie was having his own house built there, close to the Epping Forest. He was also showing an interest in cars: his first major purchase had been a Daimler convertible and now he had a Riley 1500. He also started playing golf, going round with Anne Shelton's husband, David Reid.

'San Miguel' was Lonnie's only hit song from the album. It was written by Jane Bowers, who also wrote 'Remember The Alamo', and was a single for the Kingston Trio. It's a good performance with a throbbing bass and fiery rhythm but why did Lonnie bother as the song is a one-line joke about a servant who presumably beds his mistress? Somehow, he worked this Mexican song into his pantomime, 'Aladdin', at the Finsbury Park Empire.

When you consider the ham-fisted way the Beatles' albums were released in the US, it is bizarre to report that 'Lonnie Rides Again' was issued with far better packaging by Atlantic Records in the US, where it was re-titled 'Skiffle Folk Music'. The sleeve notes by Gary Kramer were as gushing as Peter Clayton's in the UK, but he had a far better grasp of the music. He writes, "In bringing the songs to us, via Britain, he makes us keenly appreciative of our rich American folk heritage." He emphasises the simplicity of skiffle, but adds, "Very few will ever be able to sing these songs with his excitement, incomparable charm and artistry."

The remaining track from the sessions was a sea song recorded by Woody Guthrie, 'The Golden Vanity'. Sometimes known as 'Lowlands Low', the song was first heard in the seventeenth century and it told of the conflicts between England and Spain. A cabin boy is entrusted to sink a Spanish galleon (!), which he does by boring holes in its side. The captain reneges on his promises of a fortune and his daughter's hand by killing the cabin-boy. Nothing wrong with Lonnie's version but it is rather truncated - it might be given ten verses in a folk club. Nick Payn: "'The Golden Vanity' was put on the B-side of 'My Old Man's A Dustman' and it was fantastic, one of his very best records. I'm sorry that we never played it live in the later years 'cause we did a good version at soundchecks. I remember him telling Chris to hit the bass drum on 'Up jumped the captain'. Lonnie should have done it again - it reminds us that we are a seafaring nation!"

For some months, Lonnie had been including a snatch of a schoolboy song in his stage act, but as soon as he was about to say a cheeky line, his band would stop him. He was encouraged to record it and the song was 'My Old Man's A Dustman'. Lonnie Donegan: "So far as I have been able to ascertain, it started as 'My old man's a fireman on the Elder Dempster Line', which was a shipping line out of Liverpool. It became a student's union song in Birmingham, and then it was picked by the troops in the First World War as 'My old man's a dustman, he fought in the Battle of Mons. He killed ten thousand Germans with only a hundred bombs.' That's how I learnt it when I was a little boy at school. We used it as a joke on stage, and then the A&R department told me to 'Write it', and so we took it away and wrote it, guv'nor. We tried it on tour and 'My Old Man's A Dustman' had about 30 verses. We performed new verses every night until we were satisfied we had ones that would work well on record. You need a lot of verses for a song like that, anyway. It's a joke song and people aren't going to keep laughing at the same jokes."

Another version of the song from World War I went:

"My old man's a farmer,
Now what d'yer think of that,
He's wearing khaki trousers
And a little gorblimey hat."

A gorblimey hat was the soft Service cap which some officers wore, Being short for 'God blind me', it showed a mock respect. A song called 'What D'yer Think Of That' was copyrighted in the 1920s and was owned by Lawrence Wright Music. Lonnie, who had updated the lyrics with his road manager Peter Buchanan, had placed the song with his own publishing company, Tyler Music. When Lawrence Wright Music threatened to sue, Lonnie agreed to pass over some of the royalties.

The group's road manager, Peter Buchanan, wrote the lyrics: "I had been writing things in the act to give Lonnie a chance to catch his breath. Little joke - 'Nick is our drummer (applause). He 's got a good head for money. It's got a slot in the top.' The girls went mad over Les Bennetts, so I had Lonnie say, 'Les brings grace and charm to the act - Charm was fine but we had to get rid of Grace.' Lon was bloody good at delivering those jokes."

The arrangement for 'My Old Man's A Dustman (Ballad Of A Refuse Disposal Officer)' had come about during a meal. One of the group had taken a fiddle from the wall of a restaurant and was clowning around. Lonnie realised that this could be used to good effect in 'Dustman', which was recorded at the Gaumont Cinema in Doncaster in February 1960. Lonnie performed the song at the time of its release on his fifth appearance on 'Sunday Night At The London Palladium', and the effect was such that it became the first UK single to enter the UK chart at Number 1 - the only other record to have done this was 'Jailhouse Rock' for Elvis Presley in 1958. Lonnie says, "We had no idea that would happen, but who knows how a record will do. Throw it in the air and if God picks it up, whoopee. We had built up a market for our records and every one was a big hit and when we made 'Dustman', we assumed that it was going to be a big hit. The dealers ordered more than they usually do and that put it in the Number 1 position before it even got in the shops." Lonnie is playing down the effect of that record as his last two singles had only reached the Top 20. 'My Old Man's A Dustman' caught the public's imagination like nothing else he had recorded and it sold 250,000 copies in its first week, removing Johnny Preston's 'Running Bear' from the top.

Dressed as dustmen, Lonnie and his musicians filmed the single. So many of these vintage clips have been destroyed but Lonnie chasing the dustcart has been preserved and frequently shown in nostalgia programmes. Unbelievably, the song and film were controversial as the dustman's union complained about its irreverence and typecasting. Lonnie also filmed a promo for 'The Battle Of New Orleans', but this does not appear to have survived.

Pete Huggett played drums on 'Dustman': "I never liked 'Dustman' and I thought it was a waste of time, but when we recorded it on a Sunday concert in Doncaster, it brought the house down. Then it was played on 'Juke Box Jury' and the panel was ecstatic. When it went in at Number 1, I said to Lon, 'I'm sorry, I was wrong.'"

'My Old Man's A Dustman' was the first single to drop the word 'skiffle' from the billing, Lonnie Donegan and his Skiffle Group. That three minute single changed Lonnie's life and nothing was ever the same again. The folk songbooks were put back on the shelf: "I think we reached a limit. We brought an American sound into Britain and soon everybody was singing folk songs. But we were scraping the barrel once the first flood of novelty wore off. We had to appeal to the whole public and so we couldn't just sing folk songs per se. We had to sing folk songs which would appeal to everyone. That's a very different thing. Not all Leadbelly's songs are like 'Rock Island Line'."

Peter Buchanan found that he had to write new verses for 'Dustman': "I wrote 87 verses in all. When he went to Australia, I got a book from the library and I found that they had an animal called a platypus, and that stuck in my mind. He went to the Sydney Opera House first and this stopped the show:

'The animals in Ozzie are very very strange,
They've got one called a platypus, you'll find it on the range,
You'll always recognise it, just like you would your brother,
Cause his plat is on the one end and his puss is on the other.'

They clapped and cheered and stood up when they heard that."

After writing several jokey hits for Lonnie Donegan and the scripts for his TV series, Peter Buchanan turned to TV comedy series, notably the sitcom '…And Mother Makes Three' for Wendy Craig. He now lectures on creative writing and he says, "When students ask me to how to get started, I say, 'Go to Glasgow'. They say, 'Why Glasgow?' and I say, 'That's where the end of the queue is.'"

Pete Appleby: "I would come on with a dustbin which had been tuned to G, and I would thump it and hit the cymbal on top. Later on I would put things inside the dustbin, there wasn't a lid on it, and it seemed to please the public though I'm not sure why. I'd fish in the dustbin and suddenly I would pull out a tennis ball with green raffia hanging from it and Lonnie would say, 'What's that?' I would say, 'It's a spring onion' and he would say, 'No it's not'. And I would bang it on the ground and catch it. And there was a vivid red pair of old lady's bloomers with one leg cut off, and he would say, 'What's that?', and I would say, 'Half a knicker'."

'My Old Man's A Dustman' was as much a millstone as a milestone and it can be viewed in the same light as Chuck Berry's 'My Ding-A-Ling'. Drummer Pete Merrick: "I remember him saying in the 1970s, 'You may be fed up with 'Dustman', I am fed up with 'Dustman', but it is paying the mortgage. We are booked 'act as known' and we have to do it."

LONNIE VERSUS KINGSTON TRIO AGAIN

LONNIE DONEGAN

IT seems that The Kingston Trio are fated to be in continual opposition to Lonnie Donegan. Lonnie has just recorded "San Miguel" on Pye, also "done" by the trio on Capitol.

This is an unusual Lonnie, giving a "character" performance—not a beat, skiffle or rock job, but a plain Spanish story that achieves its considerable effect as much by implication as by the facts related in the lyric.

KINGSTON TRIO

While being restrained and controlled, Lonnie's performance is more energetic and forceful than the Trio's and gives him a good chance of a big seller.

Do, however, listen to both versions before buying. It may be that you, like me, will prefer the cold, unemotional, almost sinister singing on the Kingstons' disc.

"Talking Guitar Blues" will amuse Lonnie's fans as he offers a fairly Cockney monologue about a lad who bought a guitar, and the troubles that followed this purchase.

'CORNY' COMEDIAN

LONNIE DONEGAN
"My Old Man's A Dustman"
"The Golden Vanity"
(PYE 7N.15256)

★★★★ I MAY BE WRONG, mind you, but I think Lonnie has yet another hit to his long list. "My Old Man's A Dustman", subtitled "Ballad of a Refuse Disposal Officer", was recorded at the Gaumont Cinema, Doncaster, and features Lonnie and the group with new words and music by Mr. D.

TTT

It's an unpretentiously "corny" comedy number which always goes down like a bomb on Lonnie's personal appearances. With the enthusiastic reaction of the audience to add to the atmosphere, this disc could well be a really big hit for Lonnie.

Again Lonnie has provided new words and music for a song, "The Golden Vanity", the story of a sailing ship from the history books. Lonnie tells the tale in typical form while the boys provide the excellent accompaniment we have learned to expect from them.

DONEGAN WOWS 'EM AT THE VARIETY CLUB

ONE of the big hits at The Variety Club of Great Britain's Luncheon last week at the Dorchester Hotel, London, in honour of the artistes who've sold millions of records was LONNIE DONEGAN. He didn't go on stage like the rest of the other guests of honour; he did his party piece from the top table . . . and, of course, he wowed 'em with "My Old Man's A Dustman"—R&SM Picture by Stan Lee.

MIKI & GRIFF
THE LONNIE DONEGAN GROUP
RALPH DOLLIMORE AND HIS ORCHESTRA

ing on
Donegan
erpt from James Brennan's
ving summer show

s Theatre, Blackpool
NG

NNIE DONEGAN
S O'CONNOR
TER GOODWRIGHT
E CLARK BROTHERS
E KESTRELS
.L WESTLAKE
E TILLER GIRLS
en Moule and his Orchestra
NCE DIRECTION BY DENNY BETTIS
EVISED AND PRODUCED BY
LBERT J. KNIGHT
ELEVISION DIRECTION BY
LBERT LOCKE
TV Network Production

Donegan's 'Dustman' hopes to clean up in America

LONNIE DONEGAN'S sensational No. 1 hit, "My Old Man's A Dustman," was released in America this week. Widespread interest is reported by the Atlantic label, and the record is already selling well in Canada.

Because of its humorous Cockney flavour the disc was not expected to be issued in the States. With the record, U.S. disc-jockeys will be supplied with a detailed glossary explaining slang expressions featured on the record.

The American coupling will remain the same as in Britain—"The Golden Vanity." The record is also to be released soon in Scandinavia. There is particular interest in it in Sweden.

"My Old Man's A Dustman" will be featured in at least two of the six "Putting On The Donegan" ATV shows which Lonnie is currently recording. Guest star Alfred Marks will sing the number with Lonnie on a show to be taped tomorrow (Saturday).

NIE DONEGAN with his e, presented to him on Monday he Wholesale Clothing Manu- rers' Federation for being one ritain's ten best dressed men on and every occasion". He was ng a plum checked suit (cost white shirt, horizontal striped gold guitar cuff links (present wife Maureen) and dark brown dile-skinned shoes. Lonnie was ated for the honour by NME editor Andy Gray.

LONNIE DONEGAN WILL STAGGER YOU!

A SONG of the homesick sailor—that's a nutshell description of "I Wanna Go Home", recorded for Pye by Lonnie Donegan. And this is going to be a staggering shock for all listeners, whether they be Lonnie's fans or not.

For the accompaniment is a dreamy, string arrangement directed by Wally Stott. The tempo reflects the gentle swell of a calm sea, the mood is relaxed, the overall effect is delightful.

When you think about it, this is "normal" material for Lonnie, who has waxed many quiet folk songs—this one is broadly in the same category. It's Lonnie singing so differently (at moments reminiscent of Dean Martin!) and with such an unexpected backing.

Let's hope he won't suffer the same fate as The Everly Brothers did when they had an orchestral backing.

Lonnie deserves success, because this is a very good record. The flip finds Lonnie back with his skiffle group, singing in his usual style about "Jimmy Brown The Newsboy".

All ready to step out in their top hats, white ties and tails for the finale—CLIFF RICHARD, ADAM FAITH and LONNIE DONEGAN.

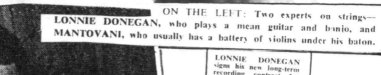

ON THE LEFT: Two experts on strings—
LONNIE DONEGAN, who plays a mean guitar and banjo, and
MANTOVANI, who usually has a battery of violins under his baton.

LONNIE DONEGAN signs his new long-term recording contract for Pye in the dressing room of his theatre in Nottingham, where he is playing Buttons in "Cinderella."

TED HEATH, PET CLARK and LONNIE DONEGAN got two big receptions at the new Brighton Palladium, when it presented the first of a series of twice nightly Sunday pop concerts last weekend. This Sunday, Johnny Dankworth and Marion Ryan are featured

DONEGAN, BASS COMO'S GUESTS

SHIRLEY BASSEY and Lon Donegan are both in line appearances in Perry Com famed U.S. TV show, cables N Hentoff.

The Columbia songstress, w is currently in cabaret in Ne York has attracted widespread a tention on this trip, and the Com show is only one of many offe she has had.

Donegan, who visits America o his way to New Zealand nex month, will probably guest in the first of the new series of Como shows.

Shirley had to miss her appearance last Saturday, as she was suffering from a sore throat. She recovered at the weekend.

on the DONEGAN " returns to ATV for six weeks from next
Above is LONNIE with his banjo, belting out the final line
with ROY CASTLE during the telerecording of the show
see on July 28. Roy's latest disc is reviewed on page 4.

THREE of the many stars who were honoured guests at the Variety Club of
Great Britain "Golden Disc" lunch last Thursday (May 11) are pictured
above—MATT MONRO, JOAN REGAN and LONNIE DONEGAN.
Lonnie was one of the hits of the day, without singing a note. He made a very
witty speech and then turned serious to make a very sincere plea on behalf of
youngsters trying to break into show business. He praised the recording companies for encouraging new talent but criticised the agents and promoters for a
certain amount of "closed shop" practice.

LONNIE DONEGAN

"Have A Drink On Me"
"Seven Daffodils"

(Pye 7N.15354)

NATUR-
ALLY, a
TOP TWENTY
TIP. The only
disc Lonnie has
made in the last
years that hasn't
apt into the Top Twenty was
st Christmas' "Virgin Mary",
d if "Lively" hadn't been
ing so well at the time it too
ght have been a hit for him.
"Have A Drink On Me" (an
d "Leadbelly" Leadbetter
ber) has additional lyrics
Messrs. Donegan and
chanan as Lonnie and the
s bouncily romp through
happy ditty. A simple
ation: Donegan=a hit.
Seven Daffodils" is a slow
sy number, Lonnie rather
ning the unusual words to
unusual melody. Again Mr.
s managed to find material
grasps your interest, and
nts it in a delivery that
ins that interest.

BING, LONNIE and those Gold Discs.

ABOVE: MAX MILLER and LONNIE DONEGAN in the studio as they recorded 'The Market Song'.

8. THE PARTY'S OVER
I. 'Lonnie Donegan Presents…'
II. 'Putting On The Donegan'
III. Final hits

I.

As well as Lonnie Donegan's own releases, a number of Pye releases were labelled 'Lonnie Donegan Presents…'. It was a short-lived operation but the acts involved had long careers. In the 1950s the husband and wife team of Barbara MacDonald Salisbury (born 1920) and Emyr Morus Griffith (born 1923) came from the George Mitchell Choir and, as Miki and Griff, were a comedy act on variety shows. They were captivated by an album of folk songs by the Everly Brothers, 'Songs Our Daddy Taught Us' (1958), but did not include any of the material in their stage act, which included comedy routines around 'Cleo And Me-O (And The Baby Crocodile)' and 'Old McDonald Had A Farm'.

One night a supporting act couldn't appear in a Lonnie Donegan show at Norwich and Miki and Griff were recruited as last minute replacements. Lonnie Donegan recalled, "I saw Miki and Griff in Norwich. They had what would now be thought a terrible comedy act but it was effective in context. I thought that they were very nice people and I put them on the bill with me. Miki had a natural ear for country music harmonies and when we sang together - me with my high voice and she with her low one - you'd swear you were listening to the Everly Brothers. I produced an EP called 'Rockin' Alone (In An Old Rockin' Chair)' on which they were accompanied by my group. They also sang on a number of my hit records like 'Virgin Mary'."

Lonnie had Miki and Griff as regulars on his TV series, 'Putting On The Donegan', which is considered in the next section, and they were featured on many of his hits including 'Jack O'Diamonds', 'Ham'n'Eggs', 'Tom Dooley' and, Miki alone, 'My Dixie Darling'. Miki says., "There was one song that I sang, 'I Never Will Marry', where Lonnie just plays acoustic guitar and whistles. The whole effect was so pretty and that was all due to Lonnie, it was completely his idea."

Accompanied by Lonnie's group, Miki and Griff were, for a time, very successful. Both 'Hold Back Tomorrow' and 'Rockin' Alone (In An Old Rockin' Chair)' made the Top 50. Their EP, actually called 'This Is Miki, This Is Griff', made Number 2 on the EP charts. Griff: "We recorded a country song called 'Hold Back Tomorrow' and when our friends told us it was nice, we said, 'Okay, but you should listen to this one, it's fabulous' and we would play the original by Wynn Stewart. They would think it was terrible - and it wasn't, of course, it was fabulous. We realised though that people over here don't like the out-and-out country sound and so we always did our own versions of these songs."

Whatever it was, and it was probably Griff's ridiculous moustache, Miki and Griff always seemed old and unfashionable. When the hits, such as they were, stopped, they concentrated on albums and established a considerable following. They had a comfortable career in country music clubs and as a support act on country music tours with Slim Whitman, George Hamilton IV and Don Williams. Miki said, "The fans know we're an old married couple. We live in a little house and sleep in an ordinary bed. There is nothing glamorous about us." Miki died from cancer in 1989. Griff was devastated to lose his companion, but he took on hospital visiting and cheering patients up. In 1992 he made a guest appearance with Lonnie Donegan and Chris Barber, but his spirit was broken and he died in 1995.

Another of Lonnie's discoveries was Kenny Ball and his Jazzmen. Lonnie said, "In those days you had to audition to get on to the BBC and those audiences were like Nazi war tribunals. Three old men would sit grimfaced and serious at a table in the middle of a room while you performed. If you were a comic, you died a death. Kenny Ball and his Jazzmen were auditioning one day and as I happened to be around, one of the panel said, 'We're a bit out of our depth here, Mr Donegan? Can you tell us if they are any good?' I said, 'Yes, they're very good' and then they asked me if they would be suitable for the BBC. Of course they were but they were put on 'Children's Hour' or something like that. I took the band to meet my record producer, Alan A Freeman. He said, 'Let's record them straight away.' That's what we did. They were put under contract to me and their very first record, Samantha', was a hit."

Kenny Ball's memories are similar but differ in details: "We were auditioning for a children's programme on ITV and Lonnie Donegan was rehearsing his TV series in the next room. He heard us playing and wandered in. He was asked if we were any good and he said, 'Yeah, they're bloody good. Can I put them on my television show?' It was as easy as that. Then he got us a contract with his label, Pye. It was amazing. We had been knocking our bloody heads together, we'd been to Germany playing from eight at night to six in the morning, and we'd lived in and out of vans. I can rememeber going to play the Cavern and the door fell off the van in the Mersey Tunnel, which is like a bleeding racetrack."

John Bennett, who played trombone for Kenny and still does, remembers: "It was up in Liverpool at the Iron Door club that we learnt 'Samantha'. We were packing the gear away and the club's piano player was tinkling away with 'Samantha' as a ragtime piece. Ken said, 'That sounds good, we'll have a go at that.' We rehearsed it, and when we went to the studio, Lonnie was the A&R man. We had a list of tunes Ken wanted to do like '76 Trombones', and we played through the list until we got to 'Samantha'. Lonnie didn't want '76 Trombones' but he thought 'Samantha' had something. He said, 'I don't like the ragtime bit, it wants a bit of dunga, dunga, dunga', and our banjo player had no idea what he was talking about. Lonnie borrowed his banjo and showed him what he wanted. It changed the whole thing and it was completely different from the way we played it originally."

'Samantha' made the UK Top 20 in February 1961 and led to a succession of hit records. Lonnie maintained his friendship with Kenny Ball, playing banjo on their version of 'Dinah' and making a single with them in 1973. Kenny Ball: "Lonnie was a terrific banjo player who swung like the clappers, and he did 'til the day he died. One night in the early 60s we were at the 100 Club and my banjo player was sick. I phoned Lonnie and asked him if he could come and play with us. He said, 'How much is it worth?' I said, 'A fiver', and he said, 'Okay'. We had a great night."

Lonnie also promoted another trad band, Ian Menzies and the Clyde Valley Stompers, and twelve hours of sessions were booked for the 'Have Tartan Will Travel' LP. Lonnie, being somewhat more exacting than for his own sessions, insisted that they stayed in London until they got it right. A session that was meant to end at midnight lasted until 5am and then the band made the 300 mile trek to Morecambe for a concert date that evening. The gig went well but straight after it they were returning to Scotland and one of their cars overturned, putting the clarinet player, Forrie, and the singer, Fiona, in hospital. They postponed their homecoming show in Broomhill for a week when they played right through the album to tumultuous applause. The album is a good one with Lonnie joining Fiona for two songs, 'Just A Closer Walk With Thee' and 'Ice Cream', but the LP jacket is abominable. Miki and Griff look positively cool when you consider the Stompers' garish tartan outfits.
The only other act to be accorded a 'Lonnie Donegan Presents...' byline was his replacement in the Chris Barber Band, Johnny Duncan, for a single of 'Tobacco Road' in 1961.

¶.

Supremely confident, Lonnie Donegan was a natural for TV. The public warmed to him and he was, for example, used to increase the sales of 'Sugar Puffs'. He performed on one TV variety show after another and, in 1959, he was given his own ATV series, 'Putting On The Donegan'. The half-hour programmes, screened at the peak time of 8pm, ran until 1962 and it was one of the first TV variety shows to concentrate on music. In 1963, it became 'Donegan's On Again' and slightly changed its format, using the Grandisons gospel group rather than Miki and Griff. The original title was restored in 1964 for what was to be the final series, this time with the Clark Brothers.

Talking about a video compilation in 1992, Lonnie said, "We dug back into the old 'Putting On The Donegan' series and made a compilation of tracks for a video. It has come out extremely well: it is black and white, but it is nice and crisp and clear and the sound is actually better than on the records that were released at the time. Nowadays you go into a recording studio and you spend a year on the first click track, but in those days we went to a mike, stood around it and sang our songs. That is what we did in television, but they had slightly better equipment than they did in the studios because it was newer."

Whereas Lonnie is ebullient, his group (guitar, double-bass and drums) display little of their personalities. 'Brother Leslie', Les Bennetts, plays excellent guitar solos, but he is mostly chewing gum and looking bored. The arrangements differ from the records - Lonnie never sang a song the same way twice and 'Gamblin' Man' includes a drum solo.

The set may be cheap and perfunctory (Anne Shelton is given a set of steps which lead nowhere), but the budget did include Jack Parnell and his Orchestra. Some weeks they do little more than accompany Lonnie in his closer, 'So Long, It's Been Good To Know You', but the opportunity to sing standards is usually taken - 'Alright, Okay, You Win', 'Chesapeake Bay', 'Makin' Whoopee' with Sheila Buxton and 'Ac-cent-tchu-ate The Positive' with Alma Cogan and Ray Ellington.

The low budget affects the guest list. There are no A-list celebs. Lonnie keeps joking about Tommy Steele, but he is nowhere to be seen. The celebs are of the Glen Mason, Stan Stennett and Dallas Boys ilk. Lonnie and Hughie Green become song and dance men, and there are no concessions to rock'n'roll, which Lonnie lampoons with hip-shaking movements. He has a rock'n'roll pompadour though, but he is always smartly dressed, usually in bow-tie and dinner jacket. In 1960 he was listed as one of the ten best dressed men in Britain by the Wholesale Clothing Manufacturers' Association. Also in the list were the water speed record holder Donald Campbell, the MP Gerald Nabarro and the cricketer Peter May, but the magazine, 'Tailor And Cutter', was not impressed with this concession to modernity (or Millets). "Lonnie's imaginative and neat," said its editor, John Taylor, "but not, I think, material for my list." When Lonnie attended the awards ceremony, he wore a navy suit with pearl buttons on the cuffs for which he paid £25.

Lonnie told Steve Jones in 1986, "Right from the beginning, we wanted to give the impression of being professional musicians. We didn't want to be labelled snotty-nosed amateurs and so we tried very hard to be professional in our conduct, our appearance and our performance. These days the amateur is glorified and any hint of professionalism is frowned upon."

Lonnie really was puttin' on the style. He gave the 'Hit Parade' readers a lesson in how to dress. "In my view, the most important part of a man's dress is around his neck. Surprising? Look at it this way. When you're talking to a fellow, his face and neck are always in direct vision, and are never out of sight. So if a fellow sports a neat tie and a clean, well fitting shirt, half his battle to appear smart is over."

He comments on fashions of the day: "Take the Italian style pointed shoes. In moderation, this style is fine. But it can go haywire, and the pointedness can get out of hand. To my mind, they were obviously not designed for the comfort of the feet. Yes, I know your toes don't reach right down into the points. In which case, what a waste of leather!"

The best moments on 'Putting On The Donegan' are often at the start of the second half as Lonnie sings a tender ballad such as 'Times Are Getting Hard' and 'Nobody's Child'. Miki and Griff - Miki made her own clothes, incidentally - are regulars, performing a range of country standards. The filming, restricted by black and white, is generally very good and fine use is made of shadows, particularly when Monty Sunshine performs 'Lonesome' in silhouette.

There is one sketch with Chris Barber, who is as uncomfortable as Lonnie is at ease. The links and sketches were written by Lonnie's road manager, Peter Buchanan, who also wrote many of Lonnie's comic verses. There is a running one-line Jack Benny gag concentrating on Lonnie's meanness. Lonnie won't work with the Barber band until he knows how much they will cost. "Haven't you seen my money before?" he asks Chris. "No," says Barber. The repartee in 'Putting On The Donegan' is typical on Lonnie's own life. Many of the band members have anecdotes relating to conversations between Lonnie and Les Bennetts. Pete Merrick :"I can remember them being in armchairs, supping tea, and Les goes, 'Give us a bit of your bacon buttie, Lon.' 'No.' They go on reading the papers and Les says, 'Donegan?' 'What is it, Les?' 'Give us a bit of your bacon buttie.' This goes on until Lonnie is down to the last piece of bread: 'Lon, you're not going to eat that last piece of bacon buttie, are you?' 'For Christ's sake, Les, of course I am.' Les then says, 'Bev, do me a bacon buttie, will you?' She says, 'Can't, Les, I'm out of bacon.' 'In that case,' says Les, 'I will have to eat my own.' He puts his hand in his pocket and brings out, wrapped in aluminium foil, a bacon buttie that he had bought on his way to the flat."

In 1956 Chris Barber's Jazz Band had started the skiffle craze and, in 1959, they began the fad for Trad with 'Petite Fleur', a Top 3 record featuring Monty Sunshine's clarinet. Lonnie Donegan: "Nick Nicholls didn't want to leave me but he was promised a prince's ransom by Monty Sunshine when he left Chris Barber after 'Petite Fleur' made the charts. I've kept in touch with Nick and he did a pantomime with Mary Hopkin and me."

Nick Nicholls: "This is not quite true. I had known Monty socially for years and we had always agreed that we were going to play together someday. He asked me to join him and I felt the timing was right because I sussed that Lonnie really wanted to be a single. It was getting to be more like a vocalist in front of a trio instead of a group performing together. Nothing wrong with that of course, but it did lead to Lonnie recording songs that weren't right for him. He wasn't really suited to standards like 'The Party's Over', but I did love the way he did 'Lemon Tree'."

His replacement on the drums was Pete Appleby: "Lonnie rang me up and I had known him since his Chris Barber days. I was working with Mick Mulligan and George Melly, and I wasn't sure about joining him. I didn't want to get dressed in tights and do pantomime. He mentioned the money and I thought, 'Okay, I'll be Bob the Baker's man.' I'm glad I did it. It did take me away from jazz which was my first love, but it did open my eyes to a wholly different way of life. This was show business."

What comes across most in 'Putting On The Donegan' is Lonnie's confidence. Learning new lyrics or repartee does not phase him and, indeed, in 1960 he even included a 'controversial' verse about the Palace bins in 'My Old Man's A Dustman' for the Royal Variety Show in which he was featured in a pop sequence with Cliff Richard and Adam Faith. On a special Scottish Command Performance in Glasgow, Lonnie was pushed into a swimming-pool after performing, causing one critic to remark that it was "a most unfair way to end his act." Not that Lonnie minded, he would do anything for a laugh.

III.

With a view to having a lasting success with Lonnie Donegan in the American market, Ahmet Ertegun, the founder of Atlantic Records, invited him to New York in March 1960. He was assigned to Jerry Leiber and Mike Stoller, who had written many hits for the Coasters and Elvis Presley, and expectations were high. Lonnie's manager, Cyril Berlin, said that the sounds would not be achievable in the UK.

The intention must have been to release an album, but only nine tracks were recorded - four US singles ('Take This Hammer', 'Beyond The Sunset', 'Lorelei', 'The Wreck Of The John B') and a UK single ('Lorelei') and EP ('Yankee Doodle Donegan'). The single made the UK Top 10, but commercially, the trip did not achieve its intentions. Lonnie, too, must have been unsure of the results. In the liner notes for 'Yankee Doodle Donegan', he writes, "There they are. They are all experimental and the verdict now lies with you. I hope you are going to like them. Tell your friends to book early to avoid disappointment!!!"

The experimental nature would have come as no surprise to a viewer of 'Putting On The Donegan'. Lonnie is working with orchestral backings for the first time on record and, on the whole, doing very well. He is right in swingin' Sinatra territory with 'Nobody Understands Me' which has a cod Nelson Riddle arrangement from Stan Applebaum, while the string-drenched 'In All My Wildest Dreams' works very well.

The strings at the start of 'Corrine Corrina' resembles the swell at the start of the Drifters' 'This Magic Moment', but then settles into an easy-paced version of the folk song. Lonnie's second daughter, Corrina, had been born on 24 August 1958 and it is surprising that Lonnie did not seek to personalise the lyric. The big band version of the drugs song, 'Junko Partner', with King Curtis on sax also works very well. The full-blown 'Take This Hammer' with 'Chain Gang'-like groans does not work as well as the version with his group. Luke the Drifter becomes Lon the Drifter as he performs 'Beyond The Sunset' complete with narration.

Leiber and Stoller did not contribute, or offload, many of their own songs. Lonnie takes a 1958 Coasters' B-side, written by Leiber and Stoller, 'Sorry, But I'm Gonna Have To Pass', removing their novelty arrangement and treating it as an middle of the road ballad. (In view of Lonnie's marital problems, which we will be coming to, the lyrics of this song must have rung true, or rather, untrue.) The only new song that Leiber and Stoller gave Lonnie was the tall tale of 'Lorelei' in which he falls for a mermaid.

A West Indian calypso, 'The Wreck Of The John B', had been recorded in 1927, but Lonnie heard it on the Kingston Trio's first album in 1958. He had tried the song on the American sessions, but dissatisfied with the results, he reworked it in a new arrangement with Wally Stott and his Orchestra in April 1960. At over four minutes long, it had a verse removed before being released on a single. Now called 'I Wanna Go Home', the pop ballad made the UK Top 5 but the record is near perfect and deserved to make the top. The song was revamped as 'Sloop John B' by the Beach Boys in 1966 for their 'Pet Sounds' LP and became an international hit.

After adventurous singles with 'I Wanna Go Home' and 'Lorelei', Lonnie returned to familiar territory with 'Lively!', but it only reached Number 13. The construction was similar to 'My Old Man's A Dustman' and told of the escapades of a burglar: "I sang this song at a policeman's dance," says Lonnie, "but I was only singing for coppers." Halfway through, Lonnie adds some scat singing and some deliberately slurred vocals, suggesting that he is already fed up with the song. It was backed by a very swinging 'Black Cat' recorded in London with Ralph Dollimore and his Orchestra with a very overpowering drummer.

The Christmas single was 'Virgin Mary' with Miki and Griff. Lonnie said, "I was extremely disappointed that wasn't a big single as I thought it was the perfect song for the time. The BBC banned it as they considered it bad taste. Nobody heard it, so nobody bought it. It came from Jamaica, it was a Christmas carol and I sang it exactly as it was." The BBC's ban is mystifying and this song should have become a Christmas classic. Even now it cries out for someone to revive it. The B-side was a second arrangement of 'Beyond The Sunset', this time with Ralph Dollimore and his Orchestra.

The first single of 1961 was a ballad with Trad overtones, '(Bury Me) Beneath The Willow', but what song of suicide ever makes the charts? The song was written by the Pulitzer Prize winning writer, George Walker, but despite its pedigree, it was Lonnie's first single to miss the charts since 'Diggin' My Potatoes'. The B-side, Ray Charles' 'Leave My Woman Alone', which had also been recorded by the Kingston Trio, would have been a safer bet, but it was taken too fast and the arrangement was too show-biz.

The hit-making Adam Faith asked Lonnie Donegan for a song. Lonnie gave him 'Have A Drink On Me'. "Lonnie wrote that for me and brought it to me in pantomime in Wimbledon. It was different from my other hits so I didn't do it. He recorded it himself and had a huge hit with it and he put a little dig in it, 'You can make a fortune writing Adam Faith's songs'."

Lonnie Donegan: "Adam asked me for a skiffle song like 'The Wreck Of Ol'97'. I took 'Have A Whiff On Me', which originally referred to cocaine sniffing, and changed it to 'Have A Drink On Me'. Same song, same message really. Adam said it was too much like a Lonnie Donegan song. I said, 'Adam, that's what you wanted.' He said, 'I know, but I realised that I would only sound like an imitation.'" Much has been made of the importance of the scouse accents of the Liverpool bands, but was it such a cultural revolution? Lonnie Donegan, Adam Faith, Tommy Steele, Anthony Newley and the Vipers were working class London lads, who often emphasised their roots.

The B-side of 'Have A Drink On Me' was a beautiful ballad which had been recorded by the Weavers, 'Seven Daffodils'. it created some interest in its own right and it was revived by both the Mojos and the Cherokees in 1964.

'Have A Drink On Me' restored Lonnie Donegan to the charts, making the Top 10 and it was, incidentally, the first record that Rick Wakeman ever bought. Then something unlikely happened. Lonnie's 1959 US single on Dot, 'Does Your Chewing Gum Lose Its Flavour', was picked up by Arnie 'Woo Woo' Ginsberg of WMEX in Boston, Massachusetts, who played it incessantly. It created a demand and the single made the US Top 10. Bing Crosby, who was in the UK filming 'The Road To Hong Kong', presented Lonnie with two gold discs, one for 'Chewing Gum' and one, somewhat belatedly, for 'Rock Island Line'. It was mooted that Lonnie would make a comedy album for the US, but such tracks as 'She's Big, She's Blonde And She's Beautiful' remain unissued. On a promotional visit, Lonnie starred alongside jazz legend Stan Getz for a New York performance.

High on the US chart at the same time as Lonnie and eventually making Number 1 was 'Michael' by the Highwaymen. The campus quartet was very similar to the Kingston Trio, and Gil Robbins, a member of the Highwaymen, is the father of Hollywood actor, Tim Robbins. The UK songwriter, Tony Hiller, formed a vocal group to cover the song and made a version for Pye, produced by Tony Hatch: "We were pleased with it, but then we heard that Lonnie had decided to record it with an OB. Pye didn't want two versions so our record never got out, and we never even got as far as deciding our name."

Lonnie covered 'Michael' while he was appearing in a summer season called 'Putting On The Donegan' at Blackpool and using one of the support acts, Miki and Griff, on backing vocals. By upping the tempo, changing the arrangement and calling it 'Michael Row The Boat', he was able to place it with his own publishing company, Tyler Music. Lonnie was in the charts first, making Number 6, but surprisingly, the Highwaymen overtook him and went to the top.

That Lonnie lost the chart race is even more surprising as the record was promoted as a double-A side with 'Lumbered' from the hit West End musical, 'Stop The World, I Want To Get Off'. The performance is a hybrid of pop, jazz, skiffle and music hall - the whole essence of Lonnie Donegan in three minutes, in fact - and the comic lyrics by Anthony Newley and Leslie Bricusse are very good. Lonnie can't resist a comment of his own, reminiscent of his line about Adam Faith in 'Have A Drink On Me':

"I wrote Newley a long letter, saying why aren't pop songs better,

He put music to it and it was a hit."

Another Pye producer, Tony Hatch, asked Lonnie to cover the theme song from the western, 'The Comancheros', starring John Wayne, Stuart Whitman and Lee Marvin. This time Lonnie left the original by Claude King standing, but it only made the Top 20. He said, "I never really liked 'The Comancheros'. I did it because the record company said it was a commercial song and so on and so forth. I always felt like a second-hand Elvis Presley on that. It was never really me, I hate to admit that, but there you are." The B-side was Woody Guthrie's 'Ramblin' Round', which he had cut at the same time as 'Have A Drink On Me'. Whilst touring in New Zealand and presumably asking people to have a drink on him, Lonnie talked to a pub pianist in Timaru about songs they both knew. They improvised 'The Party's Over', which Lonnie then worked into a duet with the show's compère and comic, Des O'Connor. They closed the show with the song and Lonnie decided to record it for a single. This easy listening ballad from the 1956 musical, 'Bells Are Ringing', was recorded with Denny Wright on lead guitar and the Mike Sammes Singers and although it marked a change of style, it was so good that it made the Top 10. Purchasers found something even better on the flip, an exquisite 'Over The Rainbow', featuring vibes, which had been recorded at the same time.
Pete Appleby: "We were getting session fees for the records so it didn't affect us financially if a record was a hit or not, but I would be disappointed for Lonnie when things didn't happen. I was never sure about him doing the ballads as I didn't think he had the voice for it. 'The Party's Over' didn't gel for me, but I didn't say anything as he was the boss and could do what he wanted. On the other hand, I think his ballad singing on 'Seven Golden Daffodils' is wonderful."
Pete Huggett: "He took to the standards well, being a jazz player. I think his rendition of 'The Party's Over' is one of the best."
Lonnie and Jimmy Currie took a folk song, 'Wanderin'', which Josh White and Burl Ives had recorded and they rewrote the lyric and expanded the melody, turning it into 'I'll Never Fall In Love Again.'. Lonnie said, "I took a folk song that wasn't a very long one, and I rewrote the lyrics and added a chorus to it, the way I did with all the others. That was a deliberate attempt on my part to sound a bit like Ray Charles, who was coming to the front at that point. But I failed miserably. I didn't sound like Ray Charles and the record meant nothing to the great British public. Later on, Tom Jones was round at my house, thumbing through some of the records, and he said, 'I don't remember this one, boyo.' He played it and borrowed it and recorded it himself." Tom Jones' version of 'I'll Never Fall In Love Again' made Number 2 in 1967. It also made the US Top 10, where Sammy Kaye's treatment of the folk song had been a hit in 1950. 'I'll Never Fall In Love Again' has been recorded by numerous artists since and Lonnie was especially thrilled by Elvis Presley's version in 1976.
Donegan's B-side is a lively skiffle workout with the Kestrels of the Carter Family's 'Keep On The Sunny Side'. The next A-side, Leadbelly's musical round, 'Pick A Bale Of Cotton', was also recorded with the Kestrels, but in just 20 minutes. It had previously been recorded by the Vipers and also by Harry Belafonte. It was released as a single and returned Lonnie to the Top 20. It was a simple phrase repeated over and over again, but it enabled Lonnie to inject his personality. The B-side was a sensitive version of the inspirational ballad, 'Steal Away'.
Just to demonstrate how unhip Lonnie was becoming, he mimed to the record on 'Sunday Night At The London Palladium', so he could dance with the Tiller Girls, who included the future MP and Speaker of the House, Betty Boothroyd. By way of contrast, an intriguing performance has been preserved of Leadbelly performing the song at breakneck speed in a white hat and pastel-coloured clothes against a clear sky. See this and you will never forget

it.

In 1962 Lonnie called off a ten-week tour of the States because he wasn't allowed to take his own group. He was, however, considering a Broadway show, 'Kelly', which was about Steve Brody, an aggressive little Irishman who jumped off the Brooklyn Bridge for a bet. Towards the end of 1962, those former skifflers, the Beatles had their first hit with 'Love Me Do'. Lonnie noted with some irony, "The week they went into the charts, I went out. That's too much of a coincidence. Their first records sounded like all the rest of the stuff that was being bandied around at the time. What I did find attractive was their vocal harmony sound and they got better and better and better still as they went along."

By 1962, Lonnie had been three years without a new LP, although the hit compilations, 'Tops With Lonnie' and 'More Tops With Lonnie' (both with hideous covers) had done well. Inspired by 'Michael Row The Boat', Lonnie investigated the legacy of black gospel songs, which resulted in 'Sing Hallelujah', a brave release for a white UK artist. Apart from the rousing 'Joshua Fit The Battle Of Jericho' and the blues 'Nobody Knows The Trouble I've Seen', few of the potential buyers would know these tunes. It was a labour of love and he said, "I had been to black churches and when I sang the 'Hallelujah' songs, I really meant what I was singing."

Lonnie made the album with his group and the Kestrels but the album is not as exciting as it should have been. Donegan later performed better versions of 'New Burying Ground', while 'Born In Bethlehem' would have been preferable in an arrangement akin to 'Virgin Mary'. Part of the melody of Sister Rosetta Tharpe's 'This Train' has been lost. There is the feeling that nobody was taking much care with the LP - how else can the cough in 'Noah Found Grace In The Eyes Of The Lord' be explained? Sing hallelujah, indeed.

Lonnie greatly admired the music hall comic, Max Miller, who was known as the Cheeky Chappie. He said, "Max is so funny, he can get a laugh out of 'Good evening'." When Lonnie went to discuss a record with him, he found Max on his roof, cleaning out his gutters. Just one single was released. Lonnie and Peter Buchanan wrote the knockabout 'The Market Song', which a year earlier could have been a hit, but the fake audience laughter is irritating - the song is amusing rather than funny. The B-side, 'Tit Bits', written by Miller, was more of the same. Lonnie said, "Pye booked a hall and recorded us doing a spot together. The technical quality wasn't very good because Max wasn't used to recording. He'd move away from the microphone. We later recorded 'The Market Song' in a studio and that was released. Somewhere in Pye's vaults are two hours of Max Miller in concert accompanied by Lonnie Donegan's Skiffle Group."

This contrasts with Pete Huggett's memories: "I booked Star Sound as it was the only studio in London which had seating for an audience. Max Miller would only work with his costume on and he did a warm up, which was funny in itself, before we cut the single. I got the Tiller Girls to come along and sit in the front row. They were all wearing short skirts and when Max came on, they crossed their legs at the same time. Max nearly collapsed and then he tore the place apart. We did the single there and then and it was a good evening."

Max Miller had undertaken a tour of the Moss Empires and, despite warnings, he had constantly overrun, leaving the producer Val Parnell with an overtime bill for the theatre staff. After taking an extra eight minutes on a Royal Variety Performance, Parnell banned him from working for him again, to which Max retorted, "You're £40,000 too late." Lonnie planned to use Max on 'Sunday Night At The London Palladium' so that they could plug the single. As soon as Val Parnell heard of Lonnie's intention, he said no and Lonnie was left performing the song without him. Lonnie and Max never worked together again as Max died shortly afterwards, and Lonnie attended his funeral.

Although 'The Market Song' is an entertaining keepsake of their work together, it can also be viewed as another variation of 'My Old Man's A Dustman'. Lonnie was also facing competition from another Pye artist, Benny Hill, who drew on the same music-hall tradition for his smutty, comic songs. Indeed, Benny's 1961 hit, 'Gather In The Mushrooms' (1961), aped Donegan's frantic style. Lonnie said, "Songs like 'My Old Man's A Dustman' were fun to do because they were often recorded live and there weren't many acts who were up to doing that. But it was too successful. I found I was writing 'Son Of My Old Man's A Dustman Rides Again'. The record company wanted more of the same. 'Lively!' was one of those songs, but I was flogging a dead horse and things got overdone. The public stopped buying my records and effectively I'd thrown two careers away."

'pick a bale of cotton'

PYE 7N15455

LONNIE AT HIS BEST

ON the Pye label, "Losing By A Hair" is the latest from Lonnie Donegan and his Group. A sort of c-and-w number about a guy who came home late one night for his wife to discover some wrong-coloured hairs on his jacket.

Nothing new, then, about the story; main asset of the disc is the Donegan performance.

Lonnie is at his exhilarating best, building the song to a great climax.

"Trumpet Sounds" is a semi-spiritual and a very good one. As a song it's ten times better than the top side.

And the atomically explosive arrangement will shake your record player to its foundations!

LONNIE DONEGAN'S a keen motorist and usually has at least one high-powered sports car in his garage. But even he's discovered there are times when it's quicker—and fitter—to go by bike! This picture was taken at a cycle rally Lonnie helped organise in Great Yarmouth.

LONNIE GIVES ALL HE'S GOT AT BLACKPOOL

"LONNIE Gives All" could well be an alternative title for "Putting On The Donegan" which started its 22-week summer marathon at the Queens Theatre, Blackpool, last Saturday. He worked like a Trojan himself, and expected the whole talented cast to do the same.

Result? A loud, brash, but fast and entertaining family show in which Lonnie suffers everything except the traditional custard pie in his face.

But don't think for a minute that it is all Lonnie! There's The Kestrels—great! The Clark Bros.—those superb coloured American dancers and singers. Peter Goodwright's uncanny impressions. Miki And Griff with their folk songs and more comedy. The sweet voice of newcomer Jill Westlake and a real comedian Des O'Connor. And a fine on-stage band directed by Ken Moule.

Great seaside entertainment.

'500 Miles' will work steadily for Lonnie

Lonnie Donegan
500 Miles Away From Home; This Train
(Pye N 15579) ★★★

WHILE you're reading this review, Lonnie expects to be in Bermuda lolling in the sunshine, enjoying a holiday after spending 22 weeks entertaining other holiday makers in Blackpool. He leaves this disc behind to work for him. Which it will do steadily, no doubt.

I prefer Lonnie's treatment of **500 Miles Away From Home** to Bobby Bare's disc, reviewed last week . . . probably because of the absence of narration.

This Train—a familiar track from one of his long-players—shuffles along merrily on the turnover.

LONNIE—Now on holiday in Bermuda.

What next for Lonnie?

WHAT comes next for Lonnie Donegan —the man who only a few years ago was billed as "The King of Skiffle" and who has developed into one of this country's most polished and versatile entertainers?

This is the question that pop-fans are asking now that Donegan has surprised everyone once again by recording "A Very Good Year"—a song which is completely different to the zingy, swinging folk songs with which disc-lovers normally associate him.

In Blackpool, where he is having a highly successful season at the Queens Theatre, I asked Lonnie what had persuaded him to record this haunting ballad and what his plans were for the future.

"My first consideration was the song itself," he told me. "It was composed by an unknown writer on the West Coast of America where I first heard it and I really think it is one of the loveliest songs I have ever heard.

"Secondly, I wanted to try something which was as far removed as possible from the idiom in which I usually sing.

"The success of 'The Party's Over' proved that disc-fans would appreciate my singing a standard ballad, so I thought I'd try a slow-tempo number which was completely unknown.

"I'm delighted with the reception it has received because 'A Very Good Year' is one of the most satisfying records I have ever made."

I put it to Lonnie that many DISC readers would like to know whether there were any plans for old - style Donegan records, especially the comedy discs in which he is unsurpassed.

ALWAYS LOOKING

"I'm always looking for record material but, quite frankly, it's a tough job," he said.

"There is only a limited number of good folk songs and finding a top-class comedy number these days is like striking oil.

"As soon as the right number presents itself I'll record it.

"You see, I think the record-buying public are intelligent enough to know when a performer makes a disc just for the sake of making one.

"I'd rather wait until a song comes along which really excites me."

At the moment there are many thrilling plans being made in the Lonnie Donegan camp.

It is possible that he will make a British film in which he will have an acting part as well as singing role, and negotiations are going on for him to star in an American musical on Broadway.

If this latter deal comes off, he will be one of the first British light entertainers to star in a Broadway musical.

"I want to extend my horizons as much as possible," said Lonnie. "The idea of a musical has always appealed to me and the possibility of appearing on Broadway would thrill any performer."

Those who watched Lonnie's recent TV series and who see his current summer show will also notice that he is doing a great deal of comedy—and doing it very well.

Comedian Des O'Connor, who stars in the same show says, "If Lonnie wasn't first and foremost a singer he could probably be one of the best comics in this country."

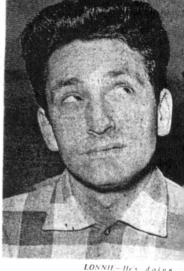

LONNIE—He's doing great deal of comedy

WE HAVE A LOT OF FUN

Says Lonnie, "Comedy has now become a very important part of my act. In fact, I've even got my group, Peter Huggett, Pete Appleby and Denny Wright telling gags now. We set out to have a lot of fun while we're working and I think we succeed."

Offstage, Lonnie is also keeping very busy. A keen footballer he plays regularly with the team of show-biz stars who are appearing in Blackpool for the summer and has won his place as the right winger.

"Won" is the right word, for competition is great to play for the team, which includes the Dallas Boys, Fred and Jeff Mudd, of the Mudlarks, Don Arrol, Des O'Connor and other top names.

They take their football very seriously and anyone who isn't playing bang on form finds himself dropped.

BIT OF A GIGGLE

"It's crazy," laughed Lonnie. "From being a bit of a giggle the team has suddenly started playing every match as though it's the world Cup Final.

What little bit of spare time Lonnie does have, which isn't devoted to cars or soccer, is given over to, as he puts it, "the noble art of stud-poker."

"The way things are going right now," he said. "If the American trip comes off I'll have to go to the States as a stow-away. My drummer, Pete Appleby, wins every time we play cards. In fact, I might even finish up working for him."

The next 12 months looks like being a decisive and important one in the life of Lonnie Donegan. His many thousands of fans will be hoping that it turns out to be "A Very Good Year."

John Peters

Lonnie not to play 'Kelly' on Broadway

RICHARD HARRIS, star of the film "Sporting Life," has been signed for the lead role in the Broadway production of "Kelly." Lonnie Donegan was in the running for this part.

"Naturally I'm disappointed," Lonnie told DISC.

It now seems likely that Lonnie will take up the offer to star in Anthony Newley's "Stop the World"—in Australia.

"I can't comment on that until I have further discussions with my manager, Cyril Berlin, who returns from holiday this weekend," said Lonnie.

ΟΝΝΙΕ DONEGAN

Beans In My Ears; It's A Long Road To Travel (Pye 7N 15669).

ΟΝΝΙΕ'S version of the Serendipidity Singers U.S. click should beat them over here, ainly because Lonnie's version far more angled at the British arket. It's a jolly little folk voured number with a never-let-guitar backing, and a repetitive vour about the lyric. Should be re popular with the Mums and ads. Flip is a gospel flavoured st affair with plenty of beat, d old time Donegan singing.

TOP FIFTY TIP

NIE DONEGAN (Pye) sings a sad d wistful ballad with whispering cking group and strings, "Get Out My Life." Sincerely handled, but ot hit material. Mid-tempo "Won't ou Tell Me" is dual-tracked with rgan.

NIE DONEGAN: **Auntie Maggie's Remedy; My Sweet Marie** (Pye : A rival to the Fourmost — Lonnie sells like a good 'un on the George Formby song, retaining all the old spirit. ★ ★ ★ ★

LONNIE DONEGAN

Reverting to his old swinging style, **Lonnie Donegan** enthusiastically gives out with a gay, snappy bouncer "Louisiana Man" (Pye), which he waxed in Nashville —with harmonica, banjo, clattering piano, driving beat, group joining in, and Lonnie occasionally going into falsetto.

It's an old Cajun number (half-Indian, half-French), and his most commercial for ages.

"Bound For Zion" is even faster. It's gospel-styled, and swings along at a breath-taking pace, with spirited chanting adding to the excitement.

John D. Loudermilk

The Lonnie Donegan Folk Album

NPL 18126

LONNIE DONEGAN

" World Cup Willie "/" Where In This World Are We Going " (Pye)

A music-hall personality routine—you can almost see Lonnie Donegan strutting across the stage as he sings it.

A Dixieland backing, complete with tuba and banjo, and a male group joining in the chorus complete the picture.

It's a bright-and-breezy jingle which will appeal to football fans (it's about the 1966 tournament to be staged in Britain), but I doubt if the girls will dig it.

Flip: He's in poignant, mildly protesting mood here, with guitar backing.

9. PUTTIN' ON THE AGONY
I. Family life
II. Working in the 1960s

I.

Much had been made of Lonnie's private life - he had had a house built at Woodford and he doted on his two children, Fiona and Corrina. But the image of family life was a charade as Lonnie was constantly busy and leading his life his own way on the road. Lonnie and Maureen split up in 1961 and divorced in November 1962. She was granted custody of the children and kept their house in Woodford. Because of the children, Lonnie and Maureen remained friendly. Commenting on their relationship some years later, he said, "I lived on adrenalin, which helped rot my heart and my liver, whereas I should have been living on love and affection. For the first time I had a real home of my own, but I let it go. Fame just hit me like a wave and I was swept along with it." From time to time, he commented, "She'd be with me now if she could be. I should never have bloody left her. I didn't know what I was doing."

In 1959 the 17 year old singer and dancer Jill Westlake met Lonnie Donegan when he was in pantomime in 'Cinderella' at Bournemouth. The following year they reprised their roles in Margate, and Cinderella and Buttons became an item. Lonnie said, "I wanted Jill because she was 18 and she looked just like my mother. Jill never loved me. Her mother put her up to marrying me because she wanted her to be married to a star. It was a horror story."

In 1963 Jill appeared on his TV series, 'Donegan's On Again' and also in his summer series at the Queens Theatre in Blackpool but they strove to keep their engagement secret. As Lonnie said, "I did not want my children to go to school and have all their pals saying daddy was marrying another girl." When the press found out, his daughter Fiona was distraught and refused to speak to him. Lonnie and Jill were married in June 1964.

They had two children - Anthony and Juanita. Lonnie dedicated his song, 'My Lovely Juanita', to her. Lonnie and Jill parted in 1970 and they were divorced in 1972. He said, "Just like my mother, she entirely failed to mother me. Jill wanted a father figure so it was hopeless. Things didn't go well on our wedding night, but we had two children and I stuck with it with for six years. I couldn't bear to break up another home and leave my children again."

Steve Jones recalls an accident when he was in the pantomime, 'Aladdin': "I think it was a tempestuous relationship but I wasn't there and I don't really know. The story was that he had slipped and put his hand through a plate glass door. He was the guv'nor so we believed him of course. It didn't affect him at all on stage. Dr. Showbiz, they want you on stage and that's what you do. He just did the panto with his hand bandaged."

Lonnie recorded the Jacques Brel and Rod McKuen song, 'If You Go Away', as part of his middle of the road album, 'Lonniepops', in 1970, but as he was recording the song, he realised how the lyrics applied to his own life and despite the overblown arrangement, he gave one of the best performances of his career. Lonnie said he would never sing it again. In interviews, however, Lonnie was rarely charitable towards his former wives. He told the 'Sunday Express' in 1979, "The kids are wonderful: it's the wives that are the problem. Maureen is remarried, but Jill isn't. She's very attractive, you know. Do you know anyone who'd marry her? It would cut down my alimony payments quite a bit."

II.

Lonnie Donegan was yesterday's news in 1963. The record charts were full of new beat groups and London had lost its stranglehold on the music business. Ironically, the lead vocalist, Tony Jackson, of Pye's top new act, the Searchers, was strongly influenced by Lonnie's nasal delivery. Bill Wyman recalls in 'Stone Alone' (1990): "I saw a Lonnie Donegan show and got so excited that I danced in the aisles for the first and only time in my life. He was brilliant. But he was to slag off and insult the Stones in later years, a mean characteristic of so many of the old jazz musicians we eclipsed in popularity."

Even if Lonnie had made the best records of his career, they would not have sold. And the irony of it all is that he did. Lonnie released an extraordinary single in 1963 and nobody took any notice.

Jack Rhodes, who wrote 'A Satisfied Mind' (Porter Wagoner), 'Woman Love' (Gene Vincent) and many lesser-known songs, had sent some demos of new songs to London. Lonnie was impressed by 'Losing By A Hair', which told of how a man's deception was discovered by a hair left on his jacket. Unfortunately, the song didn't fulfil the promise of its title and it was a weak A-side that would not have even succeeded in happier times. The B-side, 'Trumpet Sounds', is a terrible mess. Lonnie is drawing a link between first hearing a trumpet in a jazz club and the judgment on the final day, and although Tony Hatch's overblown arrangement is styled along Bobby Darin lines, it possesses none of Darin's subtlety and is unlistenable. Just as bad, and coming from the same sessions, was the B-side of the next single, 'Rise Up', an early Shel Silverstein composition. Donegan takes the gospel song too fast and the drummer must have been exhausted at the end of this two minute marathon.

Having made such an insensitive record, it is curious to report that, at the same time, Tony Hatch coaxed a brilliant performance from Lonnie and wrote the most sensitive of arrangements for 'It Was A Very Good Year'. This reflective song, in the same vein as 'September Song', was written by Ervin Drake, and had been recorded by the Kingston Trio on their album, 'Goin' Places' (1961). It had a sophisticated lyric in which a man mulled over the relationships of his life, comparing them to the wine he drinks. It is as though he is going into his cellar and picking out the years, 'When I was 17', 'When I was 21' and 'When I was 35'.

"When I was 35, it was a very good year,
It was a very good year for blue-blooded girls of independent means,
We would ride in limousines,
Their chauffeurs would drive,
When I was 35."

Drake, who had written 'Good Morning Heartache' for Billie Holiday, had excelled himself. Bob Shane's intimate vocal performance could hardly be bettered, but because he was the only member of the Trio featured and because it would have been too much of a change, it was not released as a single.

As soon as Lonnie heard the song, he knew it was a winner and he took the unusual step of acquiring its copyright for countries outside of America. Naturally, he wanted to record the song himself and he thought it would be better to run the verses together rather than separate them with the whistling on the Trio's version. A sleeve writer normally writes up the songs on an album, but writing about this record on 'Rock Island Line - The Singles Anthology', Stuart Colman says, "'It Was A Very Good Year' was simply outside Lonnie's league, and his cabaret-like air of indifference guaranteed scant airplay." I disagree - that air of indifference was deliberate and it made the song. This is American chanson and Lonnie is acting the part of someone who is not impressed by all he has experienced - I would put his record on a par with Peggy Lee's 'Is That All There Is'. Lonnie knew he had a great song and had made a great recording: the trouble was, at the time, the public did not know that. Lonnie liked his recording of 'It Was A Very Good Year': "The Kingston Trio recorded it before I did, but you'd hardly know we were singing the same song. After I'd done it, I was having lunch with my agent in New York and a bloke came up and asked me if I was Lonnie Donegan. He told me that he had written 'It Was A Very Good Year' and he said, 'I cried when I heard what you'd done with the song. It was beautiful.' You'd put things in there that I'd never written.' A short time later Frank Sinatra recorded the song and as his arrangement was so similar to mine, I can only conclude that he had been played my version. It's rather flattering because Tom's version of 'I'll Never Fall In Love Again' and Sinatra's version of 'It Was A Very Good Year' are very similar to mine I secured the publishing rights on the song in the UK so quite literally, I have Frank Sinatra working for me."

In 1965 Frank Sinatra, nearing 50, realised that this was a saloon song on a par with 'One For My Baby' and Gordon Jenkins' ultra-slow arrangement gets more dramatic as the singer reflects on his older years. The record is more significant than Donegan's because we can read so much of Sinatra's own life into it, but I don't think it is necessarily better, and nor does Lonnie. Pity I never asked Lonnie what he thought of Homer Simpson's version in 1995.

The gentle calypso, 'Lemon Tree', was written by the actor Will Holt and had been recorded by another US folk group, Peter, Paul and Mary. Lonnie is in good voice but he is let down by a disjointed arrangement from Tony Hatch. The B-side, 'I've Gotta Girl So Fine', was another one of Tony Hatch's big band arrangements. Why did he often make such a mess of things with Lonnie and yet do so well with Petula Clark? Still, it's amusing to hear Lonnie using a Frankie Valli falsetto and even though he wrote the song, it is no more than pedestrian words to 'This Little Light Of Mine'.

For his next single, Lonnie, now recording at Pye's new Marble Arch studios, covered Bobby Bare's country hit, '500 Miles Away From Home'. Although based on a folk song, it indicates Lonnie's growing interest in contemporary country music. In 1964 he covered a nonsense song recorded by the Serendipity Singers, 'Beans In My Ears'. The song had been banned in the States as it was felt that some silly listeners might follow the instructions and damage their hearing. As Lonnie says in one aside, "It's daft", and those daft voices predate Monty Python. An interesting curio, but a hit song it wasn't. Lonnie is battling with the orchestra on 'It's A Long Road To Travel' and both sides lost - another terrible recording, why was Lonnie wasting his time?

Wesley Rose, the head of Acuff-Rose Music, had formed a new US record label, Hickory, and he signed a licensing agreement with Pye. Lonnie had recorded a number of Acuff-Rose songs, notably 'The Battle Of New Orleans', and he invited him to record in Nashville. "I was the one in England who most looked like a country and western singer and so they asked me to go to Nashville. They sat me down with John D. Loudermilk and Doug Kershaw, the raging Cajun, and they assumed that this was the kind of music I was trying to make, and they were right. Pete Drake, Floyd Cramer, Charlie McCoy were also on the sessions. The tracks I cut in Nashville were extremely good but they meant nothing here simply because it was country music. I played the Grand Ole Opry two Saturdays running. I went on the first time and they were so delighted with me that they brought me back the next week." Lonnie is right - he sang 'Rock Island Line' both weeks and the reception was ecstatic - mind you, the audience had been conditioned to cheer everything, even the adverts. Lonnie gets a laugh when he says during the introduction to 'Rock Island Line', "unless they got certain things on board like DDT for the Beatles." June Carter, who introduces him, refers to him staying at Mother Maybelles' house.

The tracks from Lonnie Donegan's Atlantic sessions in 1960 had been issued piecemeal, largely because Lonnie hadn't made enough for an album. He should have learnt his lesson, but no, just nine short tracks were recorded in Nashville. Considering that Nashville musicians work so fast and that he was there for ten days, he should have done more. If he had released an album, 'Lonnie Donegan In Nashville', he would have done much for his own credibility, which was plummetting rapidly, and, indeed, for the standing of British country music as a whole. Lonnie said, "I loved being in Nashville and I am still proud of what we did there. It was a good professional job for its time. We were trying to copy what they are already masters of, so they must always be better and quicker and more tasteful than us, more creative." Oddly, Lonnie at times sounds more authentic than the Americans. Listen to the way he hollers and whoops on 'Cajun Joe', whilst the Jordanaires' backing vocals lack sparkle, and I defy anyone listening to 'Interstate 40' blind to say that Lonnie isn't American. However, 'Diamonds Of Dew', a duet with his wife, Jill Westlake featuring some pretty piano from Floyd Cramer, is close to Miki and Griff territory.

So, why didn't they complete an album? "Yes, it is a shame that we didn't complete one. I don't know why Wesley Rose suddenly decided to call a halt to it. With very little extra expenditure we could have had a comfortable album." Lonnie met the Everly Brothers in Nashville and a few folk songs with them could have been great.

Doug Kershaw was one of Nashville's rising stars as a result of his musical autobiography, 'Louisiana Man'. He was an excellent singer and fiddle player and a superb choice as he shared Donegan's exuberance. He described the French Cajuns in Louisiana in such songs as 'Cajun Joe', which Doug wrote with his brother, Rusty. Doug also wrote the whimsical ballad, 'Fisherman's Luck', the outstanding track from the sessions which became a single. Doug became a close friend and they were to work together again in 1978: "I didn't know much about him when he came over, but Acuff-Rose told me that he was huge in England. As soon as I heard him, I knew he was something else. He was doing my cajun songs and he did them very well."

Naturally, Wesley Rose was keen to have Donegan record songs that he published at Acuff-Rose. His top writers, Boudleaux and Felice Bryant, who had done so much for the Everly Brothers, gave Lonnie 'Lovey Told Me Goodbye', singer-songwriter Don Gibson supplied the spiritual 'There's A Big Wheel' (which he had yet to record himself), and John D. Loudermilk supplied 'Bad News' and 'Interstate 40', though both had been recorded by Loudermilk, as well as a new song, a cheating ballad 'Nothing To Gain'. Later in 1964, Johnny Cash would have a US country hit with 'Bad News'. Lonnie said, "'Interstate 40' is smashing. I love John D. Loudermilk's songs and all those songs are extremely good." 'Interstate 40' is a delightful, but poignant, song, close to a narration, about a broken but cheerful man who spends his life on the highway: "The Government's given me Interstate 40 and the Good Lord's given me a thumb."

When Lonnie returned to the UK, he continued with this theme and he had a number of songs by Billy Edd Wheeler that he wanted to record. Wheeler's songs had the same quirkiness as Loudermilk's ('She Was A T-Bone Talkin' Woman') and shared similar themes ('After Taxes'). Indeed, he had a country hit in 1964 with a song about an outside toilet, 'Ode To The Little Brown Shack Out Back'. Pete Oakman had joined Lonnie from Joe Brown's Bruvvers and he had a known affinity with the music as he had written Joe's country-styled hit, 'A Picture Of You'. A young British country musician, Pete Sayers, played banjo on the sessions.

The Billy Edd Wheeler songs are well performed - the up-tempo love song, 'I'm Gonna Be A Bachelor', the whimsical 'After Taxes' (and note how Lonnie anglicises the song in the final line), the story-song 'Reverend Mr. Black' (which was a US hit for the Kingston Trio), 'Blistered' (a Johnny Cash B-side, which would have been better served in Nashville) and 'She Was A T-Bone Talkin' Woman'. Lonnie said, "I never met Billy Edd Wheeler but his songs were damn good. 'She was a t-bone talkin' woman but she had a hot dog heart' is a damn good line. A lot of English people don't really listen to the lyrics: they don't hear what you're saying and it's a shame." Billy Edd's five songs were featured on the 1965 LP, 'The Lonnie Donegan Folk Album', which, somewhat ridiculously, had a very similar cover to 'Sing Hallelujah'.

Following Bob Dylan's lead, many folk singers were writing about the burning issues of the day - possible nuclear war ('A Hard Rain's A-Gonna Fall', 'Where Have All The Flowers Gone'), conflict in Cuba and Vietnam, and the destruction of the environment. Lonnie, who rarely took Guthrie's political songs and who, for example, had not come out in support of the Aldermaston CND march, sings Mike Settle's poignant 'Where In This World Are We Going' with the Breakaways as well as his gospel song, 'Bound For Zion'. The public was associating folk with protest so possibly Lonnie should have recorded more of the same if he was to call the album, 'The Lonnie Donegan Folk Album'. There is a Bob Dylan song on the LP admittedly, but it is only a reworking of 'The Leaving Of Liverpool', now called 'Farewell (Fare Thee Well)'. The album was completed by a Hank Williams weepie 'Wedding Bells' and a shaggy dog story with little melody about an elopement, 'The Doctor's Daughter'.

The singles were also damp squibs: 'Fisherman's Luck' had none and 'Louisiana Man' was probably too ethnic for the UK public, although Lonnie did perform a cajun set on the BBC's 'Saturday Club' with Brian Matthew. In-between them, Lonnie recorded a good-Dionne Warwick-styled ballad, 'Get Out Of My Life', which became a US hit for Little Anthony and the Imperials. Cliff Hall on organ was featured on the B-side, 'Won't You Tell Me', which found him harmonising like the Everly Brothers.

Lonnie had lost his popularity and a 1964 revamp of 'Putting On The Donegan' didn't pull in extra viewers, particularly when it was moved to a late night slot. Miki and Griff had gone and the Clark Brothers were added, and Lonnie featured songs from Broadway and West End shows. In 1968 Lonnie was featured with Leslie Crowther, Anita Harris and Peter Gordeno in 'Saturday Crowd', an early evening weekend series which ran for three months. Lonnie referred to Peter Gordeno as "your working man's Humperdinck".

Ironically, Lonnie was being discarded for his music-hall connotations and yet many of the Kinks' songs celebrate English working class life and are in that tradition. A few years later the same could be said of Lindisfarne. However, the Kinks and Lindisfarne were younger, had a more satirical edge, didn't perform in dinner-jackets and dicky bows, and weren't associated with summer seasons and pantomimes. A similar argument could be made for the demise of Trad. The public tired of the silly uniforms, and yet, in 1967, the Beatles were dressed like Trad leftovers for 'Sgt. Pepper's Lonely Hearts Club Band'.

Football singles were in their infancy in 1965, and 'World Cup Willie' is evidence of that. Lonnie wrote the song around England's mascot with the top comedy scriptwriter Sid Green, but the record deserved a green card. Tony Hatch recorded the song in a trad arrangement although it veers off into a crowd anthem at the end. Lonnie plugged it on 'The Kathy Kirby Show' but the fans ignored it, and deservedly so. England won the World Cup and yet this is surely the worst of all the official singles. Lonnie remembered the World Cup itself, "I was in Mexico and watching the match on a big screen. I was pelted with empty beer cans by the audience because there were only about four white faces in there."

Lonnie's group had now reconstituted itself as Cliff Hall (keyboards), Pete Oakman (bass) and Pete Appleby (drums) and he was using different guitarists on dates. Cliff Hall: "A lot of groups had had trouble with keyboard players, but the technology was much better by 1964 and Lonnie asked me to join with my Vox Continental. He didn't have a lead guitarist but he was an excellent rhythm player - I wouldn't say he was as good as Bruce Welch but he could have been. He was more interested in cabaret as a performance rather than shining as a musician, but it was very good band as the two Petes could really swing. He said to me, 'You sound fine musically, but smile a bit more. Look as if you're enjoying yourself', which was very good advice. Lonnie didn't have to look as if he was enjoying himself, he always was. He was a very happy guy when I knew him and full of life. He'd have liked to have been back in the charts but it didn't bother him. He loved touring and when we did some shows with the old-time comedian, Jimmy James, Lonnie was in the wings every night watching him. He was like Bob Monkhouse in that respect, a walking encyclopedia on these old comics. He could recite whole monologues by Billy Bennett."

'World Cup Willie' should have told Lonnie that he should leave the music hall behind but no. He revived George Formby's 'Auntie Maggie's Remedy', which is taken too fast and is nowhere near as strong as the album Clinton Ford made with George Chisholm, 'Clinton The Clown'. The B-side of the single, 'My Sweet Marie', sounds like a demo for the Everly Brothers and with more work, could have been an A-side.

Even worse was a single that was never issued - 'Ding Ding' which effectively was 'My Old Man's A Bus Conductor' and the jokes were feeble, ending, as if to stress the point, with a quip about a dustbin. The intended B-side was Leadbelly's 'Leaving Blues' with Cliff Hall on organ taking Lonnie into Animals territory, the closest that Lonnie had got to the new world of British beat groups. What he should have done was an album of blues covers and gone for the Rolling Stones market. Instead, he joined the casts of 'Stars And Garters' and 'Saturday Crowd'. When 'Record Collector' asked him about singing 'Where Did You Get That Hat' on 'The Good Old Days', he responded, "The later 60s were quite busy for me. Anyone who needs hot records for a living is in a precarious position." He told another reporter, "I coped very well by earning more money than I ever did before, playing all the big clubs."

Lonnie had worked in Las Vegas and observed cabaret acts like Jerry Lewis, Shelley Berman and Red Skelton. To a degree, he brought this gloss into his own act. Lonnie said, "In 1961 'Chewing Gum' was an enormous hit there. I could have stayed on but my first wife was pregnant. However, I'd learned how to cope with Las Vegas-type cabaret, so when it reared its ugly head in Britain, I was prepared. You can deride that from an artistic level, but it was very big money."

If Lonnie wanted good pop songs, why didn't he ask Roger Greenaway and Roger Cook, whom he knew from the Kestrels and were riding high with 'You've Got Your Troubles' for the Fortunes? What's more, he had seen Justin Hayward performing with Marty Wilde and recognised his potential as a songwriter. He acquired the rights to several of Justin's songs including 'Nights In White Satin', the royalties from which would see him through his lean years. Everytime it is played, some money goes to Lonnie Donegan. Donegan bought the rights for a mere £5. By 1979 the 'Daily Mail' reported that it had earned him over £100,000.

Lonnie Donegan: "Justin had written some songs and I wanted to do them but he said that he had written them for himself. I signed him up to my publishing company and to Pye Records and we made four tracks that are very rare recordings now. One of them was 'London Is Behind Me', which is a great song. He didn't really know what he wanted to do and then he joined the remnants of the Moody Blues."

And of course, why didn't he write his own material? His song, 'I'll Never Fall In Love Again', was a hit for Tom Jones in 1967 and was revived by Elvis Presley in 1976.

After ten years, Lonnie had finished at Pye and I wonder if they even noticed he had gone. The accountants may well have celebrated. His latest singles and albums had not repaid their expenses, and his hits were now available on budget-priced LPs, which admittedly were selling well.

Cliff Hall: "We all loved working with Lonnie, but he wasn't working for most of the year. He would do a six week tour and then take a couple of months off. He loved to swan off to Las Vegas. Pete Oakman, Pete Appleby and myself asked him if we could be on a retainer for the year, but he wouldn't have that. The three of us took a job at the Starlight Club in Redcar in Yorkshire, and it was regular work. Lonnie wasn't very happy about that and Pete Oakman went back to him."

In fact, Pete Appleby settled in Redcar and was only a few miles from Les Bennetts' mother.

When Les and June Bennetts were married, Pete had been their best man. Although they divorced, June often brought the children to see their grandmother. She mentioned that Pete Appleby lived a few miles away and they were married four months later. At the wedding reception, Pete showed the cinefilm of June's first wedding.

As well as the summer seasons, Lonnie was asked to support Judy Garland at the prestigious London nightspot, The Talk Of The Town. Garland was unreliable and, if the worst came to the worst, Lonnie could take over at the top of the bill when she wasn't there. The top critics came to see Garland and by giving quality performances, Lonnie garnered very good and unexpected reviews in quality newspapers. After the Garland season had finished, Lonnie starred there in his own right. Things were more humiliating at Blackpool in 1968 where he was second top to Engelbert Humperdinck and billed somewhat incongruously as 'Lonnie Donegan with Les Bennetts and the Group'.

Lonnie was proud of the pantomime, 'Aladdin', he did for the Glasgow Empire with Stanley Baxter and Ronnie Corbett in 1967. The show was written for him and the dancing was based on 'West Side Story'. Lonnie was so pleased that he repeated the panto at the same theatre the following year.

He still guested on television shows, often hosted by his friend, Des O'Connor. After some banter with Donovan on a live TV show (he accused Donovan of stealing his name!), the host Simon Dee said, "I'd heard you were difficult to work with" and Lonnie responded, "Yes, and now you're finding out that it's true."

Lonnie also played some concerts with Tom Jones in the late 60s and appeared as a star guest on his US TV show, 'This Is Tom Jones', which was filmed in the UK. Tom and Lonnie sang a medley of spirituals. He also played Las Vegas, working with Vikki Carr in 1968, Engelbert Humperdinck in 1969 and Vic Damone in 1970.

The record companies were not lining up to sign Lonnie. He didn't record at all in 1967 and his only offering in 1968 was a single, 'Toys' and 'Relax Your Mind', for EMI's Columbia label. In 1969 he did get back on television with the series, 'Lonnie', with Roy Hudd and Millicent Martin. He told the press that he saw himself as a "young Billy Cotton". He added, "I don't want to do all that jumping about anymore. My idea is just to stand still and put over a good lyric." He also said that he was tired of dustbins.

Drummer Pete Merrick: "Everything Lon was doing was pure vaudeville, and he and Les Bennetts taught me a lot about stagecraft. Lon liked to have drum effects for whatever he did. Les told me when the cowbell, the bass drum bash or the cymbol crash would come in. The drummer never stopped, so it was a good job. Lon always swung like the clappers, and his banjo playing was great. He could play banjo in one time and tap his foot in another and sing in another time against that, and that could piss drummers off. It used to piss Chris Barber off too as he couldn't do it. If we were chasing 'Rock Island Line', Lon would think nothing of dropping two beats out of a measure, but somehow or other it got tagged on the end. He had an inbuilt talent, I suppose. It was incredible to work with him."

In 1970 he recorded an album of contemporary material, 'Lonniepops', for Decca. Well, when I say 'contemporary', Lonnie wasn't going psychedelic. They were the hit songs of the day like 'Both Sides Now', 'The Windmills Of Your Mind' and, Lord above, 'Long Haired Lover From Liverpool', although Little Jimmy Osmond wouldn't sing it until 1972. By now, Lonnie was firmly entrenched in the cabaret world, which explains the full-blown, lush arrangements and the singalong nonsense of 'Hey Hey'.

Lonnie is on his best behaviour for the album and, apart from the occasional rolling r, he performs the Bee Gees' 'First Of May' and Burt Bacharach and Hal David's 'What The World Needs Now Is Love' as straight as he can. His vocal on the verses for Sandy Denny's 'Who Knows Where The Time Goes' is one of his best, but the song is ruined by a kitchen sink arrangement. 'Little Green Apples' would have sounded better with just his regular musicians.

Lonnie Donegan co-wrote the delicate 'Love Song To A Princess' and Lonnie pays tribute to his daughter with 'My Lovely Juanita', which was released as a single. The album closes with a ballad from Dave Cousins of the Strawbs, 'And You Need Me', which was recast as a pop song. He said, "I thought that was a lovely song. The title of the album was 'Lonniepops' which was its worst enemy as nobody is going to buy an album called 'Lonniepops'. The idea was that it was Lonnie singing the popular standards of the day and I had a lot to choose from and that was one of the ones I chose. As far as I'm concerned it is one of my best albums."

Although **LONNIE DONEGAN** has been keeping a bit quiet on the record scene lately, he has been drawing crowds and crowds to cabaret and night-clubs. Now he has a new single out, and it's a song of his own, 'My lovely Juanita'. It's a change from his usual style, a gentle love song with a Continental flavour, and you'll find it on Decca F 12984.

LONNIE DONEGAN: 'I've Lost My Little Willie' (Decca FR 13669) Ties in with Benny Green's book about saucy holiday postcards. Ol' Lonnie spills double-entendres about his Little Willie in Cockney cheeky chappie style. East End music hall fun.

A secret wife for the king of skiffle

Lonnie Donegan and wife Sharon . . . they met when she was 16   PICTURE BY STEVE LEWIS

SKIFFLE KING Lonnie Donegan's secret is out. He has been married for three years—to a girl less than half his age.

Sharon, his third wife, met Donegan five years ago. He was 45 and she was 16.

Her parents had taken her to see him when he was appearing in summer season at her home town, Scarborough.

A week later she went back to see the show again, and waited outside Donegan's dressing room for his autograph.

TERRIFIC

Donegan, a guest in tonight's **Lennie And Jerry** (BBC 1, 7.55) says: " I thought she was so terrific I invited her back the next day and we started going together from then on."

But when it came to proposing. D o n e g a n t w i c e divorced — was worried.

He says: "I had committed myself to two marriages and I didn't want to do it again.

" In the end it was desperate. She was beginning to take an interest in another man because she was not being promised a future with me.

HAPPY

" So I made the decision and now we couldn't be happier. She's my Miss Perfect."

Sharon's parents were happy with the marriage plans too, although her father was two years younger than his prospective son-in-law.

Sharon helped nurse Donegan through three heart attacks in 1976.

" I feel fine now," he says. "I've developed the philosophy of 'let 'em wait'."

JOHN DODD

LONNIE DONEGAN
BURNING BRIDGES
7N 45009   PYE

Treadin' the boards;
Above in Panto amd left at
the end of the Pier. and
Lonnie's former Pye label
mate Joe 'Mr. Piano'
Henderson
'Hey-bop-a-ree-bop'!

Lonnie decked out in
his western jump-suit for
the Wembley Country Music
Festival
(Photo; Graham Barker)

(Left) Lonnie and Adam Faith

● **Lonnie Donegan** is back on scene with a new LP on Chrysalis label titled "Puttin' The Style", issued on February 3 features up-dated versions many of his old hits, and the a star backing includes Ringo Sta Leo Sayer, Elton John, Ro Gallagher, Ron Wood, Brian Ma Mick Ralphs and Albert Lee.

Great toget
Lonnie and
Gallagher (

LONNIE DONEGAN — Sundown

All Out And Down / Home / Streamline Train / Sundown / Mama's Got The Know How / Morning Light / Louisiana Sun / The Battle of New Orleans / Cajun Stripper / Dreaming My Dreams

(Chrysalis CHR 1205)********

It's weird how you can go years without thinking of someone and then have a few things nudge your memory. Lord knows how long it's been since Lonnie Donegan crossed my mind or came up in conversation, but just before Christmas I dragged out a copy of his 1957 Nixa 10 album "Lonnie Donegan Showcase" to play the version of "Frankie and Johnny" on it to an American friend. He was amazed, as was I, at how gutsy that version sounded. So much drive and life. And now, out of the blues, comes this new LP to prove that while Donegan may have been out of the spotlight for a while (he suffered a major heart attack a year or so ago), put in the studio with the right people he can still deliver heavy goods.

Producer Adam Faith has done just that: with Albert Lee, Doug Kershaw, Emery Gordy, Mickey Raphael, Richard Bennett and Ray Cooper lending support, Lonnie Donegan fires on all cylinders to come up with an album I can only recommend in the highest terms. The same old hard, high voice is there, the same attack on lyrics, the same bubble of fun just beneath the surface. Highlights must include a tremendous "Streamline Train", which features an astounding guitar solo from Albert Lee, two roaring cajun specials in "Cajun Stripper" and "Home" (although Doug Kershaw's sawing fiddle work on "Battle of New Orleans" adds more than a touch of the bayou to re-working of what, in Britain, became a Donegan classic), and a haunting and atmospheric version of Gordon Lightfoot's "Sundown". This is the second 'revival' album for Chrysalis by Lonnie Donegan. I urge you to check it out. I know I'm going to get the first.

D.S.

10. CHRYSALIS
I. Sharon
II. Comeback albums
III. A comeback show

I.

An unguarded moment from a live interview with Ken Bruce on BBC Radio 2 in 1999. Lonnie was there to promote his new album, but the conversation turned to other things.

Ken Bruce: "There is a bit of a debt that you owe to Sharon, your third wife, and she says that at age of 40 you were completely lost. Now she was 14, you were doing a bit of a Bill Wyman here. How come you weren't on the front page of 'The Sun'?"

Lonnie Donegan: "Well, because I kept my big mouth shut. She lied. (laughs)."

Ken Bruce: "Did you go to her mum and dad and say, 'I would like to take your daughter out.'"

Lonnie Donegan: "Yeah, in the normal way. I thought she was 16, to be honest. She said she was 16 and she was at work. I was doing a summer season at Scarborough and I had seen her at work in the shop. I went into the shop and bought dresses for my daughter. I took her out for a meal and then took her home and her dad was waiting outside. He said, 'Bit late is this.' I said, 'Sorry'. It was half-past eleven. I said, 'What's the problem?' and he said, 'She has to be up in the morning for school.' I said, 'No, she's at work.' He said, 'Oh, ay, back in summer, but she is back to school now.' I said, 'Back to school! How old is she?' He said, 'How old did you think she was?' I said, 'She's just had a birthday, she's 16.' 'No,' said her father, '14.' Oh, Jesus…(Ken Bruce laughs) Backed off sharpish."

Ken Bruce: (laughing) "Yeah, I had an irate dad do that once."

Lonnie had an active love life and he often succumbed to the temptations of the road. Whilst starring in a summer season in Rhyl in 1966, for example, he was living with an ice-skater, although still married to Jill Westlake.
In 1972 Lonnie was playing a summer season at the Floral Hall, Scarborough with Freddie 'Parrot Face' Davies, the Dallas Boys and Isla St. Clair. A plumber and his wife took along their daughter, Sharon, who had no idea who Lonnie was. She was transfixed and asked for his autograph. Lonnie said, "She was very sweet and innocent, quite unlike any girl I had met." He was two years older than her father.
When Sharon was 15, she left home and went to work in a hotel owned by Lonnie. He admitted to Jane Kelly of the 'Daily Mail' on 10 May 1996 that "She was under age when we started sleeping together. Bill Wyman didn't get away with it, but I did because I am much smarter than him."
In the same feature, Sharon said, "He was very lonely, he missed his four children and we had similar problems. My parents were not affectionate to me. We were both in a bad way when we met, so we just clung to each other. Lonnie always told me that he didn't want to get married again because he had had two bad experiences."
Lonnie Donegan was breaking the law and the fact that it worked out so well in the end does not condone it. Everything that follows could have turned out very differently. Lonnie Donegan could have been arrested and could have gone to jail.
In 1974 his daughter, Fiona, was married on Cup Final day. Lonnie chose to watch

Southampton beating Manchester United. He didn't respond to the wedding invitation and didn't turn up.

As well as inheriting Lonnie's family problems, Sharon also had to cope with his ill health. Lonnie Donegan: "I had my first heart attack in 1976, and I had to stop work then. That's why I went to live in California, because no one could tell me if I'd ever get better, so I went out there and contemplated my navel."

Sharon said, "As he has matured, he has become a total father to me, the one I never had. And I am like a mother to him. When I met him he was 40 and still like a confused little boy." In spite of these reservations, Sharon's parents were on the front row when Lonnie was the subject of 'This Is Your Life' in 1991.

Lonnie and Sharon had a log cabin built in Lake Tahoe. Lonnie had been reluctant to remarry but in 1979, they were married on the lawn of their home. His best man, Peter Allan, was the manager at a casino he played at in the area. As part of the ceremony, they received a blessing from an elder of the Washoe tribe: "You feel no cold., for you will be warmth for the other. There will be no loneliness for you, although you are still two bodies, there is only one life before you."

Together Lonnie and Sharon raised three children, Peter (born 1983), David (born 1988) and Andrew (born 1990). Andrew was a surviving twin and the Donegan family had a worrisome time as he was just two and a half pounds when he was born. Lonnie described it as traumatic as having a heart attack or losing his mother.

The US folksinger, Oscar Brand, visited Lonnie in Lake Tahoe: "I knew about him and I had often played his recordings on my radio programmes, especially when they coincided with American folk music. I was a judge in Reno, Nevada on the subject of whistlers, and when I learnt that Lonnie was nearby, I got someone drive me over to where he was. I was fascinated by his great interest in Leadbelly, who was a friend of mine. He had had a tremendous influence in England but he had withered. It bothered him because he thought that as an innovator and really an inventor of British rock'n'roll music, rhythm and blues, that he should have had a much greater position in English society and at least he should have been acclaimed in the books as an important influence. He was rueful whereas he shouldn't have been. He was not so important in the States and the reason he believed, and I do too, is that he wasn't Leadbelly. He had attached his star to the aura of one of the great American singers."

II.

By 1970 it looked as though Lonnie Donegan's career would settle into one long anti-climax. He was yesterday's news, getting the work and doing well, but there was little creativity involved. He would do club dates throughout the year and then appear in pantomime. Some of the pantomimes had remarkable casts. In 1971 he was again Buttons, this time to Mary Hopkins's 'Cinderella. Also in the cast were Arthur Askey, Peter Butterworth and David Essex. I imagine that he was complaining that he was only paid buttons. He wasn't all showbiz though - when he appeared on 'New Faces' as judge, he gave zero to one of the acts. Could he have become a Simon Callow or Pete Waterman? Any new records that Lonnie Donegan made were having to compete with reissues of his best-known tracks. He returned to Pye for a few singles, the Lalo Schifrin story-song from the Clint Eastwood film, 'Kelly's Heroes', 'Burning Bridges', the R&B ballad, 'Till I Can't Take It Anymore' (1970) and 'Speak To The Sky' (a Rick Springfield spiritual but not distinctive enough for a single, 1972). In 1973 there was also a cheerful rave-up with Kenny Ball's Jazzmen, 'Who's Gonna Play This Old Piano (When I'm Dead And Gone)?', an odd choice as Lonnie was no pianist.

In 1972 Lonnie appeared on 'Opportunity Knocks', not, I hasten to add, as a contestant but as a guest star performing 'Keep Britain Tidy' in a Jimmy Durante voice. The recording was played as the opening song on 'Children's Choice' the following week, but it was never released. A few months later he sang Nilsson's hit, 'Without You', with a full orchestral backing on Radio 4, but this, too, was not released. Quite a change from his appearances on 'The Wheeltappers And Shunters Club'.

In December 1972 Lonnie went to Germany for concert dates with the promoter Karsten Jahnke and he loved telling the story of what happened next. "I got a call from a promoter to come over 'und do der skiffle'. The first night in Kiel, I went straight into my Vegas act - (sings) 'Flyyyy me to the moon' - and someone shouted, 'Ve haff come to hear der skiffle. Vhere ist your vashboard?' The Germans had regressed, they were back at the beginnings of skiffle with very definite ideas of what skiffle should be - no washboard, no skiffle. After the concert, the promoter said that my act was all right for Vegas, but it didn't mean a light in Germany as the audience wanted skiffle. And they didn't want me in a tuxedo. I'd never worn jeans on stage in my life, but I realised I would have to do that the next night. I was playing at Hamburg's Musikhalle and we made no big entrance, just wandered on with our beers and plugged in. And the Germans loved it."

The supporting act for Lonnie Donegan was the German skiffle band, Leinemann, whose lineup included two Star-Club veterans, Uli Salm on bass and Ulf Kruger on washboard. Lonnie worked with them on stage and they recorded an album, 'Lonnie Donegan Meets Leinemann', for the German branch of the Philips label in 1974. The result was a mixture of the 50s Lonnie with the current version. They recorded some fine but rather restrained (for him) versions of his hits (with a really good 'Diggin' My Potatoes'), but the album also shows Lonnie's love of contemporary country music. There are good versions of Kris Kristofferson's 'Me And Bobby McGee' and 'Casey's Last Ride', and he also performs Leadbelly's 'Becky Deen'. And what could be more middle of the road pop than his own song, 'Tops At Loving You'?

In 1976 there was a second collaboration, 'Country Roads', although, the title notwithstanding, this was not a collection of country songs. The title track was John Denver's 'Take Me Home, Country Roads', but much of the rest was familiar skiffle material - 'Midnight Special', 'Lost John' and 'Have A Drink On Me' (with Tom Jones replacing Adam Faith in the lyric). The band doesn't have enough drive to make Lonnie's raving 'Rock Island Line' work but better versions were to come. He also does Joe Brown's song about a drunken Irishman in Liverpool, 'Dublin O'Shea' (published by Lonnie), and Elton John and Bernie Taupin's tribute to a showboat, 'Dixie Lily', from Elton's 'Caribou' album. Leinemann worked as a contemporary skiffle band and also made their own single, 'Lonnie Donegan Is The King Of Skiffle'.

In 1975 Chris Barber arranged a UK tour to celebrate the twenty-first anniversary of the Chris Barber band. The date was somewhat tenuous but the intention was to reform the 1954 line-up. Chris asked Lonnie to play banjo and to perform a skiffle set. They planned to record a live double-album at the Fairfield Hall, Croydon, but the concert was interrupted by a bomb scare. The musicians entertained the audience with an impromptu concert in the car park and then marched them back in. Because of the delay, not all the intended repertoire was recorded so further tracks were added in the studio to make the double-album, 'The Great Reunion Album'. Lonnie performed 'Jenny's Ball' with Chris Barber's Jazz Band, and did three more songs in a skiffle set, 'On A Monday', 'Bury My Body' and 'Lost John'. Lonnie said, "That was a miraculous event. We hadn't rehearsed and I hadn't played those banjo parts in years. I was very nervous but Chris said it would all come back to me, and it did. 'On A Monday' is an American negro work song. around Georgia and Alabama and it is typical of the songs I sing. Probably 50 per cent of the songs I sing are of that nature."

Many acts were working the UK club circuit and Lonnie followed the trend of having an album which would be exclusive to the gigs. In 1976 he made 'Lonnie Donegan' for his own Tyler label, purely for sale at his shows, although a cassette version with slightly different tracks was later put into the shops.

Although it has its moments, this cheapo-cheapo release was not thought out much beyond cost considerations. Lonnie has the rights to his singles, 'Burning Bridges', 'Till I Can't Take It Anymore', and a massively overblown ballad, 'Don't Blame The Child'. He revived a few old hits - you can sense that 'Rock Island Line' is becoming the tour de force that it became, while 'My Old Man's A Dustman' with a Salvation Army drum and feeble jokes is a travesty of the original. The revised 'Chewing Gum' is surprisingly good, the new verses being superior to the original ones. 'I Lost My Heart On The 5.42' is a light-hearted love song set in London, while Lonnie recorded his own version of 'Come To Australia (Great Uncle Albert Is Dead)' (with Vikki Brown prominent). He had previously backed his bass player, Steve Jones, on a single for the Australian market.

Lonnie recorded a novelty, also associated with Joe Brown, 'Hit Me Across The Head With A Spoon, Mama' and the ballad, 'Beyond The Shadows', which had been recorded by Miki and Griff in 1961. The best of the new tracks is a touching version of Cyril Tawney's folk song, 'Ballad Of Sammy's Bar'. As an example of how difficult this album was to acquire, Cyril Tawney told me in the early 80s that he couldn't find it anywhere and he wanted to hear how Lonnie performed his song.

In 1976, Lonnie Donegan, was still playing football for showbiz teams. The journalist, David Charters, recalls saying to Les Bennetts after one game, "Lonnie seems a regular guy" and Les said, "That's because you don't know him."

Pete Merrick: "I was driving Lon's car and we were in Skegness, and I went round to the hotel and Sharon told me that Lon had been ill during the night. They hadn't got a doctor because they wanted me to drive him down to Dr. Sinclair in Marble Arch. I said, 'We've got to be in Glasgow tonight', and he said, 'That won't make any difference.' It was an estate car and we put the seat down in the back and wrapped him up with blankets and pillows. We took him to Marble Arch and he got out of the car quite calmly and went to see Dr. Sinclair. I was driving round in circles until he came out. Dr. Sinclair told him, 'Remember Lonnie, start eating sensibly, start sleeping sensibly, don't keep having soup and potatoes late at night, just have a light meal and you should be okay.' Then we had to drive like hell up to the Glasgow Rangers supporters club. We worked okay that week at Glasgow Rangers. We didn't realise he had had a heart attack."

In fact, the doctor had told Lonnie that he had probably had a heart attack, but Lonnie was reluctant to scrap five weeks of club dates. He agreed to cut out the strenuous parts of his act (that would be a first), cancel some Australian dates and then go to California on holiday.

Before he went, Lonnie also made a single for Decca. Denis King of the King Brothers had become a noted TV and film composer, but neither distinguished themselves on 'I've Lost My Little Willie', the title coming from one of Donald McGill's comic postcards. :The singer loses his brother at a racetrack and a ravishing blonde finds him:

"I've seen your little willie and he's growing rather fast,
He looks distinctly larger than the time I saw him last."

Lonnie presumably thinks the song is beyond redemption as he slurs and mumbles many of the words, and the track isn't helped by canned applause and laughter. Peter Buchanan and Lonnie Donegan wrote another jokey song, 'Censored', for the B-side, but again this is nonsense rather than wit. I showed Lonnie the single, which I had bought for 10p. "You were done. It is not worth anything at all. I recorded it the day before I went to live in the States and that may explain things."

After his myocardial infarction, it looked as though Lonnie would go into retirement or at least semi-retirement. But was there anything left for him to do - he had been there, done that and got the dress-shirt?

Well, yes, there was. The early 60s pop star, Adam Faith, was now a record producer, having hits with Leo Sayer. Adam Faith: "I was in Los Angeles and I spent the day with Paul McCartney when they were on tour with Wings. They did the show at the Forum and after the show, there was a party in the green room. We had a table fenced off from the rest, and there was Paul and Linda, John Bonham, Elton John, Cher, Harry Nilsson, Ringo Starr, Leo Sayer and myself. Paul and Linda started doing impressions of me and Charlie Endell in 'Budgie'. That set them off on my songs and I said, 'Never mind 'What Do You Want', what about Lonnie Donegan?' That got them all on fire as they were all influenced by Lonnie and before long, we were all singing Lonnie Donegan songs. I got them to promise that if I went back to England and found Lonnie, I would produce an album of his old hits featuring top rock musicians and they would play on it. They all agreed and when I got home, I flew from Heathrow to Glasgow, where Lonnie was doing a gig for one of the supporters' clubs. I told Lonnie what we were going to do and we had a marvellous 18 months. We had some wonderful people on that album."

The album, 'Puttin' On The Style', was mostly made in London, but Lonnie had become a tax exile and so could only visit the UK for three months in the year. In addition, his health was poor and he wasn't wholly enthusiastic about the project: "I wasn't too keen at first because, to be quite honest, my old hits are a pain in the arse. They don't mean anything to me anymore. I thoroughly enjoyed making that album but if I'm booked anywhere, don't expect me to sing 'The Grand Coulee Dam' and 'My Old Man's A Dustman' all night. I do about fifty - fifty and that's about right. The album was good for me in that it made me think about them and think of different ways to approach them. I still do 'Rock Island Line', only now I do it better. Chiefly, the album was a calling card to get me noticed again. And it worked. It was picked up by the papers which was lovely."

The media loved the album as it featured Gary Brooker, Rory Gallagher, Elton John, Albert Lee, Brian May, Zoot Money, Leo Sayer, Ringo Starr, Klaus Voormann , Pete Wingfield and Ronnie Wood.. No Paul and Linda as they had other commitments. Lonnie said, "It was really nice working with them all. They all worked for nothing too. They had to. How could I afford to pay Elton John? I enjoyed having Adam Faith produce the album, but even with that line-up, they couldn't make me a star again. The prime reason was that it was aimed at America and the record company didn't know how to market it. They were too busy promoting Blondie, I think."

However, when you listen to the album now, it is disappointing. The arrangements are brash and cluttered and it sounds like one rave-up after another, perhaps because everyone had to have a chance to shine. The string arrangement on 'I Wanna Go Home' only makes a mishmash worse. Its shortcomings are all the more surprising as Adam Faith was calling Lonnie one of the world's best blues singers. Why didn't he manage to capture it?

Lonnie said, "The album did not come out as well as it should have done. An awful lot of talent went into that record, just about the best talent available in Britain. What came out was too much variety of sound. It would have been better to have selected a group from all those great talents and gone through the album with them, and that would have evolved into a sound that you could recognise and sell. As it was, it came out like a series of jam sessions which had no great appeal." In 2002 Lonnie had plans to remix the album and possibly there were bonus tracks to be added: for example, Lonnie mentioned that Brian May had asked to do 'I'm Just A Rollin' Stone'.

Individually, several of the tracks are very good. The rockin' 'Rock Island Line' with Rory Gallagher on lead guitar was deservedly chosen as a single and became the template for Lonnie's subsequent performances. Lonnie and Rory did consider touring together and certainly the combination of the two of them on stage could have been electrifying. They did cut Rory's Leadbelly-styled song, "Goin' To My Hometown" during the album sessions and then again in the early 1980s. It's a good homage to skiffle but they didn't work on it seriously enough. In 1997, the rock manager Donal Gallagher presented some tribute concerts to his late brother featuring Lonnie, Peter Green and Paul Jones.

Not everything, or everyone, worked at the 'Puttin' On The Style' recordings. Lonnie Donegan: "Graham Nash was in such a state that he never played on the sessions. He was such a bundle of nerves and he said there was no way he could play guitar with me. He was convinced he was hopeless at the task."

One of the recording engineers, Colin Fairley, seized his chance on the title song. Lonnie Donegan: "The drummer didn't turn up. The tape boy had his drums in the cupboard and so they used him. I said, 'All you have to is to keep the tempo', but he turned out to be great. We offered him a job the next morning. He had arthritis in his hands and needed injections so he couldn't play regularly."

Rev. James Cleveland arranges some beautiful background harmonies for the Southern California Community Choir on 'Nobody's Child'. The new recording had been Lonnie's idea. Lonnie Donegan: "I had recorded the song for Pye but I didn't do it all that well. Well, it was quite respectable for those days. I love my new version on this record but when I sing it on stage, I do it differently again. It's more like the old version, but slower." The religious vocal group can also be heard, rather incongruously, on 'Have A Drink On Me'. Leo Sayer plays harmonica like Sonny Terry on 'Ham'n'Eggs'. The only surprise in the track selection is the Sleepy John Estes blues, 'Drop Down Baby'. Lonnie said, "Adam refused to let me do any new material with the exception of 'Drop Down Baby', an old blues number I have always wanted to do."

Lonnie promoted the album at every opportunity, talking it up wherever he could. He told 'The Sun' in January 1978: "The result is way beyond my wildest dreams. I am delighted with the way the album has turned out. I don't know much about the rock scene, but I like what I hear and I am very impressed by all the people I have worked with."

The album sold respectably and it was evident that an album of new material was the next step. "It all fell into place very well. Shortly after I'd finished promoting that album, I bumped into Doug Kershaw, the cajun fiddler. 'You're a fine friend,' he said, 'not including me on that album with the biggies.' 'But son, you misunderstand,' I said, 'I'm saving you for the next one.' 'Fine,' said Doug, 'When do we begin?' Then I got in touch with Adam Faith and he said it'd be okay if I fixed up the sessions. Doug and I both do 'The Battle Of New Orleans' in our acts and so we did it together as a warm-up. It sounded all right so we included it on the record. Doug does 'Cajun Stripper' in his act which he sings in French. He gave me some English words and I marvel at the way he plays accordion on that. It was electric. Well, of course it was. He'd plugged it in."

Adam Faith: "The second album should have been the first as that was where Lonnie really wanted to be. He went along with the first album, but it wasn't the trip down Memory Lane that it was for me. I know he was much happier with the second album."

Doug Kershaw: "I knew Lonnie well by then. He and Sharon had seen my show when they were at Lake Tahoe. Those showrooms are great venues and Lonnie wanted to get into that. I knew he would do well as he is such an entertainer. We played golf and he asked me to go to LA with him for the album." I found, curiously, that although Lonnie and Doug knew each other well, they did not know a lot about each other's past catalogue. Doug was unaware that Lonnie had had a UK hit with 'The Battle Of New Orleans' and Lonnie had only heard the French version of 'Cajun Stripper', unaware that Doug had also recorded an English one.

'Sundown' is a lively, entertaining album. His version of Gordon Lightfoot's original does not fall far short of the original, and Donegan is on top form for three Doug Kershaw songs -

'Louisiana Sun' , 'Mama's Got The Know How' and 'Cajun Stripper', which Kershaw had recorded in French on his 1970 album, 'Spanish Moss'. Among the other songs is Leadbelly's 'I'm All Out And Down', John D. Loudermilk's 'Home' and Chris Andrews' 'Morning Light'. The musicians include Doug Kershaw, Mickey Raphael (from Willie Nelson's band), Emory Gordy (from Elvis Presley's) and Albert Lee. Kai Winding's son, Jai, is on piano.

My reservations come when Lonnie slows down the pace for 'Dreaming My Dreams' and contributes some shaky vocals. Doug Kershaw is in superlative form and the album is as good as any of Lonnie's albums. Lonnie Donegan: "It was an out and out country album, and Chrysalis said, 'It's a great record but we just don't know how to promote it.'"

Lonnie himself had the best idea: he would appear at the International Festival of Country Music at Wembley in 1979. He told me at the time, "I'm hoping Doug will come over and that will make it a big event. It'd be my record home and dry, it would be me home and dry, and it would be Doug home and dry as well. I'm hoping that it all works out. Country music is so popular in Britain and yet there is no big British artist. I'm hoping that it's going to be me. If I'm wrong, I'll be asking Chris Barber for my job back." Doug Kershaw didn't come, which is a pity because the sight of the two extroverts on stage would have been something. Still, the event went well and Lonnie returned to Wembley in 1982.

In 1979 Lonnie recorded some songs with George Harrison and Chas and Dave. The songs were 'Everybody's Makin' It Big But Me' (a Shel Silverstein song for Dr. Hook), 'Massage Parlour' and 'Punchy And The Willer Warbler' (both written by Chas and Dave). They have not been issued, but he did perform the first two songs on Canadian TV with the Irish Rovers and the first one on 'Pebble Mill At One'.

III.

In November 1978 Lonnie Donegan returned to Britain for a six week variety tour called 'The Lonnie Donegan Spectacular'. It wasn't the most auspicious of comebacks. I suspect that the only spectacular element was the money the tour lost. When I bought my ticket for one of three nights at the Liverpool Empire, I asked for one as near to the front and as central as possible. "Have what you like, love," was the reply. "We haven't sold any yet." The audience was equally grim on the night. I sneaked a look at the house plan and noted that complimentary tickets were rife. Many organisations were given handfuls. Even with these freebies, I doubt if there were 300 there. This in a theatre that holds close to 3,000. A crucial reason for the show's failure to attract an audience was the nature of the bill. Lonnie Donegan had been recording with some musical heavyweights and also been recording country music in Nashville, but he saw himself as a jobbing musician who would take whatever would come his way. He was still doing his old hits: "Doing the old hits can be very limiting. The only way I could get out of it is to go somewhere where they don't know me at all and evolve a whole new act. I just wish they wouldn't park their wheelchairs outside the stage door."

Lonnie could never make up his mind. With his crocodile grin, he looked like an end of the pier entertainer and he couldn't make up his mind whether to be Roy Orbison or Boxcar Willie. This was the start of the punk era, and that music had similar do-it-yourself qualities to skiffle.

His lead guitarist, Jackie McAuley, recalls, "There was no demand for Lonnie during the punk era, but it wasn't just Lonnie - it happened to a lot of artists. We played restaurants and a lot of the places were simply glorified boozers. Lonnie had the attitude of taking the gigs whenever and wherever they were."

The venue this particular night was an excellent one, the Liverpool Empire, but the presentation was all wrong. Here was Lonnie in an old-style variety show, the kind that TV killed off. The bill wouldn't appeal to anyone under 40. It was just as well that there weren't many to witness the débâcle. I watched the show with an open mind but it was embarrassingly bad. Lonnie apart, I didn't clap once.

The show opened with the vocal duo Stirling Silver. John Stirling was a director of the company promoting the tour and when he referred in the programme to the "very talented company", I wondered if he included himself. John Stirling and his partner Diane Massey sang pop hits with as much enthusiasm as strap-hangers on a morning train, but compared to the rest of the show, they were good or at least, all right.

Grahame McClean did what Lionel Blair does, only not as well. He and four girls went through some stereotyped dance routines. The Mistins featured Roger Mistin who, according to the programme, was the world's greatest xylophone player. I shouldn't think there's much competition, but to prove the point he was harnessed to a large xylophone, which he played spinning around on roller-skates. Now that's what you call a speciality act. Tricky, I agree, but entertaining, no.

Joe 'Mr. Piano' Henderson closed the first half. Those of us who were still awake saw him come out in evening dress waving to the audience as though he had received a tumultuous welcome. Was this Joe Henderson? He was much larger than his publicity pictures showed. His waistline was the only thing that had changed. He flashed a wide smile and went into "Hey-bop-a-ree-bop", which signified that it was time to "Sing it with Joe". Joe doesn't sing much himself and the response to 'I'm Forever Blowing Bubbles' was nil. It was a brave choice as the words would only be known to West Ham supporters. Still, he didn't fare badly considering several of the piano's notes were missing - as indeed were most of the audience, who had gone to the bar. I suppose I should mention the show's comedian, Dev Shawn, and having done so, we'll move onto the second half and Lonnie Donegan.

In the interval I talked with some friends and we hoped that Lonnie Donegan would restore some sanity to this shambles. Would he? Could he? Sadly, no. Donegan had ditched the evening dress and he wore a tight-fitting electric blue suit decorated with Indian motifs. Presumably what he thought a country star might wear, but it looked like cut-price Elvis. The sound was so atrocious that I couldn't even hazard a guess as to what the first song was. The balance was sorted out but Donegan didn't sound much better when you could hear what he was doing. He rushed through the songs like a man determined to catch the 'Rock Island Line', and anyone hearing that particular song for the first time would wonder what it was all about. Normally, I love Donegan hollering and screaming, but I also expect him to sing properly. But not tonight. He may have derived satisfaction from converting his hits into meaningless noise, but I doubted that the audience did. There was no encore.

To be fair, there were good moments when Lonnie performed some songs from 'Sundown' including an electrifying 'Cajun Stripper', but the audience was not too pleased. "Okay, you want the old ones," said Lon, following lukewarm applause.

The audience was so small that I could have conducted my interview during the show. Then I would have missed the backstage hassles. The next gig was in Doncaster and Lonnie wanted his group to travel with him. He wanted to rehearse. They wanted to stay on for a football match. The band won. Lonnie didn't tell these youngsters that he was the boss. The incident tells a lot for, despite all the bravado, I found Donegan a tragic figure. He never admitted that times might be a little hard. He denied any responsibility for the tour. He'd been called up and asked to do it. The content of the show and the promotion had nothing to do with him.

My first moments with Lonnie were awkward. How could I compliment him on his performance? Instead I praised his new album, 'Sundown', and asked what brought about this change to country music. "I'm a singer of folk songs and that includes country music. Country music has changed a lot in the last ten years and I'd call what I am doing now 'modern country-rock'. Ten years ago I would have said 'No' if someone had asked me I wanted to be a country singer. It meant Jim Reeves, Hank Locklin and Porter Wagoner and that wasn't my scene at all. Now I'd say, 'Oh yes' because there's a new category of country music that's come about. I see myself in line with Kris Kristofferson, Gordon Lightfoot and Waylon Jennings."

THE PETERBOROUGH COUNTRY MUSIC FESTIVAL

SATURDAY MATINEE AT 3 PM

CHAS 'N' DAVE

Buddy Holly's
CRICKETS

New USA Recording sensation
DWIGHT YOAKAM

RICKY VALANCE and the VALENTINES

FREDDY WELLER

HOST AND M.C. LONNIE DONEGAN

LONNIE DONEGAN

MORE THAN 'PYE IN THE SKY'

FORTUNE THEATRE

LONNIE DONEGAN
CHRISTINA MATTHEWS
MR CINDERS

A MUSICAL COMEDY

Directed by TONY CRAVEN
Costumes by PETER RICE
Designed by NORMAN COATES
Choreography by KENN OLDFIELD
Lighting Design by MARK HENDERSON

by CLIFFORD GREY & GREATREX NEWMAN
Additional Lyrics by LEO ROBIN
Music by VIVIAN ELLIS & RICHARD MYERS
Musical Supervision MICHAEL REED
Assisted by DICK HNATOWICZ

Lonnie onstage in Woolwich with Albert Lee & Hogan's Heroes December '88

MULESKINNER BLUES

LONNIE DONEGAN
Muleskinner Blues
RCA

THOUGH JUST as seminal a veteran as James Brown (in 1956, his "Rock Island Line" served alongside "Heartbreak Hotel" in both the UK and US Top Tens), Lonnie Donegan displays a much firmer grasp of his craft on this, his first studio album in over two decades. It's an enjoyably animated outing which finds him trying out new material like Paul Kennerley's cheerfully sardonic "The Welfare Line", and revisiting old skiffle chestnuts like "Stewball", "Muleskinner Blues" and "I'm Alabammy Bound [...] the company of Van (the fan) Morri[...] Lonnie's old trad-jazz boss Chris Ba[...] and virtuoso guitarist Albert Lee. D[...] gan's voice is as keeningly flexible as [...] – surprisingly similar to Van's on [...] duets – and he slips with ease betw[...] folk, skiffle, slower blues number[...] even cajun stylings. It's nice to note [...] "Rock Island Line", the original vo[...] invocation of British rock'n'roll, re[...] every bit of its peculiar pied-piper p[...] more than 40 years on.

THE ROOTS OF BRITISH ROO

DONEGAN

WITH LONNIE

ONNIE
DONEGAN
AND HIS SKIFFLE GROUP

SQUARE PEG PRODUCTIONS PROUDLY
PRESENT THE BIGGEST GATHERING OF
SKIFFLE MINDED MUSICIANS AND FANS TO
CELEBRATE A THOROUGHLY BRITISH
INSTITUTION

HAS N' DAVE'S
RSESHOE SKIFFLE GROUP

HRIS BARBER
D HIS JAZZ & BLUES BAND

NY SHERIDAN DIZ DISLEY
EE WILLIE HARRIS A SPECIAL TRIBUTE TO BERYL BRYDEN

SS NANCY WHISKEY AND THE
NNIGANS SKIFFLE GROUP

COMPERE CHAS McDEVITT

Monday 7th December
Royal Albert Hall

ickets £15, £17.50, £22.50, £25 available from Box
ffice or by credit card 0171 589 8212
r special boxes and catering package - contact Lesley 01705 296707
Mail: square-peg@clara.net

LONNIE AT THE CONNIE

LONNIE DONEGAN
& his Skiffle Group
FRIDAY, 2 MARCH 2001

also featuring

057
JODY STEPHENS
& OLD SWAN CONSERVATIVE CLUB
THE FABTONES

TICKET : £14.00

kiffle Party, 2000;
hris Barber, Van Morrison and Lon.

Adam & Lonnie
at the Royal Albert Hall
(photos Ron Mason)

SKIFFLE THE ROOTS OF BRITISH ROCK

Beryl
Bryden

The Lonnigans with Chas.
McDevitt And Diz Dizley

Lonnie Donegan
in person with his
7 piece band

the legendary 'King of Skiffle'

Cavern Club
Thursday 24 May 8pm

THE CAVERN CLUB
10 MATHEWS STREET, LIVERPOOL
THU 24th MAY 01   8:00 PM

LONNIE DONEGAN

TICKETS £ .00 plus booking fee

REVOLUTION MAKES HIS DEBUT AT THE CAVERN CLUB

□ PIONEER: Lonnie
Donegan at the
Cavern Club last
night. His exciting,
driving music
inspired the
Beatles, *inset,
above*, and many
other groups

Main picture
COLIN LANE

All roads lead to Lonnie

By David Charters
Daily Post Staff

HE WAS just another tourist walking the cobbles of fame last night, gazing at the names of rock 'n' rollers inscribed in brick outside The Cavern Club.

B u t when the camera was on him, he became the entertainer again.

This was Lonnie Donegan, spiritual "daddy" of the Beatles and thousands of other groups; the man who brought folk songs to suburban Britain from the swamps, the railroads and the plantations of America.

And he called his music skiffle, the name given to house parties where the poor men and women played their home-made instruments for friends and neighbours.

As they picked out the tunes, drumming their feet to the rhythm and taking deep slugs from the whisky jar, someone would hand round a cap for donations to pay the rent.

In January, 1956, Lonnie had his first big hit with Rock Island Line. Soon, pale English boys were learning to play guitars and banjos. And the sound of thimbled fingers rapping down washboards was heard in bedrooms and church halls across the land.

Skiffle was the biggest teenage craze this country had ever known.

Among the boys listening to Lonnie was John Lennon. Soon he was shaking his greased hair with a skiffle group called the Quarrymen. In 1957, he was joined by Paul McCartney.

Of course, Lonnie knew all about this, but last night he was happy to hear the stories as he stepped down Mathew Street, legendary home of Merseybeat.

The debt owed to Lonnie by the beat groups of the 1960s can never be measured, but it's good for him to be recognised as the man who started it all.

So, at the age of 70, he is making his debut at The Cavern tomorrow night. Yesterday, he flew in from Spain to have a look at the old place and feel the atmosphere, to get in the mood for his concert.

He had been there before in the late 1950s to hold a meeting of his fan club, but he has never performed on the stage.

In those days, he was too popular to play in a cellar which could only hold a few hundred people. He's too modest to emphasise the point, but it's true.

Maybe these days it's a little different. But the men and women on the street smiled and whispered knowingly, one to the other. Perhaps the midriff has swollen a little as befits a man of his years, but the face is just the same.

And then Lonnie met Neil Bee. The Cavern Club's DJ in the café over the road. He's only 26, yet he knew all about "the king of skiffle". In the NBC film about John Lennon, *In His Life*, currently on show in the USA and Canada, Neil is Pete Shot ton of the Quarrymen.

In the movie, he plays the washboard on Don't You Rock Me Daddy-O, Railroad Bill and Cumberland Gap, the Donegan numbers John was playing when he met Paul at the garden fete at St Peter's Church, Woolton, in 1957.

"It's harder to play than you think, the washboard," said Lonnie. Neil nodded appreciatively.

Lonnie was born to Irish parents in Glasgow. His own background was in jazz and he played banjo with the Ken Colyer and Chris Barber bands.

"Straight away I disliked rock 'n' roll because in its first incarnation it was a kind of bastardisation of the folk music I was doing," he said. "It was the 12-bar blues played in an exaggerated manner purely for commercial benefit.

Yet, there's a hint of self-mockery here. "I considered myself in those days to be a purist who didn't do anything for money which was a load of nonsense," he said. "I was earning a bloody good wage.

"But you think of yourself as being some kind of high priest of folk music. I was only young then you have to forgive me.

What about all the other big groups, The Beatles, the Rolling Stones etc, where do they fit in? The little man grins broadly. "All roads lead to Lonnie really, because in the beginning was skiffle and the word was made rock," he said.

"In fact, all the basic American music comes from the same source which is where I got all my songs, the blues and folk songs. Woody Guthrie, Huddy Leadbetter, Big Bill Broonzy. We all drink from the same fountain.

"The Beatles went on to create their own sound, their own style and their own vocabulary and you can't take that away from them.

Lonnie finished his tea and went to look at the names of all the stars who have appeared at The Cavern. Many of them are there because they heard him sing the Rock Island Line when they were little.

And then the man who gave them that moment walked down the street and waved farewell.

■ A few £15 tickets for the concert are still available at the club.

david charters@dailypost.co.uk

11. AND THE CROWD CALLED OUT FOR MORE
I. The great showman
II. The Albert Hall celebration
III. Lonnie on Merseyside

I.

Lonnie Donegan had been used to 16 week summer seasons and 12 week pantomimes - yes, pantomimes extended into March in the 1960s - and the rest of the year would be taken up with variety tours, one-night stands and TV shows. After his heart attack, he knew that he could never work at that pace again. In the 1980s he was touring about three months in the year and was restricted by tax considerations as he now lived abroad. Until they had a family, Sharon was his road manager. The 'Puttin' On The Style' album had created a new interest in his work, and he said, "I was doing enormous business again. We were doing two cabarets a night and having to travel 60 or more miles between them. It was bloody hard. It was the hardest period of my life. I was decisive, hard, a total bastard. I felt I didn't have much time left and I wanted everything to be right."

Sharon said, "People asked me why I put up with his abuse, but I understand that was how he had to be when he was on the road. He is a perfectionist, and I was his security blanket. I wanted to prove to him just how much I loved him."

Josh White Jr. recalled a show with Lonnie and the Irish Rovers: "Lonnie was a most jovial and happy man. He was very approachable and enjoyable to talk to. He put on a great show and he had nothing but nice things to say about my old man. I can't remember our conversations, but then there are pictures of me on Paul Robeson's knee and I can't remember anything about that." Lonnie liked a Tom Paxton song that the Irish Rovers had recorded, 'Wasn't That A Party', and he recorded it with Joe Brown and his daughter, Sam. Unfortunately, they couldn't find a label to release it, although they did perform it on TV. One of Lonnie's best television appearances was with Albert Lee on 'Rhythm On 2' for the BBC in 1980. Lonnie, looking reasonably trendy in his black shirt, flared trousers and white choker, performed 'Streamline Train', 'I Wanna Go Home' (narrating one verse very effectively), 'Cajun Stripper' and 'The Battle Of New Orleans' (Lonnie always said 'bloody British' in concert);. Lonnie played banjo while Albert sang 'Country Boy' and did his magical guitar runs, and they treated 'Come Up And See Me Anytime' as a duet. Lonnie loved the show and he did once amuse Brian May by telling him he was no Albert Lee. Lonnie was hitting out in all directions, jumping down and turning around all over the place. In 1981 he celebrated 25 years as a solo act and recorded a jubilee concert with Ken Colyer and Chris Barber. This was issued as a double-album on Cube and the second LP was also released separately on Rio Digital. Lonnie talks about "the audience coming on the stage to shake my hand at the end of three hours of happiness. As I said at the end of 'Goodnight Irene', it was worth waiting 25 years for." It is, incidentally, the only time that he recorded 'Goodnight Irene' although he often sang it. 'New York Town' and 'One Night Of Love' were also new to his recorded repertoire, and he was reunited with Ken Colyer for 'Take This Hammer'.

He took part in the Royal Variety Performance in November 1981 and he appeared, knowing that his mother had died earlier in the day. The sequence, hosted by Tim Rice and celebrating 25 years of British popular music, was very successful and he performed a medley of 'Wabash Cannonball', 'Don't You Rock Me, Daddy-O' and 'Cumberland Gap'. The other performers were Marty Wilde, the Searchers, Donovan, Acker Bilk, Alvin Stardust, Lulu, Adam Ant and Cliff Richard, reunited with the Shadows. Lonnie's guitar break was the hardest rocking part of the show. In 1984 he returned for a Royal Gala, but wearing his dinner-jacket and with his banjo, to play 'Does Your Chewing Gum Lose Its

Flavour' on a much more restrained sequence featuring the 50s stars, Ruby Murray, Craig Douglas, Lita Roza, Bryan Johnson, Anne Shelton, the Beverley Sisters, and Pearl Carr and Teddy Johnson. It was hard to believe that Lonnie was once contemporary with these performers and he was the only one to bring his music into the 80s.

For all that, Lonnie had no truck with the punk movement, making jokes that he was going to record as Lonnie Donegan and the Expectorates. However, in 1981 he was asked to record with a contemporary rockabilly band, the Shakin' Pyramids. The single, produced by B.A. Robertson, was a medley of 'Cumberland Gap', 'Wabash Cannonball' and 'Don't You Rock Me, Daddy-O'. Lonnie is so enthusiastic that he sounds more New Wave than they do. Lonnie had a second successful appearance at the Wembley Country Music Festival in 1982. The TV performance shows details that the audience missed such as his cross-eyed look when describing the preacher in 'Puttin' On The Style'. Following that appearance, Lonnie did a UK tour in 1983 supporting the middle of the road country star, Billie Jo Spears. The intention was to record a live album at the London Palladium, but Billie Jo was taken ill. The concert went ahead with Lonnie and a smaller audience, and it was still recorded. Unfortunately, the live album has never been released.

Lonnie was playing to full houses on the Billie Jo Spears tour but some solo concerts were not as successful. A concert at the Civic Hall, Connah's Quay only attracted 110 people, and Lonnie quipped, "Never have so many played for so few." The 'Liverpool Echo' reported that the theatre needed 300 people paying £3 a time to break even, and that both they and Lonnie lost money as it was a joint promotion.

Chas and Dave wrote a tongue-twisting tribute to their hero, 'Lonnie D', and they performed it in their 'Knees-Up' series for ITV in 1983. Lonnie appeared with them for 'Pick A Bale Of Cotton', 'Midnight Special' and 'Puttin' On The Style', but it was not well rehearsed as, at times, they were not sure who was going to sing the next verse. The show was set in a bar and Lonnie commented, "I started in a pub and now I'm back in a bloody pub."

By way of contrast, Lonnie also did some successful shows at Caesar's Palace in Las Vegas. Lead guitarist Jackie McAuley recalls, "The first night was on St. Patrick's Day so Lonnie let me sing several songs with the band. For the rest of the week, we did regular shows in the lounge. The first set was at 11.15pm, and then 2.15 and finally 4.15. There were always people there. There was 24 hour gambling and there were no windows or clocks in the place so that the punters would forget what time it was."

In 1929 Vivien Ellis wrote a musical comedy for the pantomime star, Bobby Howes, called 'Mr. Cinders'. He wrote in pantomime tricks and, as the title implies, it was based upon 'Cinderella'. Mr. Cinders falls for a housemaid who is the disguised daughter of a millionaire. The musical was a big success and one song, 'Spread A Little Happiness', became a standard. The show was revived in 1983 with Denis Lawson winning an Olivier Award for his performance.

Lonnie Donegan had changed his agent, who suggested that he did an audition to take over the role. It worked very well and although Lonnie dropped the scene calling for roller-skates, he was a very good replacement, joining in February 1984. Antony Thorncroft in the 'Financial Times' said, "Donegan is, in theory, much too mature for the role, but this just helps to set him apart from all the bright young things, and he handles the comedy routines with the insouciance of an old trouper. He can also match the singing skills of Christina Matthews, the pert young oil baron's daughter, who is his reward for being nice."

He brought more romance to the role and relished the big song, 'Spread A Little Happiness'. He didn't get the song released but the song had been a hit for Sting in 1982, when it was on the soundtrack of the film, 'Brimstone And Treacle'. Lonnie played the role until April 1984 and was then replaced by Lionel Blair. He had offers of other acting work but did not take them: it was that three month rule again. Back in Lake Tahoe, he worked at a casino some 80 miles from his home and did three shows a night, six nights a week for three weeks.

In 1985 Lonnie had further heart surgery, having a quadruple bypass. His arteries had hardened and they grafted in veins from his legs. He said, "I kept having warning attacks. I went to the hospital in the States who told me to go home and take aspirin and said I had not had a heart attack. A second doctor in California said the same thing. When we were back in the UK, my wife suggested that we got a British opinion as we have never been too confident about the American medical profession. I saw a cardiologist who said that my heart was scarred and I had had a heart attack. An Australian tour was cancelled and my wife was with me the whole time, I don't know what I would have done without her." He said that his heart was now working better than ever.

News of Lonnie's illness had a surprising effect on the Japanese Stock Market. As the tickertapes announced that Lonnie Donegan had had heart surgery, the share prices plunged. Donegan was not known in Japan, and the first interpreters of the news thought that the patient was Ronald Reagan. Two months later, he was back compering a show for the British Heart Foundation, featuring Liverpool acts at the London Palladium.

After the fiasco with the doctors, the Donegans moved to Spain. Lonnie would say that you couldn't get a good cup of tea in the States and he certainly was an avid tea-drinker, consuming around 13 strong, sugary cups a day. Anything else, he called 'gnat's pee'. In 1986 he had a very successful tour in Australia but he found ten weeks of travelling exhausting.

Many of Lonnie's records had been issued and reissued by Pye and its subsequent owners, but there was little structure to what they were doing. In 1985 fans were delighted by the LP, 'Rare And Unissued Gems', from the German label, Bear Family. It collected Lonnie's Nashville recordings together, but some of the UK outtakes such as 'Ding Ding' and a frantic 'Tiger Rag' with Lonnie on banjo and Les Bennetts on guitar, were decidedly dodgy. 'Red Beret', the story of the Arnhem invasion in 1944, was also the subject of the film, 'A Bridge Too Far', and well worth hearing.

With the advent of CDs, there have been many excellent reissues. Lonnie's first two albums were combined for a See For Miles CD and his two volumes in 'The EP Collection' included many obscure tracks. Sequel's 3CD set, 'Putting On The Styles', in 1993 was the best yet, but Lonnie didn't seem too impressed when I met him. Don't you get a good rate on this, I asked. Surely you should have renegotiated your contract to cover CDs. "Well, we all know about 'should'," said Lonnie. "Artistically, yes, I love it as it means that people are still interested in me and what I do, but financially it is disastrous as there are so many songs on these CDs. They are sold for the same price as 3 LPs so the artist doesn't end up getting nearly what he should get in royalties."

The most important reissue package was the superb Bear Family release in 1993, rather ridiculously titled 'More Than Pye In The Sky'. It was a box set comprising 209 tracks over 8CDs with a lavish booklet. Lonnie himself was uncertain about all this attention, but it really depended on which day you caught him, or, more to the point, whether he had recently received a royalty statement. He told me, "You asked me if I minded my old records being rechannelled for stereo but that's a minor point. I'm embarrassed by them being there at all. Of course there are a few goodies but I would say that I am embarrassed by 85 per cent of my old records. I don't like my performance, most of the songs, the production, in fact, everything. They were all recorded so fast. The company would be very upset if you didn't cut at least two songs in a three hour session. Now it takes three hours to tune up."

Paul Pelletier, the researcher for many of the reissues, had had more than his fill of Lonnie Donegan. He sent a circular to the fans about the Bear Family set, concluding "It was not a happy project, partly because of complications in my personal life but mainly because Mr. Donegan was less than helpful, something he has been very good at for most of his career." Lonnie's hits are now often on rock'n'roll compilations and it's ironic that such a fervent opponent of the music should now be under Rock'n'Roll in HMV. "Don't mind," he says, "We should dispense with labels as they don't work, there are too many soft edges. Everything should be judged without a label. You either enjoy the song or you don't enjoy the song - forget the label."

In 1986 Lonnie teamed up with Monty Sunshine for Donegan's Dancing Sunshine Band. The concerts went well but there wasn't enough commitment by either party to make something of it. Lonnie Donegan: "I got up and sang with Monty and liked it. I went back and sang with him again, and we gradually got the idea of putting a band together which involved the old New Orleans sound, plus my modern country-rockish sound, and just seeing if something would come out of the blend of it. We play for dancing audiences as I like the idea of seeing people enjoying themselves." The concerts became a two-part affair with Lonnie playing the banjo in the first part and taking over in the second. "I'm a silly bugger," he told Sheridan Morley, "I can't soft pedal. I have to be screaming my lungs out for a living." The single was purely a catchy signature tune to get them on and off, coupled with Leadbelly's 'Leaving Blues'. There was no Donegan's Dancing Sunshine Band album, but Lonnie did contribute to a Monty Sunshine album, produced in Germany by Frank Dostal. Dostal, who had been a member of the Rattles beat group and was the writer of the disco hit, 'Yes Sir I Can Boogie', produced a good album which deserves wider acclaim. Lonnie took part in the police drama, 'Rockcliffe's Babies' in 1987, and he was going to be in 'EastEnders', although that didn't come off. He deputised for David Hamilton on his BBC Radio 2 afternoon show. In 1988 he played to a full house at the Royal Festival Hall and undertook a UK tour with Kenny Ball and Acker Bilk. He also did some concerts with the blues singer and pianist Champion Jack Dupree, who had moved to Yorkshire. Also in 1988, he played the Appendix on a curious LP project, 'Body Work', written and partly performed by Richard Stilgoe. His contribution about the redundant appendix, 'Life Passes Me By', has shades of the Ink Spots, but the album is too knowingly clever to be fully enjoyable. He sang an impromptu 'My Grandfather's Clock' with Guy Mitchell on a UK chat show and he also sang a distinctive version of 'John Peel' on the soundtrack of 'Bellman And True', a film about bank robbers and computers starring Bernard Hill and Francis Tomelty.

Lonnie found himself with the 60s beat groups on package shows for holiday camp weekends - ironically, all the acts would be performing American classics. Lonnie Donegan: "If I got up on stage with Willie Nelson in America, they would view me as a pleasant novelty. They wouldn't take me as seriously as Willie because he is talking their language and knows what he's doing, whereas I'm copying. They're not daft." There was still skiffle in Germany but "nowadays you'd have to scour the length and breadth of Britain to find two skiffle groups."

In 1989 Lonnie toured the UK with his one-man show, 'This Y'ere De Story'. "It was based on what I was going to write in my autobiography," he told me, "but I turned it into a stage production. I sat on a stage, told a few stories and sang some songs, but my bass player joined Ray Davies and he nicked the whole idea." I told Lonnie that Ray Davies had completed his book, so it could be sold in the interval. "Well, he's obviously much more organised than me, and that's certainly the way to do it." The show was broadcast as a 90 minute special on BBC Radio 2, and he talked about his health problems for 'The Human Factor' on Granada. No doubt it all made things easier for the researchers of 'This Is Your Life' as Lonnie was a subject in 1991. The guests included Bruce Welch, Roger Daltry and the Spinners, and Chris Barber and Beryl Bryden performed 'Rock Island Line' with Lonnie. In 1989 he told 'The Independent' that his next single would be a Brian May song, 'Let Your Heart Rule Your Head', and he said, "It's a typical Lonnie Donegan song - gospelly, but not gospel." The record, if it was ever made, was not issued. In that year, he became a grandparent for the first time when Juanita had a child. An illustration showing that Juanita had inherited her father's genes came in 1996 when she received three noise abatement notices from her neighbours in Ramsgate. "I am only singing along to my stereo," she said. Lonnie continued on the road, performing intermittently between bouts of bad health, but his midriff was spreading too much. In 1989 the family moved to Malaga in southern Spain and lived in a relatively modest villa called Casa Guitara. Lonnie and Sharon sold their home in Lake Tahoe, but they returned in 1998 with their children to renew their wedding vows on a cruise ship. It was for a feature in 'Hello' and then 'Saga' magazine and although it is easy to be cynical, renewing their vows was definitely something that they wanted to do.

In 1990 two of Lonnie's songs - 'Chewing Gum' and 'Dustman' - were included on a Top 20 single by Jive Bunny, so theoretically Lonnie was back in the charts. Lonnie didn't seem to mind too much as he undertook some publicity with Jive Bunny, even though another snippet came from Peter Sellers' first Donegan parody, 'Any Old Iron'.

In 1992 Lonnie had further surgery but he was soon back on the road, this time with Chris Barber's Jazz and Blues Band. "It's work, my left hand was paralysed after the operation from a pinched nerve 'cause I was under the anaesthetic for over five hours," he told me at the time, "The way they had me lying down pinched a vertabrae at the back of my neck and that travelled to my fingers and I didn't think that I would ever play the guitar again. I was psychologically under a lot of pressure but I got the rubber ball going and I squeezed and squeezed night and day and walked and walked and walked to get the circulation back into the legs. If you don't do that, you just sit and feel sorry for yourself. It is awfully easy to feel sorry for yourself because you've been an inch away from death - if somebody pulls a wire out, you are dead. If somebody makes a mistake, it's 'Goodnight, nurse.' That is a terrible shock to the system and it takes a long while to get back. I haven't got my energy level back, nothing like it, and it has been eight months. I spoke to the specialist recently and he was amazed that I was going to start work. He said, 'This is early, it is usually about 18 months', but I can feel where the limitations are. I am also 61. Most blokes are thinking of knocking off now, not going on another tour, never mind the heart operations, not one but two."

He continued, "I haven't worked at all for a year until last week. It's not that I have got to have the smell of the crowd and the roar of the greasepaint, although I do like that, it is just that I have got to do something, I can't sit in a rocking chair and read Shakespeare and Agatha Christie, I've got to do something and the only thing I can do is entertainment, that's all I know about. Chris Barber rang up and said, 'I know the situation and if you want to do a handful of shows, we'll do it, there's no responsibility, you do how many songs you want and the way you want it. You just feel the water. If it doesn't work, it doesn't work and if it does, we all win.' This is the perfect way for me to creep back in. I am not allowed to belt them out though, Chris doesn't like belting, gives him a pain in the ear, he says, 'Turn that down, turn that off'."

Since he had first heard his father's records in the 1950s, Van Morrison had been passionate about Leadbelly and other blues singers, but he also loved the way Lonnie had interpreted their songs. Lonnie Donegan recalled a gig at the King's Hotel in Newport in South Wales: "Van came to see me and that was the first time we met. We came from the same background and we had everything in the world to talk about and Van said, 'We will have to get into a studio and make a record'."

In 1995 Lonnie was asked to provide a cabaret for the Ivor Novello Awards and when he heard who was going, he said that he would work with Van Morrison and Albert Lee.

Lonnie was surprised to find himself receiving an award for his Outstanding Contribution to British music. "It was a total shock," said Lonnie, "and one of the people behind it was Van. The set we played was so outrageous that Van said we had to record: 'How about Thursday in Reading?'"

Everything worked so well that Lonnie Donegan and Van Morrison started doing concerts together - and it led to them recording 'Muleskinner Blues' and 'I'm Alabammy Bound', which were both included on Lonnie's 1999 CD, 'Muleskinner Blues', his first studio album since 1978. Van, who is normally evasive when it comes to media interviews paid tribute to him on 'Jack O'Diamonds', the 1998 BBC Scotland documentary about Lonnie's life. It also included footage of them doing 'Muleskinner Blues' live.

Lonnie said, "I like to think I've influenced him not only way back when, but over the past couple of years. When we recorded 'Jools Holland's Millennium Hootenanny' for New Year's Eve, he did 'Philosopher's Stone' and people were crying with emotion. He played the harmonica like I've never heard it played - and I've been round the block a few times."

'Muleskinner Blues' is an exceptional album. Lonnie said, "My major problem was selecting the material to go on the record. It had been 20 years since I made a studio record. I was assuming that my old record-buying public had not seen me performing live in recent years and wouldn't realise that me singing 'Rock Island Line' today bears no resemblance to me singing 'Rock Island Line' in 1956, and so on. I decided to sprinkle a few of the oldies and goldies in there but done the way we do them on stage and add some new stuff ."

Lonnie recreates 'Rock Island Line' and 'Stewball' again and also sings his own 'Skiffle'. He said of 'Stewball': "I just felt like doing 'Stewball' that day. We got the most gospel sound on that, there is just drums and bass nothing else. The girls' response is typical of the gospel manner of singing." There is also a great gospel style revival of 'Fancy Talkin' Tinker', and while 'All Together Now', a tribute to skiffle, had been written by Peter Sarstedt and first recorded by the Sarstedt Brothers.

The English country musician Paul Kennerley wrote 'The Welfare Line'. Lonnie Donegan: "He's from Hoylake, I met him in Chelsea and he wanted to make a record with me here but he wanted to do it bit by bit by bit, taking each line and stitching it all together and I can't work like that. I get my inspiration from doing it as a performance, and then he went to Nashville, and contined to write and married Emmylou. He sends me songs which are always fabulous and I am so pleased to have done one here. This one has been done by Willie Nelson but I haven't heard his version."

Lonnie wrote 'When I Get Off This Feeling' : "When I was on the road with Chris Barber in Germany, I was trying to remember old blues and this came into my mind, it is so typically 30s urban blues and it just poured out. I went into the studio and my guitarist was there as well and I said, 'Listen to this, that's great' and we recorded it, just the two of us. The other guys wouldn't stay off and they all joined in and we didn't want them, we wanted it to sound very lonely, and now I do it on stage alone for the first half and at the first guitar solo, the band comes in very gently and then we finish it off with the full band. So if I recorded it now, it would sound different from the way I did it three years ago."

Another recent composition, 'Please Don't Call Me In The Morning', was written with his lead guitarist, a former country musician from Swindon, Paul Henry. Paul Henry: "We were recording in Reading and Lonnie said, 'What we need for balance is a blues number' and I said I had one that was partly written that I had been planning to put to him. He said, 'Bring it along tomorrow', and so I did. He changed a few words and then we did it. It seemed to work."

Lonnie Donegan: "The title comes from my wife as my constant rejoinder to people who are going to call me tomorrow is 'Please don't call me in the morning'. She said, 'Why don't you use it as a song title as it's what you say most in life?' The song fell into place very naturally."

John Ward wrote 'Spanish Nights' and Lonnie said, "It was written about me by a dear friend of mine who played fine guitar but didn't have the self-confidence to play professionally. I nagged him on this and he wrote this song. Shortly after writing it, he was found drowned. So it is very important to me, apart from the fact that it is about me and touches me in that respect. The writer's involvement touches me too. If you listen to the lyrics, the song is complaining about the road, but when you get on the stage, they want to hear the old songs. I am in a fortunate position where the audience wanting to hear the old ones is an enormous crutch to lean on, you know you have ten songs that everybody wants to hear so you can slip in what you want as the next one is one that they are going to scream for anyway. That is a very safe feeling to have on stage and Joe Brown envies me this position of security."

There is also Tony Harper's ballad, 'Always From The Heart': "This is beautiful, the nicest ballad I ever sung. I couldn't better it. The more times I would sing it the worse I would get. I hit it on the head with this particular version and I am very proud of it, I have done a great job with it. The first take sounded like Willie Nelson so I had to do another take and un-Willie Nelson it, but it still sounds like Willie. "

And as for the writer. "Tony Harper lives in Rotherham and has been writing the most beautiful songs since I met him 30 years ago. He was in one of these horrible pubs doing a competition and he was streets ahead of everybody else as he had written his own material. Since then he has been sending me these songs and I vowed to record one of them one day." This led to a second CD, 'The Skiffle Sessions', with Van Morrison and Chris Barber which was recorded in concert in Belfast. though I prefer to call it 'My Old Van's A Dustman'. The concert also includes a guest appearance from Dr. John so this has to be the world's most expensive and most polished skiffle group, which I suppose defeats the objective. Lonnie and Van sound good together and it isn't altogether easy to determine who is singing what. The album is very enjoyable and it is rare to hear Van Morrison so relaxed. The comments back and forth are tremendous and it sounds as though they didn't rehearse too much, relying on their own innate talent.

"Van's been very very good to me and I do enjoy working with him," said Lonnie. "We think along the same artistic lines. He says that I get him at it: I raise his level of musical awareness and if he sings with me, he has got to try and top me, which ain't easy. We sound alike at times and sometimes when we mixed the tracks, I wasn't sure whether something was him or me. We are very compatible vocally and in every other way too as we are a pair of grumpy old men."

But, I said, you are an extrovert on stage and he is introverted, at least he has been when I've seen him. Lonnie Donegan: "Yes, he doesn't feel that a show is necessary, he wouldn't be comfortable doing it, and both approaches are correct. By the time he has been on stage ten minutes, it isn't necessary for him to do anything if he doesn't want to. In my case, I do want to. Even when I had my own Tony Donegan jazz band, I still did it. I react physically to what I am singing."

As usual, Van Morrison was hiding behind his dark glasses. Chris Hunt: "Lonnie and Van were grumpy old men but in very different ways. Van Morrison appears to be a deeply unhappy person for some reason or other, but Lonnie was never like that, he would have his curmudgeonly ways and we would laugh at it. I never saw Van Morrison outside of the shows, he wouldn't turn up at the soundchecks, but he did come alive on stage, I can't deny that. I only spoke to him once in the two years I was working with him." Which is more than the rest of the band spoke to him.

Russell Gilbrook: "Lonnie would say, 'Don't worry about him, I'm running the show, you're my band.' Lon and Van were two extremes of the scale, which worked very well for both of them, but I would rather be on Lonnie's side because it is such a wonderful thing to be so expressive. It didn't really matter because Lonnie's Lonnie, and Van so thought so much of him. Van was sometimes the shadow because Lonnie had so much aura about him."

Always wanting to wind people up (even if it was Van The Man doing you a favour), Lonnie referred to him as Fat The Hat. Jackie McAuley who played with Van in Them and with Lonnie in the late 70s says, "Van never seemed to have much time for anyone, but he really did a lot for Lonnie. I think he must have really liked him."

Paul Henry: "It worked a treat but it was like an unexploded bomb when he and Van were on stage. I always felt that something might set it off and we would be the innocent bystanders who got injured."

Nick Payn: "One night in Belfast, Lonnie had gone into his 'act' - you know, 'I say, I say, I say', and Van Morrison came on and said, 'Cut out the fucking cabaret, Donegan.' Of course, he took no notice. As far as he was concerned, the audience was bowing at the throne of Lonnie. It was his stage, it was his set, and Van was coming on with his group later on."

Saxophonist Nick Payn: "When they did 'Goodnight Irene', Van sang it in a gospelly soul way, but Lonnie would do it as a country folk blues. With Van's vocal, I did some King Curtis blues licks, and I carried this through when I was with Lonnie alone. One night he said, 'Stop playing all that Gerry Mulligan stuff.' That showed me that he knew a lot of jazz, but he had also missed a lot out."

Amongst his gigs, Lonnie played Glastonbury, now more of a family festival, and received eight encores. Paul Henry: "Glastonbury was great fun. It took hours to get in and get out but his performance was great. Some people may have been watching him for the novelty value, but they soon realised he was a living legend."

Nick Payn: "Playing at the Albert Hall was an occasion, but the show for me was at the Flower Festival in Finsbury Park about three years before he died. It was electrifying even before we started. He performed great that night, going on after John Martyn. It was a pretty young audience and he could cross that divide. We might play a supper club to 150 covers and it would still be exciting. He could charm an audience, he knew how to pace things with the right number at the right moment."

Lonnie played the Labour Party Conference. "I'm the darling of New Labour," joked Lonnie. Sticky Wicket: "I only remember him doing 'Dustman' once and that is a tribute to the persuasive powers of Mo Mowlam - what a great politician she must be to get Lonnie to do 'Dustman'. It was a private do that the Party had organised, not the conference, and Mo had become a close friend of Lonnie's in many respects and certainly was a fan. We were all flabbergasted when he said we were going to do 'Dustman'."

Lonnie Donegan: "It's not the stage that wears me out, it's the travelling. I can go onstage and sing with no problem, but I just can't take the travelling. I've got to have a full night's sleep or I just can't function the next day. It's essential." Lonnie played gigs on alternate days. "It's financially limiting, but it's more expensive if I die."

The payment for Lonnie's gigs contained an element of farce. When he was booked in Liverpool in 2001, the fee was £5,000. First of all, he had to be paid £2,000 and then a week before the gig, he had to receive another £,2000. He would receive the remainder on the night, presumably to pay the band. Lonnie's fee was always £5,000. The Merseysippi Jazz Band asked me to see if he would sing with the band at their annual jazz festival. They expected it to be considerably less as he had only had to turn up with his guitar, but no, with or without the band, it was £5,000, and, of course, nothing came of it.

Chris Hunt; "Lonnie would play for anyone who came up with the money. He would play gigs for rich fans, people who had followed him since they were young and would be the same age as Lonnie. They had made their money and they would put a marquee in the garden and show off to their rich pals. I have played in village halls and there was no messing about - Lonnie always gave a full show, everyone would get the same. The Albert Hall or the village hall in Duncton in Sussex, he would never skimp on that."

The final Lonnie Donegan band was excellent, perhaps the best he had ever had. It comprised Paul Henry (lead guitar), Pete Oakman (bass), Nick Payn (saxophone), Sticky Wicket (percussion) and Chris Hunt (drums). 'The Battle Of New Orleans' surpassed Lonnie's original and 'Rock Island Line' was so ferocious that I marvelled that a man at 70 could perform with such passion. Lonnie didn't waste his time with 'My Old Man's A

Dustman' or 'Does Your Chewing Gum Lose Its Flavour', but went instead for raunchy blues like "Rocks In My Bed".

Paul Henry: "He would say that we were the best musicians in the world but we knew we weren't. He said, 'No, it takes good musicians to follow me as I'm doing something different every night. As opposed to knowing the chords, you have to be listening all the time.' That was true - he went off on tangents and that kept it fresh. I don't think that we were ever happier than when it was just us on stage. It's partly from the fact that Lonnie wanted to rely on people. A lot of the big names wouldn't have rehearsed and wouldn't be used to him changing in mid-song. With his band, he could do what he wanted. We would encourage him to go out on his own sometimes - as a solo singer and guitarplayer he was superb."

Russell Gilbrook: "Lon didn't want perfect time, he wanted people on his wavelength. Because I got on with Lonnie well, it was easier for me to read the situations and if I didn't read it right, he would alight on it and he would see I got it the second time and have a big grin on his face. He allowed enough spontaneous action on stage to keep that energy alive. His bugbear was that no one wanted to perform anymore, there is no entertainment in the music business. He wanted us on stage, looking flamboyant with big smiles, and that transmits to the audience. He wanted the people around him to be giving off the same sort of fire, and that made it far more enjoyable for him and the audience would love it."

I asked his bass player, Pete Oakman if Lonnie ever surprised him on stage. "Yes, if the atmosphere is right and someone shouts out some obscure song that he hasn't done for years, he will go into it if he remembers it. Nine times out of ten, we follow through and pick up on it. There have been some great players with Lonnie over the years like Denny Wright, Les Bennetts, Jimmy Currie, Micky Ashman, Pete Huggett, Pete Appleby and a few others. They were very good musicians who made sure that the arrangement never got cluttered. The current day Donegan band is one of the best, everyone is so sympathetic, everyone is listening and picking up on everyone else, and that is the key to a good band. I hardly ever take my eyes off Lon as I'm never entirely sure what's going to happen next. There are certain songs where I just sing the odd line with Lon and I'm watching him so the harmony is as close as I can get it."

He added, "I admire the guy so much for his energy. I wish I had half of the energy that he has when he gets on stage. I'm very static, always have been. His vocals are better than ever now. His voice has really matured and the quality is so much better. He did lose his way a few years ago but then Van Morrison came along and he realised there's a lot to do out there. He's found a new audience in addition to his old audience and it's been like a tonic for him."

Nick Payn: "Lonnie had an incredible vocal range. He could sing very high without going to a falsetto, and he had an incredible bass voice as well. He was very cheeky, he would sometimes come down on to my bass part or even lower, and he would look across with his cheeky little look that said, 'I can do it all.' He was a natural performer so you allowed Lonnie that freedom to go wherever he wanted to go. He would throw songs in. Sometimes on a major concert he would play 'Lemon Tree' or 'Love Is Strange'. He said that you couldn't please everyone because if we did everything, we would be there all night. He would always squeeze something humorous out of a request."

Paul Henry: "The energy levels were very high, seriously very, very high. On a good night he had more energy than the whole band put together. Of all the people I have worked with, he is the oldest and definitely the one with the most energy. He would be revving himself before he went on. If his life had been getting out of a box, playing and getting back into it, he'd have still been happy. His daily life was not good as he would get into rows and arguments, but put him near a stage and he was absolutely golden."

II.

RAVE ON LON.DON
Royal Albert Hall, 1998
(This section is adapted from a feature I wrote for 'Record Collector' in February 1999.)

If you want to promote a prestige evening of rock'n'roll, country, folk, soul or rap, you would have no difficulty in finding key names to perform. But skiffle? Who are going to be your star attractions? Lonnie Donegan and - er, that's it. And let's face it, Lonnie struggles to fill 1,000-seater theatres when he tours the UK.

All praise to Square Peg Productions for having the courage to stage 'Skiffle - The Roots Of British Rock' at the Royal Albert Hall in December. Naturally I went by train - with 'Rock Island Line', 'Midnight Special', 'Last Train To San Fernando' and 'Freight Train', it's the only way to travel and I was hoping that some witty skiffler might update them to mention Richard Branson. Nothing to do with the show, but the seat I was allocated from Liverpool to London had a black bin-liner over it: the previous occupant had urinated on the seat, and so the servicing staff placed the bin-liner over the mess, stuck on the reserved ticket and expected me to sit on it! I'd rather be with the pig-iron on that freight train.

With the vast majority of the seats sold , the Skifflefest was a great success. Most of the audience were in the late 50s and many were former members of skiffle groups themselves - I know this because Chas McDevitt requested a show of hands for old skifflers. I wasn't sitting next to some old-time skiffler though, I was sat by the newsreader, Moira Stuart. When I went into the Hall, I saw Chas McDevitt signing and selling copies of his book, 'Skiffle - The Definitive Inside Story'. He'd be compering the show in half an hour's time and his behaviour illustrated the homemade approach to skiffle music. No room for prima donnas here - at least, that's what I scribbled at the time. Later, I discovered that Lonnie Donegan had threatened to pull out half an hour before he performed because the stage setting wasn't to his liking. ("But, Lonnie, Mal Roberts has agreed it on your behalf, so please get out there and do it.") Even better was Ray Bush of the Avon City Skiffle Group, who had come over from Canada, ostensibly for the finale but insisted on a song of his own. He had no stage presence or presentation to speak of, yet even his "Fishing In My Pond" was preferable to the appalling vocal from Bob Weston of the Horseshoe Skiffle Group whose 'Good Morning Blues' with Chas and Dave was the most unmusical performance I've ever heard on a stage, let alone at the Royal Albert Hall. The show needed a tougher stage manager and I felt sorry for the good-natured Bill Wyman who dutifully arrived at 2pm for the rehearsal. He went through some songs with Lonnie and expected to play on several songs, but in the end was relegated to the final number. (Wyman, a generous-spirited man, took it in good heart. He invited Lonnie to join the Rhythm Kings on stage in Malaga in 2001 and they did 'Frankie And Johnny' and he narrated the Radio 2 tribute to him.)

If a Martian (or to be just as unearthly, my late father) had come to the show, could he have made any sense of it: would it show what skiffle was and explain its attraction? As the first half hour, with no explanation, was devoted to Chris Barber's Jazz and Blues Band, the Martian (or my dad) would have thought that skiffle was performed by eight-piece bands emulating New Orleans jazzmen. It was very professional and I know that the skiffle craze developed from Chris Barber's original band, but why didn't he perform more suitable material? Duke Ellington's 'Mood Indigo' and Scott Joplin's 'Maple Leaf Rag' have no connections with skiffle, so why play them? The only appropriate number was Sonny Terry and Brownie McGhee's 'Cornbread Peas And Black Molasses', but the twin sax break was more R&B than skiffle. I confess, however, that I disliked Chris Barber's set, not for the music, but for the fact that he kept shaking his trombone and enormous globs of spittle would drop to the stage. Disgusting.

A contemporary band, the Lonnigans, gave an excellent impression of what a large skiffle group in 1957 looked and sounded like. Bonnie, Connie, Donnie, Johnnie and Ronnie Lonnigan (presumably their real names) are young and enthusiastic and the ten-piece lineup includes double bass, cowbell and washboard. The washboard was played an old hand, Derek Mason, a Jimmy Savile lookalike who had appeared in New Station Skiffle Group on the BBC's first teenage show, '6.5 Special'.

The Lonnigans played a sparkling bluegrass arrangement of the show's theme music, which was recorded by the late skiffler, Bob Cort. They also paid tribute to the UK's best-known washboard player, the blues singer Beryl Bryden, who died in 1998, with 'Kansas City Blues' and 'He Knows How To Rock Me'. To be honest, they could have sung anything as her repertoire has bypassed me completely. Have I missed much though? Steve Voce's obituary in 'The Independent' said, "Sitting next to her myself at a concert by Count Basie during the Fifties, I lost the subtleties of Basie's rhythm work as Bryden tried to clap her hands in time with the band throughout the whole concert." No such trouble with Moira Stuart, I might add.

Most British lads never worked in the fields, but it was on Chas McDevitt's mind as his first number, backed by the Lonnigans, was 'Pick A Bale Of Cotton', and his second, 'Cotton Fields'. Chas was going to open with 'It Takes A Worried Man' but he heard Lonnie perform it at rehearsal and dropped it. A second Chas, Chas Hodges of Chas and Dave, also heard Lonnie sing something they were planning but said, "Who cares? We're on first."

Chas McDevitt paid tribute to another late skiffler, Ken Colyer, before introducing his brother, Bill, better known as Bilko. Bill is a testimony to the preservative powers of alcohol. Now an old man, he sits under his brother's plaque at the 100 Club. "I'm Bill Colyer," he says pointing upwards, "and that's my brother." People have been joking about Bill's intake for years, but he continues on and looked very happy playing washboard for Chas on 'Goin' Home'.

Ken Colyer himself was a sorry character: perhaps a symbol for skiffle music itself. I interviewed him late in life and his house was a terrible state: the oranges in his fruitbowl were so old that the pips rattled inside. Derek Vaux, who plays with the Merseysippi Jazz Band, played with Ken Colyer but was quickly disillusioned: "It was playing the same thing over and over again, very boring chord sequences, and I never liked the way he played his instrument. His old seafaring friend, Ron Ward, played bass for him for many years. One night the drummer's bass pedal broke and for the first time in ten years, Ken Colyer actually heard what Ron Ward was playing and he sacked him immediately. That typifies his approach to the music he was playing."

Chas McDevitt's former singing partner, Nancy Whiskey, took the rostrum with the leading jazz guitarist and ex-skiffler, Diz Disley, for an affable but short set, performing 'Dark As A Dungeon', 'Casey When She Moans' and, with Chas whistling, the inevitable 'Freight Train'. She said of her relationship with Chas, "We were never married and we never even had it off." Kindly leave the stage, we do not wish to know that. By reuniting for "Freight Train", Chas and Nancy were the only artists on the bill, outside of Lonnie Donegan, to perform their own skiffle hit. Nancy Whiskey has a fine voice and you wonder why she never consolidated her initial success. Perhaps the answer lies in Mike Dewe's book, 'The Skiffle Craze', which states that Nancy only received one-twelfth of the record royalties.

Before Screamin' Lord Sutch, there was Wee Willie Harris, and before Steve Murray became Wee Willie, he ran a skiffle group which performed at the central stomping-ground, the Two I's coffee-bar in Soho. Willie, now in his late 60s but he's looked that way for years, performed soberly in a long dinner jacket: that is, until he turned round and 'WEE WILLIE HARRIS' was written in red capitals on the back. With some Lonnigans and Mike Wilsh of the Four Pennies on double-bass, he paid tribute to Wally Whyton of the Vipers with 'Maggie May', then Johnny Horton with 'North To Alaska' and finally Lonnie Donegan (why? Lonnie isn't dead and was on the bill!) with 'Diggin' My Potatoes'. It was a good set but I was hoping for 'Rockin' At The Two I's'. Still, I should be glad that he didn't wear his leopard-skin and chase young girls with his polystyrene club while singing 'I Go Ape'. Incidentally, have you noticed how many entertainers have names with sexual overtones - Wee Willie Harris, Dickie Pride, Little Richard, Roger Moore and, I suppose, Googie Withers?

Chas and Dave closed the first half of the show. Chas and Dave? Well, the one resembling the Hairy Cornflake, was in a skiffle group, and to show their credentials, they introduced 'Rabbit' as "a sort of skiffle number". Sort of. This duo has more rabbit than Sainsbury's. They paid tribute to Lonnie but not with their fine 'Lonnie D' but 'Bring A Little Water, Sylvie'. Chas introduced 'You're The One Rose', somewhat incongruously, as "Jerry Lee Lewis' father's favourite song" and after performing 'San Francisco Bay Blues', Dave said, "It's all coming back to me." As the first half had already lasted over two hours, I thought, "God, I hope not."

As Chas remarked in his book, 'The Rock And Roll Years Of Chas Before Dave' (Lennard Publishing, 1987): "Skiffle played its part, and an important part. It got me started. Throughout pop history, a relatively simple type of music every now and then becomes popular. It is good because it makes the kids think, 'Perhaps I can do that', and they do, and in a short time some of them are sounding as good as the records. The serious ones move on from there, but that start is important."

Tony Sheridan joined Chas and Dave for 'It All Depends (Who Will Buy The Wine)' and 'Money Honey', and I know from past experience that Tony has good nights and bad nights. This was a bad one and I was wondering if he had even rehearsed.

There could be no show without Punch and Lonnie Donegan, Punch-like in profile, topped the bill. He came on, dressed in black, and acknowledged the applause with a John Travolta pose. He said, "Don't know how long it took you to reach the Albert Hall tonight, but it's taken me 45 years." All this from a man who was thinking of going home. Lonnie had a six-piece band including sax and they rocked so hard that you could imagine Bruce Springsteen as the vocalist instead of Lonnie.

In an 80 minute set (this was a long show), Lonnie performed such skiffle favourites as 'It Takes A Worried Man', 'I Shall Not Be Moved' and 'Corrine Corrina' and his own hits such as 'Puttin' On The Style', 'Michael Row The Boat' and 'Lost John'. Lonnie shunned 'My Old Man's A Dustman' and 'Does Your Chewing Gum Lose Its Flavour', but he did feature material from his new CD, 'Muleskinner Blues', advertised in the programme as 'Mulskinner Blues' (sic). This is a record company that knows what it's doing.

Lonnie had rehearsed 'Tom Dooley' with Joe Brown, but he performed the song without him. Joe was left backstage, wondering what was going on, but he was eventually summoned to play fiddle on 'The Battle Of New Orleans'. Even though Peter Oakman, a former Bruvver and writer of Joe's hit 'A Picture Of You', was in Lonnie's group, Joe was not invited on to the rostrum to sing with Lonnie. The reason? Seems that Lonnie, a smallish man, didn't want Joe, a tall one, towering over him. He didn't object to the pint-sized Adam Faith, who joined him for 'Have A Drink On Me' (originally written for, and rejected by, Adam) and 'Railroad Bill'. Adam told us he'd been looking forward to working with Lonnie for some weeks, but if that's true, why didn't he learn the words? I suppose he figured, quite correctly, that whatever he sang, Lonnie would drown him out. As Adam can't say his r's, I was listening for "Wailwoad Bill", but all I heard was Lonnie.

All the time I was watching Lonnie Donegan, I was thinking "This is remarkable. This is the best advertisement for heart surgery there could ever be." Lonnie performs like a man possessed and his frenzied 'Rock Island Line' turns the goods train into a thundering Virgin express . His set was full of highlights including 'New Burying Ground', 'I Wanna Go Home' and 'Seven Golden Daffodils'. Lonnie once told me that he could get audiences crying with 'Nobody's Child', but although he performs the country ballad immaculately, I didn't see anyone with their Kleenex. Lonnie took his name from the blues singer, Lonnie Johnson, and he performed one of Johnson's standards, 'Rocks In My Bed', with great feeling. Bruce Welch came out of the Shadows for the encore but the song Lonnie chose, 'Frankie And Johnnie', wasn't appropriate for the backing vocals of Adam Faith, Chas and Nancy, and Wee Willie Harris, who weren't sure what to do.

This was the biggest gathering of skiffle since the 1950s - not that there has been much competition - but the highspots had little to do with skiffle at all. Lonne said it was "the greatest concert of my life. If I never do another show, I will die a happy man."

III.

FANCY TALKING TINKER
(This section is adapted from a feature I wrote for 'Now Dig This' in May 2001.)

Lonnie Donegan has such a long schedule of concert and club dates for 2001 that you could see it as a death wish. Why else would he put himself under such strain? Well, firstly, he regards himself as The Man Who Should Be King. Several critics have dismissed him as a novelty singer and there is an element of wanting to ensure his place in rock history. Another factor is to give his touring band regular work as otherwise he could lose them to other performers. However, the prime consideration is easyJet. Lonnie is careful with his money (not tight - he bought me dinner) and discovering easyJet means he can commute back and forth to his home in Spain quickly and economically. In the Liverpool area alone, his dates include the Old Swan Conservative Club (March 2), Pontin's Holiday Village, Ainsdale (March 24), the Cavern (May 24), the Mathew Street Festival (August 27) and Parr Hall, Warrington (November 2). Lonnie is everywhere - look at the festivals supplement in 'Folk Roots' and marvel at the hardest working pensioner in show business. (Three of those Merseyside dates were played - his fee could not be met for the free Mathew Street Festival and the Warrington gig was cancelled due to ill health.)

Lonnie Donegan plays superbly and he has shaken off the cabaret blandishments he had when playing for chicken-in-a-basket crowds. The music comes first and even in a small club, Donegan attacks the songs like a rock superstar. Most of all, he is singing better than ever, and knows it: "You could say that I've been practising a long time so I bloody well should be better - just like Tom Jones. My voice has gone deeper at the bottom end, it has broadened, it has dropped a bit at the top and I have learnt to breathe properly. The only lesson I've had is from Anne Shelton who saw me at the Prince of Wales in 1956 and said, 'Lonnie, that was wonderful, but you've got to learn to breathe.' I thought, 'What is she talking about? I'm breathing.' I realised I should hold my breath so that I can hold notes. I can now hold notes longer than almost anybody on the stage."

Fortunately, Lonnie has not priced himself out of the market. He will play small clubs if they can meet his fee. Hence, his appearance at the Old Swan Conservative Club, affectionately billed as 'Lonnie At The Connie'. The Old Swan Conservative Club sounds like an oxymoron as I didn't know there were any Conservatives in Old Swan. The club is a favourite with taxi drivers and is bigger than I thought. The capacity is still only 325 and the club's manager, Frank Furlong, has to charge £14 a ticket. Part of the bar profit would have to go towards Lonnie's fee and the likelihood of even a small profit was slim. "I don't mind," says Frank, "Lonnie has been my idol for years and I'm so proud to be presenting this."

Being an ardent Europhile, I'm not keen on entering a club covered in 'Keep the pound' billboards, but that's the Tories for you. The noticeboard announces future bookings - anyone with a record contract would look like a star in this plethora of tribute acts. As friendly as the surroundings are, I wondered if Lonnie had accepted something beneath his dignity: "No. What matters is the money. If someone phones up and says that he will pay the fee, I will be there." So if I come up with the money, you'll play in my front room? "Certainly. I play 60th birthday parties, no problem."

Towards the end of the afternoon, I arrive for an interview with Lonnie at the Connie. Lonnie and his band are already there, and what other 69 year old looks like this? He is wearing a black and red check shirt with a brown track suit bottom held up by braces. With his substantial belly, he resembles a circus clown. Facially though, he doesn't look 69 and indeed looks younger than his sometime partner, Van Morrison, 14 years his junior. The sound-check is marvellous, a show in itself, with ten of us applauding the numbers. It begins with an acoustic 'Grand Coulee Dam', which becomes more intense as the song goes on. I want to say, "Lonnie, this is only a sound-check, there's no need to exert yourself" but nobody could ever tell Lonnie that. He attacks the lyric with such gusto and I wonder if anyone hearing the song for the first time would have a clue as to what it's about.

The band join him for 'Linin' Track' and a slow, creeping 'Cajun Stripper' is next with the emphasis on the sibilant "s". Carl Jones, a Lonnie Donegan collector from Mold, is entranced, "Lonnie stayed with me last night and I showed him a video of the Wembley Country Festival in 1979. That was the time of the 'Sundown' LP and so that must have put 'Cajun Stripper' in his mind. I haven't seen him do this for ten years." Lonnie has fun with 'It Takes A Worried Man' and he sings 'I Wanna Go Home' with all the poignancy of a concert performance. It is my first Lonnie Donegan show of the day, and I was reminded of a soundcheck in Southport ten years earlier. Lonnie was on stage with Chris Barber's Jazz and Blues Band, and Chris said to me, "Once Lonnie gets on that stage, he'll never get off and we won't get round to the other numbers."

Before Lonnie went on stage, he asked Carl Jones to show me his new publicity material. Lonnie had done this on his computer and it looks impressive. "But don't point out any spelling mistakes", warns Carl. "I told him it was Ronald Reagan and not Ronald Regan and he said, 'You can spell it like that.' 'Yes', I said, 'but Ronald Reagan doesn't.'" I decide to tell Lonnie that it looks good and not ask him who Rolph Harris is. I give Lonnie my new book, 'Brother, Can You Spare A Rhyme?', which covers a hundred years of hit songwritng. He flicks through it and alights on a photo of himself. "Why am I in 1924?", he asks. "It's the year 'Chewing Gum' was written," I say. "No," he replies, "That's 1931." I nod, sure I had checked the fact but not wanting to disagree with Lonnie before I had even switched on my recorder.

Lonnie is telling us how Liverpool becomes Louisiana for a night: "'Rock Island Line' is the archtypal Afro-American folk song with its slow rhythm, ponderous feel, speeding up and growing excitement. It has wonderful imagery with a great storyline of a guy smuggling stuff through on a train. I enjoy the first part immensely and I like to get it really atmospheric: I like to look into the faces of the audience and see them down there in Louisiana with the sweat trickling down their temples as they feel the heat and see this great train in front of them. Then we come to the action and the more you do it the faster you can do it. Now it's very difficult to slow down. I get excited and when I get excited, the audience gets excited, and well, we go for it, you know."

The interview has already started but Lonnie says, "Come for a Ruby Murray and we can do the interview while we're waiting." Lonnie and I get into Carl's Mercedes for the short drive to the Travel Inn, where Lonnie will be getting changed for the show. A short drive, but still an experience as Lonnie is a front seat back seat driver. "Don't drive like that, foot on the brake, swing round a little more, come on, that's more like it" and this is before we've left the car park. Carl, a retired British Steel manager, takes it in good humour: he doesn't mind being Lonnie's lackey for the day. I surmise that, as a driver, Lonnie had better control of the accelerator than the brakes.

We walk from the car and go inside the Travel Inn. Lonnie points to a bog-standard table and two chairs and says, "What a palatial reception area." The twenty-something manager ignores his comment and wecolmes him, "We have had many celebrity guests here. Atomic Kitten have stayed here and their manager is here all the time." Lonnie tells us to get a table for four at the Stag And Rainbow next door, "Pete Oakie can join us as well. I'm going to my room and I'll only be five minutes."

Five minutes to Lonnie is always twenty so I chat to Carl and then Pete Oakman. He has been playing bass on and off for Lonnie for over 30 years. He was also part of Country Fever with Albert Lee and he tells how they backed Guy Mitchell in the early 70s on an Irish tour promoted by Clodagh Rodgers' father. Guy had gone to South Africa to dry out and "if he'd come straight to Ireland to join us and perform, everything would have been all right. Unfortunately, he had three days on his own in Ireland before the tour began and he started drinking again. He was sozzled on stage and the second week had to be cancelled." I ask him to contrast working with Joe and working with Lonnie. "Neither of them has any stage fright," he says, "They don't get butterflies, but the adrenalin gets them going. Joe has a very good cheeky chappie image and I'll go and see him whenever he is working locally. Unlike Billy Fury or Marty Wilde, neither Lonnie nor Joe were selling sex, and that's done them well over the years as they get both the guys and the girls. I remember with Joe having our car blocked in and we called for some guys to lift the other cars out of the way. They did it and I don't think they'd have done it for Billy."

Pete Oakman credits some of Joe's success to his mother's enthusiasm. Mrs. Oakman was a classically trained pianist who wrote the vaudevillian 'Good Luck And Goodbye' for Joe Brown and 'My Sweet Marie' for Lonnie Donegan. "My mum would be playing 'Czardas' and Joe would say, 'Oh Mrs. O, you've got to teach me that.' She loved Italian tarantellas and that's why there are quite a few unusual songs on Joe's albums."

Lonnie joins us and immediately joins in. I ask him why he and Pete haven't written together: "We've done the odd thing, but we're lazy songwriters. We've never been encouraged to write our own songs and so it's just a sideline. I have lots of ideas, but I'm lazy about sitting down and doing the graft. I suppose I'm saying that I am not a natural songwriter. If someone wants me to do something, I do it: otherwise, I don't. I should do more. Tom Jones has told me that 'I'll Never Fall In Love Again' is his favourite song of all-time. Tom was in Las Vegas and Elvis saw his show many times. They hobnobbed and Elvis liked it too and recorded it. I always think of Elvis as a ballad singer, he really did the ballads best." Did Colonel Parker make you give up some of your royalties? "No, but now you mention it, it's quite surprising, isn't it?"

We order our meal, Lonnie wanting a shank of lamb with medium white wine and making recommendations for everyone else: "Tempos are going to be a bit down tonight. 'Tom Dooley' for the encore - after the tap-dance, that is."

"Don't you get fed up doing 'Rock Island Line'?"

"No, I said to Dickie Valentine once, 'People keep asking for 'Rock Island Line'. How long do I have to go on singing it?' and he said, 'For as long as people want to hear it."

We talk about music books - Lonnie had been reading Kitty Kelley's attack on Sinatra, 'His Way': "I believe all that stuff about the Mafia. I saw it myself. I could have worked for Sinatra in Las Vegas but it would have been working for the Mafia." When I mention Charlotte Breese's biography of the entertainer, Hutch, Lonnie takes out his handkerchief and does an impersonation of Hutch singing 'These Foolish Things', a moment I will always treasure. "Wasn't he reputed to have a large willy?" says Pete. "Not reputed, my son, he did have. I saw it at the East Ham Granada." Lonnie is so funny: "First impressions are often the best. It was instant dislike when I met George Melly and I haven't changed my mind. There aren't many people that I can't take to, but he's one of them."

I want to talk about Lonnie's forthcoming appearance at the Cavern. Outside the Cavern, there is a wall of bricks showing everyone who has played there. "I've got a brick there," says Lonnie, who visited the club the previous evening, "but they're wrong because I haven't played it yet. I was at the Liverpool Empire in 1958 and I rented it for my skiffle club one Saturday morning. Nobody in Britain knew very much about American folk music, more specifically Afro-American folk music, and so I thought it would be a good idea if I could enlighten the public. I formed the Lonnie Donegan Skiffle Club and we issued a monthly magazine in which I highlighted a different American blues singer each month like Big Bill Broonzy, Josh White and Burl Ives and gave instructions on how to play their better known songs. We also gave news of what we were doing and where we were playing. We played everywhere for a week in those days and when we were at the Liverpool Empire, which seats 3,000, we would do two shows a night six days a week. That's 30,000 people a week, a football stadium a week if you like, and we never stopped working. It's 100,000 a month and a million people a year. I did that for six years and that's a bloody lot of people. The Rolling Stones never played to crowds like that. Who plays to a million people a year now?" Quite. The boy bands complain of stress after a couple of gigs and Lonnie keeps on going. He still holds nothing back and hurls himself into it.

Quite simply, the Cavern which opened in 1957 was not big enough for Lonnie at the time. "Even when I was in a semi-pro jazz band, the Ken Colyer Jazzmen, we were too big to play the Cavern. We played the Picton Hall and that is where we always played in Liverpool." Lonnie is planning a new album but he is not sure what he wants to do: I say, "You once told me that you would like to do Hank Williams's narrations as Luke the Drifter."

"I still would like to do that. Nobody has managed to recapture that intensely emotional, personal recitative form. You not only have to have a good singing voice, but you also need a particular kind of speaking voice as well, which Hank did have. That concept was original to him, I would love to be able to do that."

"It could be an unplugged album, perhaps just you and a guitar."

"If I thought my guitarplaying was up to it, I would. Martin Guitars want to issue a Lonnie Donegan Martin, which is incredibly flattering, that's the apogee of my career. I said to my wife, 'All I've got to do now is to learn how to play the thing. I'm no Eric Clapton."

"What about a live album from the Cavern?"

"No way, the sound would be dreadful."

"It was good enough for Paul McCartney in 1999."

"But he had so many people working for him, scores of people getting it right. I can't afford that. We would have to re-do parts in the studio and it could go for a long time."

"It'd be like the Eagles' live album where the only thing left was the applause."

"That'd be the first thing to go. They want a lot of people in the Cavern and so they will be standing up. No matter how much you like an act, you can't applaud with a glass in your hand. The applause won't be that hot."

Lonnie has the drummer Jerry Allison of the Crickets playing on his 'Muleskinner Blues' CD, and he praised his work with Buddy Holly. "English drummers were very wooden, a lot of them still are, and this guy was flowing and you never knew what he was going to play from bar to bar. He had a wonderful full sound as if he were playing three drum-kits at once. I asked him what style it was, and he said, 'I guess it's Texas drumming.' That sounded funny at the time but I found out later that there was a Texas style, which had a semi-military sound to it."

Who's been the most electrifying person you've seen on stage? "Probably Mahalia Jackson way back at the Royal Albert Hall when I was 17. She filled that hall with no microphone, just her singing and an acoustic piano and a church organ. It was spine-tingling. Since then, I have wanted to sing some genuine gospel music but I've always been thwarted and 'Fancy Talking Tinker' is as close as I've got. I asked Sam Brown who is a wonderful singer to hand-pick two other girls and we tried to get this gospel sound, and we've done a reasonable job on it."

After the meal, it's into the Merc to return to the Connie. Lonnie is even worse: "What the hell are you doing, Carl? Can't you get out of this car park. Go the other way. No, you're blocking everybody now, get your arse moving. Come on, I want you to leave me this Mercedes in good condition." And so on. Line him up for the next Celebrity Big Brother. Back at the club, the supporting acts are working hard. As Lonnie had instructed, there are no comedians but the Fabtones (Frank Johns and Paul Ogden) don't take themselves seriously, although their playing of familiar oldies is good. They go down well but Jody Stevens and her backing tapes have a mixed reception. She's a belter and she has her PA too loud. She acknowledges this, pretends to make adjustments and continues as before. An elderly couple have seats at the front for Lonnie and put their hands over their ears. Jody berates them for being wimps and not being able to take the sound like the rest of the audience. If only they'd said, "We've got our hands over our ears because we can't stand you."

Lonnie comes onto the small stage to rapturous applause. They open with 'Linin' Track' and 'New Burying Ground'. I love the combination of saxophone and washboard for 'It Takes A Worried Man' and Lonnie straps on his banjo for 'Putting On The Style'. The gospel medley of 'Rock O'My Soul', 'Michael Row The Boat' and 'I Shall Not Be Moved' transform the club into a revivalist meeting.

Lonnie says, "This show is a test of memory more than anything else. See if you remember this, see if we do." Lonnie has a 12-string guitar for 'I Wanna Go Home' and hits some tremendous low notes. A powerpacked 'Grand Coulee Dam' comes next and then Donegan's own 'When I Get Off This Feeling', a highlight from his 'Muleskinner Blues' CD. He now calls it 'Brand New Man' and the live version is as good as the record. Alan 'Sticky' Wicket has a military drum for 'Battle Of New Orleans', which turns into a percussion battle with Chris Hunt, who is playing very well despite a recent illness.

Then comes the bluesy 'Rocks In My Bed' with Lonnie's own guitar solo. 'Corrine Corrina' is such a good number for audience participation that someone gets out his banjo and plays along. Lonnie imagines himself in Louisiana for his closer, 'Rock Island Line'. The applause is deafening and Lonnie returns for an acoustic 'Goodnight Irene'. This is not an easy song to perform, but he does it to perfection. Lonnie goes off and the audience starts singing 'My Old Man's A Dustman'. Pete Oakman comes out, "Give him a break. The poor sod's nearly 70 and he's knackered."

Carl calls his wife Barbara and asks her to ensure that the heating is on in Lonnie's room. He takes Lonnie to the Travel Inn to change and then takes him home. Later he tells me that Lonnie spent the early hours reading my book, 'Halfway To Paradise', and doing a lot of humming and hawing. "I don't know why," I told Carl, "I'd reproduced what he said word for word." "Oh, it's not that," said Carl, "It's what Chris Barber was saying."

I had recorded the show and I sent a copy to the noted Bob Dylan analyst, Michael Gray. He sent me an e-mail: "'Lonnie At The Connie' is a curious mixture. There's something about him that confirms that my teenage self was right in dismissing him - too British and too 'Boiled Beef And Carrots' music-hall - and yet...he's using a surprisingly good band, a lot of his material is impeccable, he's as good as he ever was, and for a man of 70, he's in fine fettle indeed: impressive."

I have a second date with Donegan on Saturday 24 March as Lonnie is starring at 'Another Fabulous Billy And Wally Weekend' at Pontin's Holiday Village in Ainsdale. It is Billy Butler and Wally Scott's 33rd promotion at the camp and they total 50,000 visitors, the majority being fans of Billy Butler's radio show who return again and again. The weekend breaks present value for money - £55 for three days' entertainment and two night's board and lodging - but, without sounding snobby about it, Pontin's is not for me.

After getting through Checkpoint Charlie and a maze of slot machines, I reach the theatre where Billy is appealing to the audience for the return of a stolen wheelchair. Looking at the gaudy décor, you might think that the designer had had a traumatic experience with a kaleidoscope, but the back wall of the theatre features large black and white murals of film stars. When you perform, all you can see is Jack Nicholson in his crazed 'Here's Johnny!' moment.

Or possibly 'Here's Willy!' I had missed the strippers, the Centurions. These men who braved the cold had a clause that they would strip to G-strings, but would do a full strip if the audience wished. What audience wouldn't? "This is a family weekend," I say to Billy Butler, "so why have you got strippers on?" "Oh, they're hilarious," replies Billy, "and the bigger the dick the better it is." "Maybe," I say, "but there'd be an outcry if you booked female strippers." I fully accept that times have changed and you can even book John Allison of the Allisons as a stripping singer. If you want the Full Monty combined with 'Are You Sure?', John Allison's your man.

Billy tells me that Lonnie has done a sound check: "He saw the forms on the tables asking who they would like to see at future events and I heard him tell the band to write down 'Lonnie Donegan'." On stage at present is the Cy Tucker band, an excellent club act. Cy was part of Earl Preston and the TTs in the 60s and his powerful, beat-ballad singing has made Cooper's Emporium the busiest pub in Liverpool. Admittedly, he always plays too loud and the best place to listen is in the street. Cy gets a very good reaction and the audience enjoys singing along. I had missed the tribute acts to Elvis Presley, Billy Fury and Doris Day, although a real life Doris Day would never have worked with male strippers.

I sit down with Lonnie's band and say this is the ideal place for 'Cajun Stripper'. The drummer Chris Hunt praises my review in 'Now Dig This'. "But I haven't written it yet," I say, "I'm combining it with this show." "No, not Lonnie," he says, "The one with Dana Gillespie at the Cavern. I was with her for a long time and she used to get 'Now Dig This'. One of the perks of the job was getting 'Now Dig This' after she'd read it." "Thank heaven you weren't drumming for Tommy Bruce," I say, "His manager thinks I've been most unfair to him. Apparently, Tommy demands respect because of all the gold, silver and platinum discs he's got at home." "Ah, but whose are they?" says Chris. Chris looks sad but he has a good sense of humour. Still, there's not much to be happy about here. The band are in Pontin's chalets and Chris's hadn't even got hot water. Go backstage and it's like entering a Third World country.

Because Lonnie is the star, he doesn't have to stay at Pontin's but he's faring little better at the Scarisbrick Hotel. He ordered Steak Diane at 7.30pm as he thought it wouldn't take long. The food wasn't ready until 9.00pm and was so stewed that Lonnie brought it up before he went on stage. Still, he's in good form when I see him. "After we spoke," he says, "I came across an interview we did in 1999. I was giving you a hard time." "You always do," I reply. I remember the interview well. I had commented quite innocently that his new CD was on RCA. He said it was on Capo. Both company names are on the record and I remember thinking, "Am I ever going to get off this topic? Who cares what label it's on?" It was a typical Lonnie Donegan interview: he's putting on the bile. His way through the boredom of regurgitating stories is to correct interviewers at every opportunity.

I assemble the group for a photograph: "Come on," says Lonnie, "Gather round. This is for 'Kerrang!'" Lonnie prepares for the stage show by singing an oldie with the band. Their voices soar on "Not for all the dreams in dreamland" and Lonnie goes into a softshoe shuffle.

At the record stall I find Mel Roberts who has been involved in Lonnie's management for 30 years. In other circumstances, I would say that he was the artist's manager, but Lonnie manages himself. Dave Radcliffe, who is running the record stall, compiled the impressive "Lonnie Donegan Discography, 1953 - 1982". It lists, for example, Lonnie's commercials -

Sugar Puffs (mid 50s), Chivers Jellies (1962), Smith's Crisps (1967), Wrigley's Spearmint (1977) and, bizarrely, Erith And Co (1981).

The holidaymakers have been drinking and are in a party mood when Lonnie goes on stage. There is dancing at the front and Carl says, "This'll be a good one. Lonnie loves it when they're dancing." There is line dancing for 'Grand Coulee Dam' and they improvise firing guns for 'Battle Of New Orleans'. A bus pass groupie walks onto the stage and, who knows, propositions Lonnie. The audience sings along with 'It Takes A Worried Man': "Let's do it again," says Lonnie, "I'll play it for you." You couldn't imagine Lonnie working with Van Morrison at Pontin's.

The repertoire is largely the same as at the Connie. When he launches into 'Rocks In My Bed', Billy Butler says to me, "This is self-indulgent, he could lose them." But Lonnie knows exactly what he's doing and the next song is one of his hits. I expect him to finish with 'Goodnight Irene' but he finds his second wind and returns for 'Have A Drink On Me' and 'Tom Dooley'. As Lonnie wipes away his sweat, he watches Billy Butler start a singalong of the hits he hasn't performed. Fancy being followed by your own tribute act. Time to leave.

Lonnie Donegan, 2001 (Brian Smith)

LONNIE DONEGAN
SKIFFLE

"THIS COULD BE THE LAST TIME" tour

Sep 14	SALISBURY	CITY HALL	01722 - 327676
Sep 16	TRURO	HALL of CORNWALL	01872 - 262486
Sep 18	WESTON S MARE	PLAYHOUSE	01934 - 645544
Sep 20	CHELTENHAM	TOWN HALL	01242 - 227979
Sep 22	JERSEY	OPERA HOUSE	01534 - 511115
Sep 24	KINGS LYNN	CORN EXCHANGE	01553 - 746846
Sep 27	ISLE of WIGHT	MEDINA THEATRE	01983 - 527020
Sep 29	BOURNEMOUTH	THE PAVILION	01202 - 456456
Oct 01	IPSWICH	REGENT THEATRE	01473 - 433100
Oct 03	TUNBRIDGE WELLS	ASSEMBLY ROOMS	01892 - 530613
Oct 05	WEYMOUTH	THE PAVILION	01305 - 783225
Oct 17	BRECON	THEATR BRYNHENIOG	01874 - 611622
Oct 19	BIRMINGHAM	ALEXANDRA THEATRE	0870 - 6077544
Oct 21	SHREWSBURY	MUSIC HALL	01743 - 281281
Oct 27-28			01599 - 895555

		ROYAL CONCERT HALL	
Oct 30	NOTTINGHAM	see Notts box - office for details	

plus guests inc..... JOE BROWN

Nov 03	YORK	OPERA HOUSE	01904 - 678700
Nov 04	STOKE	VICTORIA HALL	01782 - 213800
Nov 06	BOLTON	ALBERT HALLS	01204 - 334400
Nov 07	NEWCASTLE	OPERA HOUSE	0191 - 2320899
Nov 10	LIVERPOOL	ROYAL COURT THEATRE	0151 - 7094321
Nov 13	GRAVESEND	WOODVILLE HALLS	01474 - 337459
Nov 15	CROYDON	ASHCROFT THEATRE	0208 - 6889291
		WESTCLIFF PAVILION	
Dec 04	SOUTHEND		01702 - 351135

tour ticket-line 0845 6023 789   www.artists2events.co.uk

Sheffield City Hall

Lonnie Donegan

Thursday 25 October 8.00pm
Tickets: £17.50 in advance

Lonnie Donegan
Memorial Hall
Almost 50 years as an entertainer, the seminal Scottish blues/folk guitarist whose style influenced dozens of bands, including the Beatles and the Rolling Stones. Lonnie amalgamated folk, blues, gospel, and country years before Bob Dylan carved his new sound out of the music of the American South.

The Band;
Pete Oakman,
Paul Henry,
Chris Hunt,
Lonnie, Alan
'Sticky' Wickett
and Nick Payn

LONNIE DONEGAN
Sheffield City Hall.

Still hailed as, and I guess always will be, 'the king of skiffle' (Tony) Lonnie Donegan whose run of unforgettable songs lit the fuse for many careers in British rock with hundreds of young skifflers following this musical pied-piper. Lonnie's own career has also been dogged by ill-health surrounding heart problems, but you'd never know it watching the man at work. Lonnie's performance brought out all the elements that contributed to skiffle: blues, folk, hillbilly and gospel exemplified on "It Take A Worried Man", "I Shall Not Be Moved", "Corina, Corina", "Rock O' My Soul", and "Muleskinner Blues", the latter recorded with Van Morrison. Bombarded with requests,"Chesapeke Bay" caught Lonnie's ear and gave it a quick impromptu run-through. Also much to everybody's pleasure were many of Lonnie's chart successes; "Grand Coolee Dam", "Micheal, Row The Boat Ashore", "Puttin' On The Style", "Sloop John B." and "Battle Of New Orleans". Backed up by a solid band including original Bruvver and writer of "Picture Of You", Pete Oakman on bass, Nick Payne on harmonica and sax from Bill Wyman's Rhythm Kings and ace guitarist Paul Henry. Whilst injecting a great deal of soul and energy into his songs, Lonnie appeared very relaxed and at times the set was more like a sound-check. The song that started the Donegan story off was of course Rock Island Line dressed-up here with heavy, atmospheric intro before switching mid-way to its faster torried arrangement with some frenzied vocals from Lonnie. This led into a couple more commercial successes, "Have A Drink On Me" and the novel "Does Your Chewing-gum Lose Its Flavour". Winding things up with a moody rendition of Leadbelly's "Goodnight Irene" Lonnie was rewarded with a standing ovation from a loyal audience who all recalled those far-off days. Although his music may have come from a different age, Lonnie Donegan continues to give it quality and credibility.

JOHN FIRMINGER

LONNIE DONEGAN IS DEAD

Midway through a UK tour, Lonnie Donega the man who was alternately dubbed 'The Ki of Skiffle' and 'The Irish Hillbilly', collapsed a died from a heart attack on November 3rd wh staying with friends in Peterborough. He was

LONNIE DONEGAN 1931-2002

The first British artiste to achieve hit parade success on both sides of the Atlantic, Lonnie Donegan died at the home of a personal friend in Peterborough, Cambridgeshire, in the early hours of the morning of Sunday, November 3.

Lonnie Donegan, MBE
(1931-2002)

Order of Service

Peterborough Crematorium
Thursday 14th November 2002

Celebrants: Pauline Southam
and Ernest Fytche

"It's what he would have wanted!"

REMEMBERING LONNIE

We were so very sorry to hear of Lonnie Donegan's passing. We were fortunate enough to really spend some quality time with him and his son, Peter, when Van Morrison invited my father and Lonnie to tour with him for a few weeks in 2000. He was a genuine guy and I just sat back and listened to all the stories and notes he and dad shared backstage and at dinner.

I can recall Lonnie sitting at a table in his Las Vegas suite in January 2000 taking a lot of pills related to his heart condition. He seemed annoyed with this daily ordeal but looked and sounded very good on stage. He went through a litany of his health problems and heart surgeries. He was surprised to know I had a vinyl copy of the 'From Elvis Presley Boulevard' LP from 1976 which he didn't have a copy of. The album contains Elvis' version of 'I'll Never Fall In Love Again' which, of course, was penned by Lonnie. When I returned home from Vegas, I sent him my copy immediately.

I have some nice photos and, looking back now, I'm so glad we took them. There's no denying Lonnie's influence. I know he was a giant in the UK and many here remember, him as well. It's so disturbing each time we lose someone we admire - a performer who was so vital to millions around the world. God bless his soul!

Charlie Gracie Jr.
Drexel Hill, Philadelphia, USA

Gracie Jr., his dad, Lonnie Donegan and Lonnie's son, Peter. House Of , Las Vegas, January 2000. (Photo courtesy of Charlie Gracie Jr.)

12. TELL 'EM LONNIE DONEGAN'S BIN HERE AND GONE

In June 2000 Lonnie Donegan was awarded the MBE in the Queen's Birthday Honours List which gave Michael Caine a knighthood, Lulu an OBE, Michael Parkinson a CBE and Carol Vorderman two consonants and a vowel - an MBE as well.

In 2001 Lonnie celebrated his fiftieth year in the business. He had ideas for a 3CD set of unissued material with Reader's Digest but it never went beyond the planning stage. "I have stacks of unissued material," he told 'Record Collector', "Over the years it keeps piling up. All artists are the same. If you don't think the public should hear something that isn't up to scratch, then you don't put it out. I've got hundreds of tracks - some of them good, some of them not so good."

Lonnie had further cardiac surgery in 2002 and also had back problems but that did not deter him. The dates were announced for the fiftieth anniversary tour, starting in September. His opening act was his son, Peter, with a mixture of Spanish dancing and Elvis impressions. Lonnie's voice was as powerful as ever, and whilst on tour he filmed a few words for the awards to Elton John and Bernie Taupin at the Music Industry Trust. He agreed to be a castaway on 'Desert Island Discs' and he was also planning a DVD of his stage show for the organisers of the annual Americana Festival (another of Lonnie's triumphs), neither of which were to happen. Looking further ahead, he was negotiating to make an album with Shakin' Stevens' producer, Stuart Colman, in Nashville in 2003.

Eric Clapton invited him to perform on the George Harrison tribute at the Royal Albert Hall on November 29. Lonnie agreed, and Clapton tactfully said, "As you started it all, Lonnie, will you open the show?" "Okay," said Lonnie, "but which poor sod is going to follow me?" "Alright," said Clapton, "you can close the first half."

Carl Jones saw him perform at Shrewsbury the week he died and, as always, he was full of energy. They went to an Indian restaurant and he was full of plans. Carl said, "He said, 'What was that old joke I used to tell in the 60s? I'd like to put it back in the act. Something to do with institutions.' 'I remember it,' I said, 'What the country needs today is institution, restitution and pros - perity for all.' That's the last time I had a good laugh with Lonnie."

Finbar Furey: "You would never think he was going to die as he was always full of life. People say he had a lot of energy on stage, but he used a lot of energy even in just talking to you."

Chris Hunt: "Lonnie always had cases full of pills, and they would always work at the wrong time. When he would take his downers at night, he would suddenly come awake again. He would want to talk to someone at four in the morning. When we stayed in hotels, he would be the one with the roadbooks outside waiting to go. I have seen him change rooms two or three times a night, he was very fussy about hotels."

Lonnie couldn't do too much - it was one day on, one day off - but in the end he did do too much. He needed a day off to let his body recover, but he found it hard to rest. .Nick Payn: "Lonnie was not a good sleeper. He would be up late at night, he couldn't go back to his room, have a cup of cocoa and go to bed. He'd had all those operations and I said, 'You're like the Six Million Dollar Man, there is not much left that can go wrong with you now.' He seemed indestructible. He never said, 'I don't feel very good, we shall do the barest minimum.' On every show he gave everything he had. He was an absolute professional."

As Lonnie said, "People don't want to see me taking it easy, that's not what Lonnie Donegan does."

Sticky Wicket: "Whatever he felt before the gig, the performance was always fantastic. I can never remember a second rate performance. His old-fashioned timing when he spoke to the audience was in that lovely music hall kind of way. He would work an audience. He would tell some of the same jokes every night but because he had such fantastic comedy timing, it always seemed funny."

In common with rock tours, the 2002 tour was given a name, being, rather prophetically, 'This Could Be The Last Time'. Anthony Donegan played percussion for his father on the first show and another son, Peter, was the opening act for the whole tour. He played rock'n'roll and some Spanish numbers, and then added some piano for his father. "That was really good," says Chris Hunt, "We had never done 'I'll Never Fall In Love Again' before and it was nice to have the piano for that. Anthony is a drummer and he's as good as anybody."

Paul Henry: "We were like a family and we met on tour. We were all good friends, and it was like a party on the road. After five days on the road, things really started to happen on stage. This last show was really exciting in that respect, but they were all very good.

Sticky Wicket: "He never gave an impaired performance even on his last gig. He played one of the tour dates on minidisc and he said, 'That gig last night was bloody good. No, I don't mean bloody good, I mean bloody, bloody good.'"

Lonnie had been troubled with a bad back, but the band turned up for its soundcheck at the Royal Concert Hall in Nottingham on 30 October. Chris Hunt: "We arrived for the soundcheck at six o'clock and Lon wasn't there: sometimes he didn't make the soundcheck, so it wasn't too much of a surprise. He was still at the hotel and he had a bad back and the doctor had been called out. He gave him a muscle relaxing injection. It wasn't clear whether we were going to do the show until the last minute. About 8 o'clock, he said, 'Let's do it', and he did longer than he normally would, about an hour and a half, so he didn't make it easy for himself."

And even then he stayed for autographs. Chris Hunt: "He always stayed for autographs. He would have a shower after a gig and people would wonder where he was, but he always came out. At the last Nottingham gig, the last time I saw him, he was standing at the door signing autographs."

It had taken it out of him - he thought he would cancel the next two gigs, which were in York and Leeds. Lonnie was staying with the promoter, Mel Roberts, at Peterborough. He collapsed and died in his sleep in hospital on 3 November 2002 with his wife, Sharon, and his son, Peter, by his side.

Ron Bowden "The six of us in the Chris Barber band of 1954 - Chris, Lonnie, Monty, Pat and Jim and me on drums - had a special affinity and he rang me just a few days before he died. I found out that that he had rung Monty as well, so maybe he had some sort of premonition. He was the youngest of us and he was the first to go."

Death is a recurring theme in Lonnie's work and, indeed, his life. From the 1950s he has been singing 'New Burying Ground', 'Bury My Body', 'Gloryland' and many gospel songs. John Lennon sang, "Imagine there's no heaven", but Lonnie assumed that there was. Because of his damaged heart condition, he had felt that his time was likely to be cut short. As it happened, Lonnie made it to his three score and ten - 71 years actually - and he probably would have settled for that. His death had come at the time of a Lonnie Donegan renaissance and so he left on a high.

The tributes were generous:

"The importance of Donegan and that early hit, 'Rock Island Line', cannot be underestimated. The skiffle craze it unleashed had far-reaching effects, not just on pop music, but on the development of the whole rock genre. Rock'n'roll hits by Elvis, Little Richard and Bill Haley had an equally profound impact. The difference was that Donegan, by his example in reviving the lost art of skiffle, had shown that music need not be a passive entertainment. You didn't have to be a professional musician to play. Anyone could have a go." (Chris Welch in 'The Independent')

Robin Denselow in 'The Guardian' said, "Lonnie Donegan was the first British pop superstar, and the founding father of British pop music." He did add that "Lonnie Donegan may have been the godfather of British pop, but, at heart, he was an updated music hall performer."

Even 'The Los Angeles Times' acknowledged the debt of numerous British rock musicians and described skiffle as "a chipper, post-war precursor to rock'n'roll combining country, blues, gospel, jazz and folk music."

Mike Brocken, a lecturer in popular culture, was disappointed by the obituaries he read. He said on BBC Radio Merseyside: "I thought that most of the obituaries were putrid with no sense of his historical, cultural or social significance. They tended to concentrate on 'Chewing Gum' or 'Dustman', which admittedly are very interesting in their own right, but they didn't get to grips with Lonnie Donegan and his legacy. His legacy is absolutely vital. I would say that he is the most important popular musician of the twentieth century. Even though he never made a classic album or a series of classic records, nothing that happened subsequently could have happened in the same way without him. He is the lynch pin and without him there would not be British pop as we know it. I am talking mostly about his impact on British society and culture, but nevertheless you also find that Phil Spector got into music because of Lonnie Donegan and that Roger McGuinn was completely aware of what Donegan was trying to do with blues, country and hillbilly music."
I believe this is correct. Lonnie was a great entertainer but he is more important as an innovotator. Even the standard beat group instrumentation of lead guitar, rhythm guitar, bass and drums started in the UK with Lonnie Donegan. His contemporaries such as Tommy Steele and Tony Crombie featured saxophone. Don Lang fronted his Frantic Five on trombone. Lonnie, quite by accident, it must be said, had the rock'n'roll line-up first. It had been seen in America earlier - notably when W.S. Holland joined Carl Perkins and his brothers in 1953 and then when another drummer, D.J. Fontana joined Elvis Presley in 1955 - but in England, no.
About 100 people attended Lonnie Donegan's funeral at Peterborough Crematorium on Thursday 14 November 2002. His recording of 'Gloryland' with Leinemann was played. The impressionist Peter Goodwright wrote a touching poem for the service sheet, 'Brother Rat' on behalf of the Water Rats. The final verse was,

"Thank you, Lonnie, for your brightness and your fun,
Thank you for the skiffle sound which captured everyone,
Your Brothers here salute you with your fans both near and far,
The fountain-head of British pop - our first real superstar."

There was a one-hour Christmas Day tribute to Donegan on BBC Radio 2, 'All Roads Lead To Lonnie', presented by Bill Wyman. Adam Faith said, "Lonnie was the best singer we have ever produced in this country but the general public is not too aware of that because they are hooked into 'My Old Man's A Dustman'."
Brian May: "Lonnie Donegan is the beginning of white blues, which is a very big thing. I don't think rock music would be anything like it is today without Lonnie."
'Puttin' On The Style', a TV-advertised collection of his hits, has restored Lonnie to the album charts. It came in at No 45 and went down to No 75 the following week, but still it was something. There has been talk of dates using Lonnie's group with his sons, Peter and Anthony. It makes sense as Lonnie's group was so good and Anthony, a taxi driver, has been performing with his own skiffle group on a summer season at Margate. It begs the question of a whole tour celebrating Lonnie - I would add Billy Bragg (another Guthrie

acolyte with a big nose!), Ray Ennis (former skiffler now leading the Swinging Blue Jeans and looking more like Lonnie by the day) and, if the expenses permitted, Doug Kershaw from America. This would be an impressive line-up but I hope something is pulled together. Certainly a show with a straight Lonnie Donegan impersonator will not work. It was Lonnie Donegan that people came to see and he is, quite simply, irreplaceable. Let's close the book the way that Lonnie closed his interviews: God bless.

G · O · W · R

Lonnie Donegan, MBE
(1931-2002)

"The MONARCH of SKIFFLE"

LONNIE DONEGAN

all his FABULOUS TOP HITS on nixa

with his Skiffle Group

Putting On The Style/Gamblin' Man	N 15093
Cumberland Gap/Love Is Strange	N 15093
I'm Alabammy Bound/Don't You Rock Me Daddy-O	N 15087
Dead Or Alive/Bring A Little Water, Sylvie	N 15080
Lost John/Stewball	N 15071
	N 15036

Backstairs Session
Lonnie Donegan Skiffle Group
Lonnie Donegan Showcase

Two NEW releases by—

LONNIE DONEGAN

on 10" LP

"LONNIE"
NPT 19027

on 45 & 78 rpm

'Sally Don't You Grieve'
coupled with
"Betty, Betty, Betty"
N. 15148

exclusively on nixa

DISTRIBUTED BY PYE GROUP RECORDS (SALES) LTD., 66 HAYMARKET, LONDON, S.W.1

NOW COMING INTO THE LEAD!

PYE

LONNIE DONEGAN'S "Fort Worth Jail"

7N 15198 (45 & 78)

P Records (Sales) Ltd., 10a Chandos St., W...

LONNIE DONEGAN
" Lorelei "
"In All My Wildest Dreams"
(PYE 7N. 15275)

PARDON ME if I sound a little out of breath! Trouble is I've been trying to get this review of Lonnie's latest in print before the perishin' thing is actually in the R&SM Top Twenty. I imagine it will be a close finish. Anyway, it should be laurels for "Lorelei"!

Lonnie recorded this while in America in April this year and, according to the label, had a hand in the writing of it with the great American tunesmith team of Lieber and Stoller.

Strong banjo assists the opening, when Lonnie tells how he's been kissed by girls in Burma, Africa and London —but none of them got within a mile of the technique of "Lorelei". Of course, he later admits that she was a mermaid . . half-woman, half-fish! Which must give her some sort of advantage.

TTT

Excellent Donegan, this, with his high yodel on the word "Lorelei" guaranteed to smash pint tankards at ten paces. Mike Stoller arranged and conducted this session.

Lonnie is in restrained, quiet mood on "In All My Wildest Dreams", the backing here being by Stan Applebaum. It is a good, tuneful ballad and Lonnie takes it dead straight. No tricks; no gymnastics.

Well, that's the review! Did I manage to beat Mr. Donegan for once?

LONNIE DONEGAN

'THE VIRGIN MARY'

7N 15315

LONNIE DONEGAN
MORE TOPS WITH LONNIE

Battle Of New Orleans; Lorelei; Lively; Sal'; Got A Sugar Lip; I Wanna Go Home; Leave My Woman Alone; My Old Man's A Dustman; Fort Worth Jail; Have A Drink On Me; Beneath The Willow; Little Liza Jane; Puttin' On The Style; Camptown Races; Knees Up Mother Brown; On Top Of Old Smokey; Down In The Valley; So Long. (PYE NPL 18063.)

5

IT is a pretty safe assumption to say that just about everything is tops with Lonnie when it comes to discs. He's had them big and not-so-big—but never, I think, has the lad lost out with one of his discs.

Yes, pretty well everything Lonnie serves up on his platters is headed for success and this is just another example of an LP which will rocket off smartly hitwards.

A bundle of Lonnie's big singles are included for good measure here, so order your copy now and don't be disappointed.

A winner, fans.

(NRM Picture)

LONNIE DONEGAN *Michael, Row The Boat; Lumbered* (Pye 7N.15371)

4

THIS, Lonnie's latest rush job, has two 'A' sides, doubly a Top Twenty Tip. With the Highwaymen's record of "Michael" number one in America, Pye rushed up to the Winter Gardens Pavilion in Blackpool for Lonnie and his group to make this recording of it. With his "Chewing Gum" racing up the U.S. Charts at the moment, odds are his "Michael" will do the same here. Obviously Donegan material, a near-Spiritual (complete with "Hallelujah's") it is a sure hit.

The Anthony Newley number "Lumbered" (from his "Stop The World — I Want To Get Off") could be another "Dustman". A bright comedy number with a hatful of Donegan-style gags. Another sure winner.

THE COMANCHEROS

LONNIE DONEGAN   PYE 7N 1541

LONNIE SPRINGS A SURPRISE

SURPRISE, surprise ! Lonnie Donegan singing a coupl[e]
numbers that have been made famous by Peggy Lee
Judy Garland. Still, if Kenny Ball can play Rodgers
Hammerstein, why shouldn't Lonnie have a go, too ? An[d]
complete the hat-trick perhaps
we shall hear Chubby Checker
singing "Portrait Of My
Love"!

Lonnie sings extremely well,
capturing effectively the mood of
both these great songs. "The
Party's Over" and "Over The
Rainbow."

Tony Hatch has supplied excellent
backings, making smooth and subtle
use of the chorus.

However I fear that Lonnie can't
thrill me in the way that Miss Lee
and Miss Garland have done, do now
and always will. Label is Pye.

LOSING BY A HAIR

PYE   7N15514

Lonnie Donegan

LONNIE DONEGAN

*Lemon Tree; I've Gotta Gal So
Fine* (Pye 15564)

THIS folk tune has been recorded
by a lot of people including
Peter, Paul and Mary, but probably
Lonnie's version has the most
chance of success. It's a folksy tune
and there's some fair old vocalising
from Lonnie and the femme chorus.
It's catchy and we think it could
make the bottom half of the charts.
Rather a calypso flavour.

Flip is a spiritual type number
with a big beat flavour, and some
very loud vocal work from all concerned. It's not too bad but not
terribly commercial.

FOUR

LONNIE DONEGAN — R[e]
quests for "Lemon Tree[e"]
after a TV spot.

LONNIE DONEGAN *Pick A Bale
Of Cotton; Steal Away* (Pye 7N
15455)

WE knew what this was going to be
like before we heard it. The title
told us. And nobody could have sung
this Leadbelly number better than Lonnie
—except maybe the original.

Slow start for the extremely skiffle
number which generates more and more
excitement as it progresses.

Very repetitive and catchy, it will
appeal to just about every type of
record buyer. The group behind Mr. D.,
The Kestrels, gives him the full authentic
treatment making this as good as
Lonnie's past efforts in this his own
realm. And we believe that he's done
this one before.

"Steal Away" on the flip is much
slower and is a kind of Gospel song
arranged by Lonnie. Interesting backing
on this one, with lots of late night
listening appeal.

FOUR

TOP 20 TIP

500 MILES AWAY FROM HOME

WORDS AND MUSIC BY BOBBY BARE AND CHARLIE WILLIAMS

RECORDED BY
LONNIE DONEGAN
ON PYE RECORDS

APPENDIX 1

LONNIE DONEGAN - UK DISCOGRAPHY

A Lonnie Donegan discography covering reissues and appearances on "various artists" compilations would be a book in its own right. With a few significant exceptions, this discography concerns itself with the first appearance of each of Lonnie's recorded performances. Additionally, some performances that were first issued outside the UK are included.

The titles of many of the traditional tunes vary from release to release - for example, "It takes a worried man to sing a worried song" has been shown as "Worried Man Blues", "It Takes A Worried Man" and just "Worried Man". In all instances, I have chosen one title for consistency throughout this listing, and indeed, throughout the book.

Singles
(with Chris Barber's Jazz Band) White Christmas / On A Christmas Day (export issue - Columbia SCMC 10, 45rpm, 1954)
(with Chris Barber's Jazz Band) Precious Lord Lead Me On / Tiger Rag (Tempo A 116, 45/78rpm, 1955)
Rock Island Line / John Henry (Decca FJ 10647, 45/78rpm, 1955, No 8)
Rock Island Line / John Henry (US London 1650, 45/78rpm, 1956, US No 8)
Midnight Special / When The Sun Goes Down (Pye Jazz NJS 2006, 45/78rpm, 1956)
Diggin' My Potatoes / Bury My Body (Decca FJ 10695, 45/78rpm, 1956)
Lost John / Stewball (Pye N 15036, 78rpm, 1956, A No 2, B No 27)
The Passing Stranger / (B-side by Tommy Reilly) The Intimate Stranger (Oriole CB 1329, 78rpm, 1956)
Bring A Little Water, Sylvie / Dead Or Alive (Pye N 15071, 78rpm, 1956, A&B, No 7) *DW*
On A Christmas Day / Take My Hand Precious Lord (Columbia DB 3850, 45/78rpm, 1956)
Don't You Rock Me Daddy-O / Alabammy Bound (Pye N 15080, 78rpm, 1957, A&B, No *DW* 4)
Cumberland Gap / Love Is Strange (Pye N 15087, 78rpm, 1957, No 1 for 5 weeks) *DW*
Puttin' On The Style / Gamblin' Man (Pye N 15093, 78rpm, 1957, A&B, No 1 for 2 *Jc* weeks)
My Dixie Darlin' / I'm Just A Rollin' Stone (Pye N 15108, 78rpm, 1957, No 10) *Jc*
Jack O'Diamonds / Ham'n'Eggs (Pye 7N 15116, 45/78rpm, 1958, No 14) *Jc (Hard Travelling rejected)*
Grand Coulee Dam / Nobody Loves Like An Irishman (Pye 7N 15129, 45/78rpm, 1958, No 6)
Sally Don't You Grieve / Betty Betty Betty (Pye 7N 15148, 45/78rpm, 1958, No 11) *Jc*
Lonesome Traveller / Times Are Getting Hard (Pye 7N 15158, 45/78rpm, 1958, No 28) *Jc*
Lonnie's Skiffle Party (Parts 1 & 2) (Pye 7N 15165, 45/78rpm, 1958, No 23) *LB*
(comprising Little Liza Jane / Puttin' On The Style / Camptown Races / So Long / On Top Of Old Smokey / Down In The Valley / Knees Up Mother Brown)
Tom Dooley / Rock O'My Soul (Pye 7N 15172, 45/78rpm, 1958, No 3)
Does Your Chewing Gum Lose Its Flavour (On The Bedpost Overnight) / Aunt Rhody Pye 7N 15181, 45/78rpm, 1959, No 3)

Does Your Chewing Gum Lose Its Flavour (On The Bedpost Overnight) / Aunt Rhody (US Dot 45-137, 45/78rpm, 1959, No 5 in 1961)

Fort Worth Jail / Whoa Buck (Pye 7N 15198, 45/78rpm, 1959, No 14) *(Shorty George - unknown)*

The Battle Of New Orleans / Darling Corey (Pye 7N 15206, 45/78rpm, 1959, No 2)

Kevin Barry / My Lagan Love (Ireland only, Pye 7N 15219, 45/78rpm, 1959)

Sal's Got A Sugar Lip / Chesapeake Bay (Pye 7N 15223, 1959, 45/78rpm, No 13)

San Miguel / Talking Guitar Blues (Pye 7N15237, 1959, 45/78rpm, No 19)

My Old Man's A Dustman / The Golden Vanity (Pye 7N 15256, 45/78rpm, 1960, No 1 for 4 weeks)

I Wanna Go Home / Jimmy Brown The Newsboy (Pye 7N 15267, 45/78rpm, 1960, No 5)

Lorelei / In All My Wildest Dreams (Pye 7N 15275, 45/78rpm, 1960, No 10)

Lively / Black Cat (Pye 7N 15312, 45rpm, 1960, No 13)

Virgin Mary / Beyond The Sunset (Pye 7N 15315, 45rpm, 1960, No 27)

(Bury Me) Beneath The Willow / Leave My Woman Alone (Pye 7N15330, 45rpm, 1961)

Have A Drink On Me / Seven Golden Daffodils (Pye 7N 15354, 45rpm, 1961, No 8)

Michael Row The Boat / Lumbered (Pye 7N 15371, 45rpm, 1961, No 6)

The Comancheros / Rambling Around (Pye 7N 15410, 45rpm, 1962, No 14)

The Party's Over / Over The Rainbow (Pye 7N 15424, 45rpm, 1962, No 9)

I'll Never Fall In Love Again / Keep On The Sunny Side (Pye 7N 15446, 45rpm, 1962)

Pick A Bale Of Cotton / Steal Away (Pye 7N 15455, 45rpm, 1962, No 11)

(with Max Miller) The Market Song / Tit Bits (Pye 7N 15493, 45rpm, 1962)

Losing By A Hair / Trumpet Sounds (Pye 7N 15514, 45rpm, 1963)

It Was A Very Good Year / Rise Up (Pye 7N 15530, 45rpm, 1963)

Lemon Tree / I've Got A Gal So Fine (Pye 7N 15564, 45rpm, 1963)

This Train / 500 Miles Away From Home (Pye 7N 15579, 45rpm, 1963)

It's A Long Road To Travel / Beans In My Ears (Pye 7N 15669, 45rpm, 1964)

Fisherman's Luck / There's A Big Wheel (Pye 7N 15679, 45rpm, 1964)

Get Out Of My Life / Won't You Tell Me (Pye 7N 15803, 45rpm, 1965))

Louisiana Man / Bound For Zion (Pye 7N 15893, 45rpm, 1965)

World Cup Willie / Where In This World Are We Going (Pye 7N 15993, 45rpm, 1966)

I Wanna Go Home / Black Cat (reissue - Pye 7N 17109, 45rpm, 1966)

Auntie Maggie's Remedy / My Sweet Marie (Pye 7N 17232, 45rpm, 1966)

Toys / Relax Your Mind (Columbia DB 8371, 45rpm, 1968)

My Lovely Juanita / Who Knows Where The Time Goes (Decca F 12984, 45rpm, 1969)

Burning Bridges / Til I Can't Take It Anymore (Pye 7N 45009, 45rpm, 1970)

Don't Blame The Child / Come To Australia (RCA RCA 2128, 45rpm, 1971)

Speak To The Sky / Get Out Of My Life (Pye 7N 45184, 45rpm, 1972)

Boll Weevil Blues / (Steve Jones vocal) Come To Australia (Australia, CBS BA 221452, 1972)

(with Kenny Ball's Jazzmen) Who's Gonna Play This Old Piano / South (Pye 7N 45252, 1973)

Lost John Blues / Jump Down Turn Around (Germany, Ariola 12604 AT, 1973)

The Battle Of New Orleans / Puttin' On The Style (reissue - Pye 7N 45548, 45rpm, 1975)

(with Chris Barber's Jazz Band) Lost John / Jenny's Ball (Black Lion BSP 45105, 45rpm, 1976)

I've Lost My Little Willie / Censored (Decca FR 13669, 45rpm, 1976)

Does Your Chewing Gum Lose Its Flavour (On The Bedpost Overnight) / My Old Man's
A Dustman / The Battle Of New Orleans / Tom Dooley (Pye BD 108, 12 inch single,
45rpm, 1977)
Rock Island Line / Ham'n'Eggs (Chrysalis CHS 2205, 45rpm, 1978)
Puttin' On The Style / Drop Down Baby (Chrysalis CHS 2211, 45rpm, 1978)
My Old Man's A Dustman / I Wanna Go Home (reissue - Pye 7N46096, 45rpm, 1978)
Tom Dooley / I Wanna Go Home (reissue - Pye 7N461097, 45rpm, 1978)
My Old Man's A Dustman / Does Your Chewing Gum Lose Its Flavour (On The Bedpost
Overnight) (Pye Flashback FBS 10, 45rpm, 1979)
Puttin' On The Style / Gamblin' Man (Old Gold OG 9131, 45rpm, 1981)
(with the Shakin' Pyramids) Cumberland Gap / Wabash Cannonball / Don't You Rock Me
Daddy-O / (Shakin' Pyramids) Only My Pillow / (Shakin' Pyramids) Grab It And Growl
(Virgin / Cuba Libre VS 460, 45rpm, 1981)
Rock Island Line / John Henry (reissue - Decca F 19674, 45rpm, 1982)
(with Monty Sunshine as Donegan's Dancing Sunshine Band) Donegan's Dancing
Sunshine Band (yes, that's the song title!) / Leaving Blues (Rosie RR 015, 45rpm, 1987)
(with Jive Bunny) The Crazy Party Mixes (Music Factory Dance MFD 010, 45rpm, 1990,
No 13) (Includes snatches of 'Chewing Gum' and 'Dustman')
(with Van Morrison and Chris Barber) I Wanna Go Home / New Burying Ground /
Midnight Special (Virgin / Exile 7243 8 96497 2 7, CD, 2000, No 93)

Extended Plays
THE LONNIE DONEGAN SKIFFLE GROUP (Decca DFE 6345, 1956)
Rock Island Line / John Henry / Diggin' My Potatoes / Bury My Body
BACKSTAIRS SESSION (Polygon JTE 107, 1955) (Reissued on Pye NJE 1014, 1956)
Midnight Special / When The Sun Goes Down / New Burying Ground / Worried Man
Blues
SKIFFLE SESSION (Pye NJE 1017, 1956, Singles chart No 20)
Railroad Bill /Stackalee / The Ballad Of Jesse James / Ol' Riley
LONNIE DONEGAN HIT PARADE, VOLUME 1 (Pye NEP 24031, 1957)
Lost John / Stewball / Bring A Little Water, Sylvie / Dead Or Alive
LONNIE DONEGAN HIT PARADE, VOLUME 2 (Pye NEP 24040, 1957)
Don't You Rock Me Daddy-O / Alabammy Bound / Cumberland Gap / Love Is Strange
LONNIE DONEGAN HIT PARADE, VOLUME 3 (Pye NEP 24067, 1958)
Puttin' On The Style / Gamblin' Man / My Dixie Darlin' / I'm Just A Rollin' Stone
DONEGAN ON STAGE (Pye NEP 24075, 1958)
Muleskinner Blues / Old Hannah / On A Monday / Glory
LONNIE DONEGAN HIT PARADE, VOLUME 4 (Pye NEP 24081, 1958)
Jack O' Diamonds / Ham And Eggs / Grand Coulee Dam / Nobody Loves Like An
Irishman
LONNIE DONEGAN HIT PARADE, VOLUME 5 (Pye NEP 24104, 1959)
Tom Dooley / Rock O' My Soul / Sally Don't You Grieve / Betty Betty Betty
RELAX WITH LONNIE (Pye NEP 24107, 1959)
Bewildered / Kevin Barry / It Is No Secret / My Lagan Love
(I have used 'My Lagan Love' throughout as the song relates to the River Lagan., although
Lonnie calls it 'My Laggan Love'.)

LONNIE DONEGAN HIT PARADE, VOLUME 6 (Pye NEP 24114, 1959)
The Battle Of New Orleans / Fort Worth Jail / Does Your Chewing Gum Lose Its Flavour
(On The Bedpost Overnight) / Darling Corey
YANKEE DOODLE DONEGAN (Pye NEP 24127, 1960, No 8)
Corrine Corrina / Junko Partner / Nobody Understands Me / Sorry But I'm Gonna Have
To Pass
LONNIE DONEGAN HIT PARADE, VOLUME 7 (Pye NEP 24134, 1961)
My Old Man's A Dustman / Golden Vanity / Sal's Got A Sugar Lip / Talking Guitar Blues
LONNIE DONEGAN HIT PARADE, VOLUME 8 (Pye NEP 24149, 1961)
Michael Row The Boat / I Wanna Go Home / Lumbered / Have A Drink On Me

Albums
SHOWCASE (Pye NPT 19012, 10 inch LP, 1956, Singles chart No 26)
Wabash Cannonball / How Long How Long Blues / Nobody's Child / I Shall Not Be
Moved / I'm Alabammy Bound / I'm A Ramblin' Man / Wreck Of The Old '97 / Frankie
And Johnny
LONNIE (mono - Pye NPT 19027, stereo - Pye NSPT 84000, 10 inch LP, 1958)
Lonesome Traveller / The Sunshine Of His Love / Ain't No More Cane On The Brazos /
Ain't You Glad You Got Religion / Times Are Getting Hard / Lazy John / Light From The
Lighthouse / I've Got Rocks In My Bed / Long Summer Day
TOPS WITH LONNIE (Pye NPL 18034, 12-inch LP, 1959)
Don't You Rock Me Daddy-O / Putting On The Style / Gamblin' Man / My Dixie Darlin' /
Bring A Little Water Sylvie / Cumberland Gap / Grand Coulee Dam / Sally Don't You
Grieve / Nobody Loves Like An Irishman / Lost John / Does Your Chewing Gum Lose Its
Flavour / Tom Dooley
LONNIE RIDES AGAIN (Pye NPL 18043, 12-inch LP, 1959)
Fancy Talking Tinker / Miss Otis Regrets / Gloryland / Jimmie Brown The Newsboy / Mr.
Froggy / Take This Hammer / The Gold Rush Is Over / You Pass Me By / Talking Guitar
Blues / John Hardy / The House of the Rising Sun / San Miguel
MORE TOPS WITH LONNIE (Pye NPL18063 12-inch LP, 1960)
Battle of New Orleans / Lorelei / Lively / Sal's Got A Sugar Lip / I Wanna Go Home /
Leave My Woman Alone / My Old Man's A Dustman / Fort Worth Jail / Have A Drink On
Me / Bury Me Beneath the Willow
SING HALLELUJAH (Pye NPL 18073, 12-inch LP, 1962)
Sing Hallelujah / We Shall Walk Through The Valley / No Hiding Place / Good News!
Chariots a' Comin' / Steal Away / Noah Found Grace In The Eyes Of The Lord / Joshua
Fit de Battle of Jericho / His Eye Is On The Sparrow / Born In Bethlehem / This Train /
New Burying Ground / Nobody Knows The Trouble I've Seen
THE GOLDEN AGE OF DONEGAN (Pye Golden Guinea GGL 0135, 12-inch LP, 1962,
No 3)
Previously released material
THE GOLDEN AGE OF DONEGAN, VOLUME 2 (Pye Golden Guinea GGL 0170, 12-
inch LP, 1963, No 15)
Previously released material
THE LONNIE DONEGAN FOLK ALBUM (Pye NPL 18126, 12-inch LP, 1965)
I'm Gonna Be A Bachelor / Interstate 40 / After Taxes / Where In The World / Diamonds

Of Dew / Bound For Zion / She Was A T-Bone Talking Woman / Wedding Bells /
Reverend Mr. Black / The Doctor's Daughter / Blistered / Farewell

LONNIEPOPS - LONNIE DONEGAN TODAY (Decca SKL 5068, 12-inch LP, 1970)
Little Green Apples / Hey Hey / First Of May / Both Sides Now / If You Go Away / Love
Song To A Princess / Who Knows Where The Time Goes / What The World Needs Now Is
Love / My Lovely Juanita / The Windmills Of Your Mind / Long-Haired Lover From
Liverpool / And You Need Me

GOLDEN HOUR OF GOLDEN HITS (Golden Hour GH 514, 12-inch LP, 1971)
Previously released material plus the 1956 Pye remake of 'Rock Island Line'.

GOLDEN HOUR OF GOLDEN HITS, VOLUME 2 (Golden Hour GH 565, 12-inch LP,
1973)
Previously released material

LONNIE DONEGAN MEETS LEINEMANN (German release - Philips 6305 227, 12-
inch LP, 1974)
(with Leineman) Casey's Last Ride / Bottle Of Wine / My Dixie Darlin' / Frankie And
Johnnie / Tops At Loving You / Gloryland / Leineman's Potatoes / Me And Bobbie McGee
/ Does Your Chewing Gum Lose Its Flavour (On The Bedpost Overnight) / Becky Deen /
Jack O' Diamonds

THE GREAT REUNION CONCERT (Dutch release - Timeless CD TTD 553, 2x12-inch
LP, 1975)
(with Chris Barber's Jazz Band) Jenny's Ball
(with Skiffle Group) On A Monday / Bury My Body / Lost John

COUNTRY ROADS (German release - Philips 6305 288, 12-inch LP, 1976)
(with Leinemann) Country Roads / Rock Island Line / Keep On The Sunny Side / Dixie
Lily / Louisiana Man / Dead Or Alive / Midnight Special / Muleskinner Blues / Roll In
My Sweet Baby's Arms / Lost John / Have A Drink On Me / Dublin O'Shea

LONNIE DONEGAN (Tyler LDNH 123, 12-inch LP, 1976)
Does Your Chewing Gum Lose Its Flavour (On The Bedpost Overnight) / Burning Bridges
/ Ballad Of Sammy's Bar / Hit Me Across The Head With A Spoon, Mama / Beyond The
Shadow / Come To Australia / The Battle Of New Orleans / Till I Can't Take It Anymore /
I Lost My Heart On The 5.42 / Relax Your Mind / Grand Coulee Dam / Looking For A
Man / Don't Blame The Child

LONNIE DONEGAN'S GREATEST HITS (Bravo 2530, cassette only)
My Old Man's A Dustman / I Lost My Heart On 5.42 / Grand Coulee Dam / I've Lost My
Little Willie / The Battle Of New Orleans / Censored / Does Your Chewing Gum Lose Its
Flavour (On The Bedpost Overnight) / Beyond The Shadows / Love Song For A Princess /
Till I Can't Take It Anymore / Don't Blame The Child / Burnin' Bridges / Ballad Of
Sammy's Bar / Come Out To Australia

PUTTIN' ON THE STYLE (Chrysalis CHR 1158, 12 inch LP, 1978, No 51)
Rock Island Line / Have A Drink On Me / Ham 'n Eggs / I Wanna Go Home / Diggin' My
Potatoes / Nobody's Child / Puttin' On The Style / Frankie And Johnny / Drop Down Baby
/ Lost John

SUNDOWN (Chrysalis CHR 1205, 12-inch LP, 1978)
All Out And Down / Home / Streamline Train / Sundown / Mama's Got The Know How /
Morning Light /Louisiana Sun / The Battle Of New Orleans / Cajun Stripper / Dreaming
My Dreams.

(One song is shown as 'Steamline Train' on the cover, but Lonnie sings 'Streamline Train', which is correct.)

JUBILEE CONCERT (Cube ICSD 2001, two 12-inch LPs, 1981) (The second album was released separately on Rio Digital RDLP 1201 with the promise of the first one - the jazz set - to come. It never happened.)

(Skiffle set) John Henry / Take This Hammer / Railroad Bill / Tom Dooley / New Burying Ground / Grand Coulee Dam / New York Town / Miss Otis Regrets / Does Your Chewing Gum Lose Its Flavour (On The Bedpost Overnight) / One Night Of Love / Rock Island Line / Gloryland / Corrine Corrina / Goodnight Irene

LA GRANDE STORIA DEL ROCK, VOLUME 38 (GSR 38, Italy, 1982)

As strange as it comes, 10 tracks from Pete Best's band and two from Lonnie (70s remakes of 'Dustman' and 'Chewing Gum'), and that isn't Pete Best on the cover photo.

HOOKED ON NUMBER ONES - 100 NON-STOP HITS (K-Tel ONE 1285, two 12-inch LPs, 1984, No 25)

Lonnie sings 'Sailing' (30 seconds), 'Michelle'(31 seconds), 'Puttin' On The Style' (33 seconds), 'Cumberland Gap' (40 seconds) and 'My Old Man's A Dustman' (34 seconds), all to a disco beat, and all in a day's work.

RARE AND UNISSUED GEMS (German release - Bear Family BFX 15170, 12-inch LP, 1985)

Cajun Joe / Louisiana Man / There's A Big Wheel / Fisherman's Luck / Lovey Told Me Goodbye / Bad News / Nothing To Gain / 500 Miles / Tiger Rag / Keep On The Sunny Side / Red Beret / Kevin Barry / The Comancheros / Just A-Wearyin' For You / Ding Ding / Leaving Blues

MAMA DON'T ALLOW (German release - Pimorrekk HB 7012, 12-inch LP, 1987)

Album by the Monty Sunshine Jazz Band, and Lonnie is featured on Mama Don't Allow (vocal) and When I Move To The Sky, Corrine Corrina, Ma, He's Making Eyes At Me (vocal and banjo).

BODY WORK (First Night CAST 15, 12-inch LP, 1988)

The musical story of Dominic's body, written by Richard Stilgoe and featuring Chas & Dave, Maria Friedman, Peter Howitt, Isla St. Clair, Jake Thackray and the Chichester Cathedral Choir. Lonnie is the Appendix and sings 'Life Passes Me By'.

THE ORIGINALS (See For Miles SEECD 331, CD, 1991)

'Showcase' and 'Lonnie' albums on one CD.

PUTTING ON THE STYLES (Sequel NXT CD 233, 3CD, 1992)

77 tracks split into 'The Skiffle King', 'Ding Dong Donegan' and 'Listen With Lonnie'. Includes two previously unissued tracks, 'Hard Travellin'' and 'I'll Never Smile Again'.

THE EP COLLECTION (See For Miles SEECD 346, CD, 1992)

Previously released material

THE EP COLLECTION, VOLUME 2 (See For Miles SEECD 382, CD, 1993)

Previously released material

MORE THAN PYE IN THE SKY (German release - Bear Family BCD 15700 -H1, 8CD boxed-set, 1993)

A superbly packaged celebration with 209 tracks. The previously unissued songs are 'Hard Time Blues', 'Harmonica Blues', 'You Don't Know Your Mind', 'Baby Don't You Know That's' Love', 'Shorty George', 'My Only Son Was Killed In Dublin', 'When I Was Young' and 'Banana Split For My Baby'.

CHRIS BARBER - 40 YEARS JUBILEE AT THE OPERNHAUS N?RNBERG (Dutch release, Timeless CDTTD 590, CD, 1993)
Lonnie performs 'Worried Man Blues' and 'Down By The Riverside' with the 1954 Chris Barber line-up.
CHRIS BARBER'S JAZZ AND BLUES BAND LIVE AT THE BP STUDIENHAUS (Timeless TTD 615, CD, 1997)
Lonnie performs 'Can't You Line 'Em', 'Midnight Special', 'New Burying Ground' and 'Worried Man Blues' with the 1954 Chris Barber line-up.
MULESKINNER BLUES (Capo CAPO 501, CD, 1999)
(with Van Morrison) Muleskinner Blues / I'm Alabammy Bound
(solo) Please Don't Call Me In The Morning / Rock Island Line / When I Get Off This Feeling / Fancy Talking Tinker / Stewball / Skiffle / The Welfare Line / All Together Now / I Don't Wanna Lose You / Poker Club / Spanish Nights / Always From The Heart
LONNIE DONEGAN MEETS LEINEMAN - THE COMPLETE SESSIONS, 1974/5 (Jasmine JASCD 352/3, 2CD, 1999)
Combines two albums with Leineman.
LIVE! 1957 (Zircon Zirc 1002, CD, 1999)
On A Monday / Old Hannah / Muleskinner Blues / Precious Memories / Brother Moses Smote The Water / Ella Speed / Glory / Black Girl / I'm Alabammy Bound / Cumberland Gap / Don't You Rock Me Daddy-O / Bring A Little Water Sylvie / Gamblin' Man / Puttin' On The Style
THE SKIFFLE SESSIONS - LIVE IN BELFAST (CD Virgin / Exile CDVEDJ 945, 12-inch LP Virgin / Exile LPVE 945, 2000, No 14)
(with Van Morrison and Chris Barber) Worried Man Blues / Lost John / Goin' Home / Good Morning Blues / Outskirts Of Town / Don't You Rock Me Daddy-O / I'm Alabammy Bound / Midnight Special / Dead Or Alive / Frankie And Johnnie / Goodnight Irene / Railroad Bill / Muleskinner Blues / Jesse James / I Wanna Go Home
Also a bootleg version with additional tracks from Belfast concert.
SHOWCASE PLUS…(Sequel NEMCD 342, CD, 2000)
"Showcase" LP, "Backstairs Session" EP, "Skiffle Session" EP, singles tracks, the previously unreleased Harmonica Blues and alternate takes of Rock Island Line and I've Got Rocks In My Bed
LONNIE PLUS……(Sequel NEMCD 342, CD, 2000)
'Lonnie' LP, 'Relax With Lonnie' EP, singles tracks and six unreleased tracks - Hard Travellin' (3 takes), Shorty George, Baby Don't You Know That's Love and My Only Son Was Killed In Dublin
LONNIE RIDES AGAIN PLUS……(Sequel NEMCD 342, CD, 2000)
'Lonnie Rides Again' LP, 'Yankee Doodle Donegan' EP, singles tracks and five unreleased tracks - John Hardy, Ace In The Hole (with the Clyde Valley Stompers), Red Berets, Keep On The Sunny Side and Tiger Rag
SING HALLELUJAH PLUS……(Sequel NEMCD 342, CD, 2000)
'Sing Hallelujah' LP, assorted other tracks but despite the claim of "previously unreleased material", there is none here.
THE LONNIE DONEGAN FOLK ALBUM PLUS……(Sequel NEMCD 342, CD, 2000)
'The Lonnie Donegan Folk Album' LP, singles tracks plus three unreleased tracks - When I Was Young, Ding Ding and Leaving Blues

THE ROOTS OF LONNIE DONEGAN (Catfish KADCD 219, CD, 2002)
25 original (or very early) versions of songs that Lonnie Donegan recorded, but some major hits have been excluded. Leadbelly, the Weavers and Lonnie Johnson are strongly featured, but there's not much Woody Guthrie. The spine says "The Roots Of Lonney Donegan" (sic) and as the booklet writer, Keith Briggs, thinks 'I Wanna Go Home' was a cover of 'Sloop John B', we should be glad that the Beach Boys haven't been included. Rummaging around for the originals of Lonnie's songs is a very rewarding experience and although this is the place to start, it is really a lost opportunity. If you want to hear Woody Guthrie's versions of 'Cumberland Gap', 'Lost John' and 20 others, then the budget priced 'House Of The Rising Sun' (Music Digital CD 6255) is warmly recommended.

ROCK ISLAND LINE - THE SINGLES ANTHOLOGY (Sequel CMETD580, 3CD, 2002)
86 tracks, all previously released, in a slipcase

KING OF SKIFFLE (Castle Pulse PLS CD 539, CD, 2002)
19 tracks, mostly hits, selling at £3.99.

PUTTIN' ON THE STYLE - A TRIBUTE TO A LEGEND (Sanctuary TVSAN002, CD, 2003)
This full priced, 25 track selection of hits was TV advertised with a John Peel voiceover. It restored Lonnie to the charts, so didn't purchasers realise 'King Of Skiffle' was also in the shops?

WHEELS WITHIN WHEELS (Capo CAPO 703 82876 503872, CD, 2003)
Rory Gallagher compilation of unissued material includes Lonnie and Rory with 'Goin' To My Hometown', recorded in the early 1980s.

Skiffle Compilations
THE FANTASTIC SKIFFLE FESTIVAL (Germany, Decca 6.28422, 2LP, 1977)
32 tracks from the Decca catalogue. No Donegan but eight from Ken Colyer's Skiffle Group and seven from Bob Cort's. Includes Morris and Mitch's 'What Is A Skiffler?'.

AS GOOD AS IT GETS - SKIFFLE (Disky DO 250522, 2CD, 2000)
Bargain package of 61 skiffle recordings on a double-CD

AS GOOD AS IT GETS - SKIFFLE, VOLUME 2 (Disky 20999862, 2CD, 2000)
Seven Lonnie tracks but the best of the other skifflers is on Volume 1.

THE BEST OF SKIFFLE (Disky CB 793762, 3CD, 2002)
Bargain-priced package of 75 skiffle recordings - several by Lonnie but also the Vipers, Chas McDevitt, Johnny Duncan and many others.

" LONNIE DONEGAN PRESENTS "

JOHNNY DUNCAN
Sleepy Eyed John ; Tobacco Road
(Pye N 15358)★★★★

JOHNNY DUNCAN and his Blue
Grass Boys return to the disc
scene via the Pye label (under Lonnie
Donegan's auspices).
Sleepy Eyed John is a quick, whisk-
along country and western song which
Duncan makes into a nippy, amusing
dancer. The sort of thing Donegan
might well have performed himself.
Duncan's treatment of Tobacco
Road has a grave haunting quality
which suits the Lowdermilk story.
The singer could be returning to the
charts.

IAN MENZIES
The Fish Seller; Salty Dog
(Pye NJ2031)★★★★

SYDNEY BECHET'S famous tune,
The Fish Seller, played by
Menzies and his Clyde Valley
Stompers—presented by Lonnie Donegan in the label's Jazz Today series.
The traditional beat of the
Stompers will have many customers
for this well-known theme. It has a
fresh appeal on this record.
Vocalist Fiona Duncan is heard on
the second side and she gets the gusty
spirit of New Orleans into her performance of Salty Dog. Fiona growls
happily while the band mumble
behind her.
A breezy traditional hand-clapper
you will like.

Lonnie—minus his group

"BURY Me Beneath The Willow"
is not a very cheerful title but
don't be put off. This is the latest
Pye release by Lonnie Donegan, not
with his group, but accompanied by
Ralph Dollimore and his orchestra.
Song moves along at a steady
canter, Lonnie sings in restrained
fashion, interpreting his own lyric
most effectively.
"Leave My Woman Alone" is fast
and Donegan-furious, with a jazz-
type backing from Mr. Dollimore
and a small group. Very good.

APPENDIX 2

LONNIE DONEGAN PRESENTS

In the early 1960s some Pye records were branded "Lonnie Donegan Presents."

Singles
Miki and Griff - Hold Back Tomorrow / Deedle-Dum-Doo-Die-Day (Pye N 15213, 45/78rpm, 1959, No 26)
Ian Menzies and his Clyde Valley Stompers) - Salty Dog / The Fish Man (Pye Jazz 7NJ 2031, 45rpm, 1960
Miki and Griff - Rockin' Alone (In An Old Rockin' Chair) / I'm Here To Get My Baby Out Of Jail (Pye N 15296, 1960, No 44)
Johnny Duncan and his Bluegrass Boys - Tobacco Road / Sleepy Eyed John (Pye 7N 15358, 1961)
Kenny Ball and his Jazzmen - Samantha / Nuages (Pye Jazz 7NJ 2040, 45rpm, 1961, No 13)

Extended Plays
Miki and Griff - This Is Miki, This Is Griff (Pye NEP 24116, 1960, No 2 on EP chart)
Ian Menzies and his Clyde Valley Stompers - Swingin' Seamus (Pye NJE 1071, 1960)
Miki and Griff - Hit Parade (Pye NEP 24129, 1960)
Miki and Griff - Two's Company (Pye NEP 24145, 1961)

Albums
Miki and Griff - Miki And Griff (Pye NPL 18058, 12-inch LP, 1960)
Ian Menzies and his Clyde Valley Stompers - Have Tartan Will Trad (Pye NJL 23, 12-inch LP, 1960)
Kenny Ball and his Jazzmen -Invitation To The Ball (Pye NJL 24, 12-inch LP, 1960)
Ian Menzies and his Clyde Valley Stompers - Traditional Jazz (Pye NJL 26, 12-inch LP, 1960)
Kenny Ball and his Jazzmen - Kenny Ball And His Jazzmen (Pye NJL 28, 12-inch LP, 1961)

The Lonnie Donegan Group backs Miki and Griff on Hold Back Tomorrow, Deedle-Dum-Doo-Die-Day, I Heard The Bluebirds Sing, A New Love, I'm Here To Get My Baby Out Of Jail, Rockin' Alone (In An Old Rockin' Chair), Someday You'll Call My Name, I Never Will Marry, You Take The Table (And I'll Take The Chairs), I've Just Told Mama Goodbye, Be Careful Of Stones That You Throw and Here Today, Gone Tomorrow.
Lonnie Donegan whistles on I Never Will Marry.

Fiona Duncan and Lonnie Donegan share the vocals on Just A Closer Walk With Thee and Ice Cream by the Clyde Valley Stompers.

Lonnie Donegan plays banjo on Dinah by Kenny Ball and his Jazzmen.

APPENDIX 3

PLAYING FOR LONNIE

There are not many clean-cut divisions of when somebody joined or left Lonnie Donegan's group as he preferred to work with a pool of musicians who played according to his whims and their availability. This is particularly true in the later years when he did not tour constantly and so could not keep a permanent band together.

Ken Colyer (trumpet, vocals) - Born in Great Yarmouth in 1928 and formed the Crane River Jazz Band in 1949. If there hadn't been the ructions in Ken Colyer's own band in 1953, maybe none of the following would have happened.

CHRIS BARBER BAND, 1954

Chris Barber (trombone) - Born in Welwyn, Herts in 1930 and been playing trombone since 1948. Formed his first band in 1950. Following a breakup with Ken Colyer, has led the Chris Barber Jazz And Blues Band, the name has changed on occasion, since 1954.
Pat Halcox (trumpet) - Born in Chelsea in 1930 and joined Chris Barber permanently in 1954.
Monty Sunshine (clarinet) - Born in Stepney in 1928 and took up clarinet while in the RAF. Joined Ken Colyer's band in 1953, which soon became Chris Barber's band. Involved in many reunion concerts with Chris Barber, but has had poor health in recent years.
Jim Bray (bass) - Born in Richmond, Surrey in 1927 and took up the tuba and double bass after RAF service. Was in Tony Donegan's first band and joined Ken Colyer's band in 1953. Spent many years teaching in India and was in and out of Chris Barber's band.
Ron Bowden (drums) - Born in Fulham in 1928 and joined the Crane River Jazz Band in 1949. Went from Chris Barber's band to Wee Willie Harris (!) and then joined Kenny Ball in 1959, staying with him for 40 years.
Lonnie Donegan (vocals, banjo)
Beryl Bryden (washboard on skiffle recordings) - Born in Norwich in 1920 and guested with many bands in the 40s and 50s. Quite by chance, she became the world's best-known washboard player.

FIRST PYE SESSIONS, 1956

Lonnie Donegan (vocals, guitar)
Dickie Bishop (vocals, guitar) - Born in London in 1935 and joined Chris Barber in 1954. After Lonnie, formed Dickie Bishop and the Sidekicks. With Terry Lightfoot (1968-71) and emigrated to Germany. Still performs in the UK.
Chris Barber (bass)
Ron Bowden (drums)

LONNIE DONEGAN SKIFFLE GROUP, 1956

Lonnie Donegan (vocals, guitar)
Denny Wright (guitar) - Denys Justin Freeth Wright, born in Bromley in 1924, had worked with Stephane Grappelli (1944), Bob Navarro (1950) and Freddy Randall (1951). He was

with the BBC Show Band before he was with Lonnie.

Mickey Ashman (bass) - Michael Lewis Ashman, who was born in Kingsbury, London in 1927, was with Humphrey Lyttelton (1950-55) and then Chris Barber. He ran his own band in the 60s and was with Monty Sunshine in the 80s.

Nick Nicholls (drums) - John Michael Nicholls, born in Barking in 1929, played with many jazz and dance bands before joining Lonnie; "If I had to play old-time waltzes all night, I would play old-time waltzes.". He was released from a summer season at Ramsgate with Billy Wells to work with Lonnie. With Lonnie until February 1961 and then joined Monty Sunshine. After stints with Des O'Connor and Frank Ifield, he emigrated to South Africa in 1974.

LONNIE DONEGAN SKIFFLE GROUP, 1957

Lonnie Donegan (vocals, guitar)

Jimmy Currie (guitar) - In 1956 Tony Crombie and his Rockets became the UK's first rock'n'roll band, but they were jazzmen slumming it. Tony Crombie and his guitarist Jimmy Currie wrote several original compositions, including 'Let's You And I Rock', but I don't think it took them very long.

Mickey Ashman (bass)

Nick Nicholls (drums)

LONNIE DONEGAN SKIFFLE GROUP, 1958

Lonnie Donegan (vocals, guitar)

Les Bennetts (guitar) - From Les Hobeaux skiffle group, Les Bennetts was a "a young good-looking wizard on the guitar" (Peter Buchanan). He came and went from Lonnie's group and even managed, or rather mismanaged, the Pines Hotel in Margate for Lonnie and his second wife, Jill. When Lonnie went to sack him, he said, "You needn't bother, I quit."

Pete Huggett (bass) - Freelance musician in the 1950s, working with Stephane Grappelli, Oscar Rabin and Ted Heath. Joined Pye Records in 1965 and then managed Des O'Connor.

Nick Nicholls (drums)

Peter Buchanan (road manager), 1958 to 1962 - Ran a Glenn Miller-styled band in London with Nick Nicholls on drums, who recommended him to Lonnie as a good organiser: "Some nights it was so good that I felt like rushing on with my tenor sax to play a chorus."

LONNIE DONEGAN SKIFFLE GROUP, 1960

Lonnie Donegan (vocals, guitar)

Les Bennetts (guitar)

Pete Huggett (bass)

Pete Appleby (drums) - Was with Mick Mulligan's Jazz Band, but insists that George Melly's famed biography of the band, 'Owning-Up', was largely fictitious. The drum solos in 'Gamblin' Man' didn't bother him as he was used to being left for 15 minutes by Mulligan: "Once I heard Mick say, 'We'd better go back, he'll be running out of ideas' and he didn't realise I was standing by him. I said, 'Don't worry, I've just ordered a pint'." Pete left Lonnie in 1966, fed up with the travelling.

Lonnie's most noted but troublesome guitarist, Denny Wright, rejoined Lonnie in 1962 and played with him on and off through the Sixties. He often worked with Diz Disley and Stephane Grappelli in the 1970s and he died in London in 1992.

LONNIE DONEGAN GROUP, 1964

Cabaret time, no lead guitar

Lonnie Donegan (vocals, guitar)

Cliff Hall (keyboards) - Joined Lonnie from Oscar Rabin's band and became a top session musician (Bonnie Tyler, Leo Sayer, Cliff Richard). Spent 14 years with the Shadows. Met up with Lonnie in later years when he was in the band for Des O'Connor's TV show.

Pete Oakman (bass) - From Joe Brown's Bruvvers and had written 'A Picture Of You'. Has come and gone with Lonnie but overall the longest serving member by a long way. Maintained his own Bruvvers band whilst with Lonnie, and became Lonnie's bandleader. Still rocking and currently working with John Leyton and Jet Harris.

Pete Appleby (drums)

LONNIE DONEGAN GROUP, 1967

Lonnie Donegan (vocals, guitar)

Les Bennetts and Denny Wright (guitar)

Steve Jones (bass) - Was in a pop group, Five's Company, and met Lonnie by chance when Pete Oakman was leaving. Became a Radio 2 DJ and game show host.

Pete Mack and then Mark Goodwin (drums) - Mark left to tour with Peter Gordeno.

LONNIE DONEGAN GROUP, 1972

Les Bennetts (guitar)

Pete Oakman (bass)

Steve Jones (bass)

Pete Merrick (drums) - Met Lonnie when he was playing in the pit orchestra for a panto in Bournemouth. Lonnie invited him to drum on a gig in the Isle of Wight: "You know where the Isle of Wight is, don't you? Just drive around until you find us." Lon dropped the band in the early-80s but kept in touch: "I saw him in 2001 and he said, 'Thank god, we haven't got you on drums anymore as I couldn't do it at that speed.' I said, 'Well, I can't play at that speed either.'"

Following his heart attack, Lonnie played very few dates in 1976 and 1977.

LONNIE DONEGAN AND THE DIXIE BAND, 1978

Lonnie Donegan (vocals, guitar)

Jackie McAuley (guitar) - Played with Van Morrison in the 1960s Belfast band, Them, and auditioned for Lonnie at his sister's birthday party: "Lonnie didn't know anyone but he was singing songs in my mum's house 'til two in the morning. He loved the mandolins, the fiddles, the banjos and all the Irish stuff." Lonnie performed his songs, 'I'll Be Your Alibi' and 'Cajun Dance', but his recorded versions have not been released. After leaving John, Jackie was in Rowdy with John Gustafson and they wrote 'Dear John' for Status

Quo, a Top 10 hit in 1982. His recent album, 'Bad Day At Black Rock', contains several songs which would have suited Lonnie. He says, "I played with Lonnie about 18 months before he died. It was the final evening of a business conference, which Lonnie described as a shagathon. It was great being with Lonnie and I loved all the football matches we went to - he could get in anywhere."

Roy Davies or Big Bill Scott (keyboards) - Roy Davies went on to play keyboards for Madness but died from cancer. Ex-Stone the Crows, Bill Scott met his future wife while touring with Lonnie in Australia. He became the musical director for the country singer, Rose-Marie.

Ian Murray-Sorbie or Bob Renney (bass) - Ian did a summer season with Lonnie at Cleethorpes and met his future wife, Clodagh Rodgers. He died from a brian tumour.

Willie Wilson or Chris Hunt (drums)

LONNIE DONEGAN AND THE DIXIE BAND, 1982

Lonnie Donegan (vocals, guitar)

Paul Henry (lead guitar) - Former schoolteacher from Swindon with a background of UK country music. Joined Lonnie in 1982 as a guitarist and mandolin player. "I had never touched a mandolin before, and he was going through an Irish phase, which mercifully didn't last too long."

Bob Renney (bass)

Chris Hunt (drums) - Started 1978 and worked with both Lon and Dana Gillespie: "I'd heard that Lon was rough on drummers but he said to me at one point, 'You're all right, son,.." Often works with Pete Oakman in the Bruvvers.

LONNIE DONEGAN BAND, 1989

Lonnie Donegan (vocals, guitar)

Paul Henry (guitar)

Nick Payn (saxophone, flute, harmonica) - Started 1987, session musician, working with Barbara Dickson and Chas and Dave: "Lonnie fancied some harmonica and Jim told him that I played saxophone and flute as well Lon rang me up in the autumn of 1987, and told me he was doing 'The Des O'Connor Show' at Thames. He said, 'We're going to do a number on the show, Thames will be paying you and that way, if you're no good, it won't cost me anything.' We played one number for the show, 'Puttin' On The Style'. He then invited me to play the 100 Club with no rehearsal but a list of tunes. I thought, 'I will do harmonica on this one, that one sax, and 'Seven Golden Daffodils' would be very nice with flute. He gave me a date sheet and that was it. I was in the band."

Jim Rodford (bass) - From 1987 and through to 1996. Jim was with the Mike Cotton Sound and backed P.J. Proby on his trouser-splitting tour. Was with the Kinks for many years and latterly with Animals II. "Playing with the Kinks was like standing on a precipice as there were silly fights both on and off stage," says Jim, "but Lon was always great. It was therapy for him and it did him more good than harm. I felt privileged to be playing with one of my heroes."

Geoff Downs (drums) - Born in Blackheath in 1938, Geoff was with Dick Charlesworth (1961-4) and then Monty Sunshine. Has worked with Long John Baldry, Chas McDevitt and Beryl Bryden.

LONNIE DONEGAN BAND, 1990s
Lonnie Donegan, (vocals, guitar)
Paul Henry (guitar)
Pete Oakman (bass) -
Jim Rodford (bass)
Nick Payn (saxophone, flute, harmonica)
Russell Gilbrook (percussion) - Playing with Chris Barber's band and met Lonnie when
Chris had his fortieth anniversary tour. Joined him in 1995: "Lon used to say, "People
come and see me, but what makes me are the musicians around me."
Alan 'Sticky' Wicket (percussion) - Also met Lonnie on the fortieth anniversary tour: "It
was very refreshing to be working with Lonnie because with Chris it was working all year
long, except August."
Chris Hunt (drums)

BIBLIOGRAPHY

Historical
Woody Guthrie - A Life by Joe Klein (Faber & Faber, 1981)
The Life And Legend Of Leadbelly by Charles Wolfe & Kip Lornell (HarperCollins,1992)
Will You Miss Me When I'm Gone? - The Carter Family And Their Legacy In American
Music by Mark Zwonitzer with Charles Hirshberg (Simon & Schuster, 2002)

Books on jazz
Who's Who In British Jazz - John Chilton (Cassell, 1997)

Books on skiffle
Skiffle: The Story Of Folk-Song With A Jazz Beat by Brian Bird (Robert Hale, 1958)
Skiffle - The Definitive Inside Story by Chas McDevitt (Robson, 1997)
The Skiffle Craze by Mike Dewe (Planet, 1998)

Books on 1950s UK pop
Hit Parade Heroes - British Beat Before The Beatles by Dave McAleer (Hamlyn, 1993)
Halfway To Paradise - Britpop, 1955 - 1962 by Spencer Leigh and John Firminger
(Finbarr, 1996)

Magazines
In particular:
Fans' Star Library - Lonnie Donegan (Amalgamated Press, 1959)
Skiffle - The Roots Of British Rock (Programme written by John Pilgrim of the Vipers for
the Albert Hall event, Square Peg, 1998)

Interviews with Lonnie Donegan
In particular:
Bob Azurdia, BBC Radio Merseyside, 1981
Ken Bruce, BBC Radio 2, 1999
Alan Clayson, 'Record Collector, May 2000
Steve Jones, BBC Radio 2, 1986
Spencer Leigh, BBC Radio Merseyside, 1978, 1988, 1992, 1999, 2001
Geoff Speed, BBC Radio Merseyside, 1972
Dave Waite, 'Record Collector', May 1987